HOW TO STUDY THE BAVLI

SOUTH FLORIDA STUDIES IN THE HISTORY OF JUDAISM

Edited by
Jacob Neusner
William Scott Green, James Strange
Darrell J. Fasching, Sara Mandell

Number 37
How to Study the Bavli

by
Jacob Neusner

HOW TO STUDY THE BAVLI
The Languages, Literatures, and Lessons of the Talmud of Babylonia

by
Jacob Neusner

Scholars Press
Atlanta, Georgia

BM
503.5
.N47
1992

HOW TO STUDY THE BAVLI
The Languages, Literatures,
and Lessons of the Talmud of Babylonia

Publication of this book was made possible by a grant from the Tisch
Family Foundation, New York City. The University of South Florida
acknowledges with thanks this important support for its scholarly projects.

Library of Congress Cataloging in Publication Data

Neusner, Jacob, 1932-
    How to study the Bavli : the languages, literatures, and lessons
of the Talmud of Babylonia / by Jacob Neusner.
    p. cm. — (South Florida studies in the history of Judaism ;
no. 37)
    Includes index.
    ISBN 1-55540-688-2 (alk. paper)
    1. Talmud—Introductions. I. Title. II. Series: South Florida
studies in the history of Judaism ; 37.
BM503.5.N47 1992
296.1'25061—dc20   92-2954
                                       CIP

Printed in the United States of America
on acid-free paper

Table of Contents

Preface

When we propose to study a document written long ago, by people quite different from ourselves in language, culture, and intellectual context, we require guidance in taking the first steps toward an understanding of that document. The Talmud of Babylonia, or Bavli, ca. 600 C.E. [a.k.a. A.D.] is such a piece of writing. It is in more than one language; it is formed as a commentary to another piece of writing; it follows rules of composition different from those with which we are familiar. A first impression is that it is episodically comprehensible, but in the aggregate, is disorganized and incoherent. We may understand words, phrases, even sentences, and yet find the whole lacking in organization and cogency. Even distinguished scholars of the document represent it as a scrapbook, not as the sustained, purposive, and well-crafted writing that it is.

In this book I set forth some basic rules that will help beginners make sense of the Bavli. I pay attention to only the most basic questions. First, in the introduction, I characterize the document by placing it into the context of prior writings with which it is connected, the Mishnah, a philosophical law code of the end of the second century. Then, turning from literary to linguistic context, in Part One I explain how the multilingual character of the Bavli bears part of the message of the document. I proceed to answer the question: What is the Bavli? The answer is that it is a commentary to parts of the Mishnah and parts of the Hebrew Scriptures. In Part Two I explain how the Bavli accomplishes its principal purpose, Mishnah exegesis and amplification. I turn next to another kind of writing in the Bavli, which is of a miscellaneous character, and I set forth how cogent compositions are formed into rather discrete composites and how these hold together. In this way I mean to account for the Bavli's somewhat run-on and tedious character. I then propose to explain how the Bavli holds together, and, in Part Three, I spell out what I conceive to be one of the principal problems of a cultural character that is solved in the literary form that the document exhibits. At the same time through a work of comparison I place this solution into a broader context. In these simple steps I mean to facilitate the study, not in bits and pieces but as a whole, of the document that from antiquity to our own time has formed the principal and authoritative systematic statement of Judaism. Judaism sets forth a coherent system and statement, and so does its principal and authoritative canonical writing.

In these several chapters I put together in a single statement the results of a variety of monographs, all of which are aimed at investigating problems concerning the literary character of the document. These include the following, all published by Scholars Press for South Florida Studies in the History of Judaism (except the first, as indicated): [1] *Making the Classics in Judaism: The Three Stages of Literary Formation* (Brown Judaic Studies); [2] *The Canonical History of Ideas. The Place of the So-called Tannaite Midrashim, Mekhilta Attributed to R. Ishmael, Sifra, Sifré to Numbers, and Sifré to Deuteronomy;* [3] *Tradition as Selectivity: Scripture, Mishnah, Tosefta, and Midrash in the Talmud of Babylonia: The Case of Tractate Arakhin;* [4] *Language as Taxonomy: The Rules for Using Hebrew and Aramaic in the Babylonian Talmud;* [5] *The Bavli That Might Have Been: The Tosefta's Theory of Mishnah Commentary Compared with That of the Babylonian Talmud;* [6] *The Rules of Composition of the Talmud of Babylonia: The Cogency of the Bavli's Composite;* [7] *The Bavli's One Voice: Types and Forms of Analytical Discourse and Their Fixed Order of Appearance;* [8] *How the Bavli Shaped Rabbinic Discourse;* [9] *The Bavli's Massive Miscellanies: The Problem of Agglutinative Discourse in the Talmud of Babylonia;* [10] *Sources and Traditions: Types of Composition in the Talmud of Babylonia;* [11] *The Law Behind the Laws: The Bavli's Essential Discourse;* and [12] *The Bavli's Primary Discourse. Mishnah Commentary, Its Rhetorical Paradigms and Their Theological Implications in the Talmud of Babylonia.* All of these experimental monographs – probes of a vast piece of writing – sought to identify pieces of a puzzle and to put together one piece with several of the others. I do not think I have yet put the entire puzzle together, but I near that goal.

Support for the work on this book and the final four items above (*Massive Miscellanies, Sources and Traditions, Essential Discourse,* and *Primary Discourse*) was provided by the Alexander Von Humboldt-Stiftung, Bonn, Germany, and I acknowledge with thanks the generous grant provided by that foundation. Further, I completed this book during my service as Martin Buber Visiting Professor of Judaic Studies on the Protestant Theological Faculty of the Johann Wolfgang Goethe University in Frankfurt. I further express my genuine pleasure at the opportunity for a life of learning through both teaching and scholarly inquiry that is afforded to me by the University of South Florida. I express thanks to my University for its generous support of my scholarly work. I also thank my colleagues in the Department of Religious Studies for not only friendship but also intellectual stimulus. Finally, as always, I talked over my ideas with Professor William Scott Green, University of Rochester, and found in his responses important guidance for my own thinking.

JACOB NEUSNER

Graduate Research Professor of Humanities and Religious Studies
UNIVERSITY OF SOUTH FLORIDA
Tampa, St. Petersburg, Sarasota, Lakeland, Fort Myers

735 Fourteenth Avenue Northeast
St. Petersburg, Florida 33701-1413 USA

Introduction

The Babylonian Talmud as a Piece of Writing: The Bavli and Its Sources

The Talmud of Babylonia, or Bavli, occupies the commanding position in the formative writings of the canon of Judaism. Into it, all prior documents flowed; from it, all authoritative Judaic theology and law derived. Hence the Bavli defines the principal problem in the study, out of the canonical writings, of the formation of Judaism. Understanding the document as a piece of writing will occupy our attention to begin with, for, as is clear, only when we can say what we think a document is, can we also specify what we think a document says (if anything). And that is particularly important in the case of the Bavli, for the form as well as the substance of the document, its modes of setting forth its materials as much as the contents of the materials, dictated future discourse within Judaism, therefore also the future theology and law of Judaism. What we have first of all to ask is whether the Bavli is a traditional or a systemic writing. So before we open a page of the Bavli, we address a fundamental question: How does the Bavli relate to prior writings?

Two completed documents appear on nearly every page of the Bible, the Hebrew Scriptures, known to Christianity as the Old Testament and to Judaism as the Written Torah, and the Mishnah. Kept distinct and always marked as external to the Bavli, these are quoted and discussed. But there were other writings that reached closure before the editing of the Bavli, such as the Tosefta, various compilations of Scripture commentary called Midrashim, and the like. And, above all, there was the Talmud of the Land of Israel, written around two centuries before the Bavli and serving also as a commentary to the Mishnah. So when we ask, how does the Bavli relate to its sources, we mean, is the document traditional, compiling earlier writings, or is it autonomous, free-standing, cogent in its own terms, and making a statement in behalf of its writers? By that I mean, does the Bavli merely collect and arrange what it has received, that is, is it merely a medium of tradition? Or do the framers of the Bavli impose their own imprint upon whatever they have received, using whatever they have chosen for the purpose of making what is essentially their own system's statement? At stake in the answer to that question is whether or not the Judaism that emerged from the Bavli would be traditional or systemic. Asking the question itself represents a step beyond the received version of matters. The Bavli itself is given the form of a tradition, that is, a (mere) commentary upon a received writing, the Mishnah. It is, moreover, set forth as a stage in an unfolding tradition, for it, too, is the object of a vast commentary literature. Hence the literary form of the writing is so portrayed as to constitute a theological and legal tradition formed out of prior sources, making a cogent and authoritative statement in common and forming a continuous set of writings. That tradition formed out of prior sources, moreover, is understood to derive from a continuous process of tradition, with sayings handed on from an earlier generation to a later one until a complete and final statement came to full expression in the Bavli. Hence the Bavli is supposed to stand in relationship to prior writings as a summary statement stands to the sources that are summarized. It is supposed to respond to a received program and to restate a vast corpus of already circulating and traditional materials.

True, the Judaic system of the Dual Torah recognizes a corpus of authoritative writings, but that corpus does not form a tradition, a "tradition formed out of prior sources." The Bavli, however, does not fall into the classification formed by books that take over from the predecessors' materials to be handed on to continuators, materials that therefore are continuous with one another. The Bavli is not part of a traditional literature, each of the documents of which stand in close relationship with its neighbors, fore and after, each borrowing from its predecessor, handing on to its successor, a nourishing tradition. Since, I have insisted, the history of a religion that sets forth a canon begins with the history of that canon, let me spell out the three dimensions of any ancient text of Judaism and then specify the dimension I propose to measure here. The relationships among the documents produced by the sages of Judaism may take three forms: complete dependence or total continuity one to the next (hence "traditional"), connection, that is, intersection in diverse manner and measure, and, finally, complete autonomy. That dimension of connection provokes considerable debate and presents a remarkably unclear perspective. For while the dimensions of autonomy and continuity take the measure of acknowledged traits – books on their own, books standing in imputed, therefore socially verified, relationships – the matter of connection hardly enjoys the same clear definition.

Confusing theological and social judgments of continuities and literary and heuristic ones of connection, people present quite remarkable claims as to the relationships between and among documents, alleging, in fact, that the documents all have to be read as a single continuous document: the Torah. When we can describe the relationships between two documents or among three or more, we shall know what a given group of editors or authorities contributed on its own, and also how that authorship restated or reworked what it received from a prior group. Determining that relationship further guides us to principles of exegesis of documents, allegations and formulations of ideas and rules. If a document depends on some other, prior one, then what we find in the later writing is to be read in light of the earlier (but, of course, never vice versa). If there is no clear evidence of dependence, then the later document demands a reading in essentially its own terms. Determining the relationship of document to document forms the necessary second step. Finding out what changed and what remained the same in the unfolding of the system as a whole tells us the history of the system as its canonical writings contain that history. Seeing the documents as a continuous and final statement, we take the measure of that third dimension that takes its perspective from a distance and encompasses all of the documents: the system as a whole. It sees the documents as continuous not from one to the next but all in all, all together, all at once.

I therefore contrast thought received as truth transmitted through a process of tradition against thought derived from active rationality by asking a simple question: Does what is the most rigorously rational and compelling statement of applied reason known to me, the Talmud of Babylonia or Bavli, constitute a tradition and derive from a process of traditional formulation and transmission of an intellectual heritage, facts and thought alike? Or does that document make a statement of its own, cogent and defined within the requirements of an inner logic, proportion, and structure, imposing that essentially autonomous vision upon whatever materials its authorship has received from the past? We shall know the answer through a simple test. Specifically, if I can show that in literary terms the Bavli is not traditional, formed out of the increment of received materials, the form of the reception of which governs, but – in the sense now implied – systemic, that is, again in literary terms orderly, systematic, laid out in a proportion and order dictated by the inner logic of a topic or generative problem and – therefore – authoritative by reason of its own rigorous judgment of issues of rationality and compelling logic, then I can offer a reasonable hypothesis resting on facts of literature. Specifically I can contribute a considerable example to the debate on whether tradition may coexist with the practical and applied reason of utter, uncompromising logical rationality and compelling, autonomous order.

Every test I can devise for describing the relationship between the authorship of the Bavli and the prior and extant writings of the movement of which that authorship forms the climax and conclusion yields a single result. The authorship at hand does not pursue anyone else's program, except only that of the Mishnah. It does not receive and refine writings concluded elsewhere. It takes over a substantial heritage and reworks the whole into its own sustained and internally cogent statement – and that forms not the outcome of a process of sedimentary tradition but the opposite: systematic statement of a cogent and logical order, made up in its authorship's rhetoric, attaining comprehensibility through the syntax of its authorship's logic, reviewing a received topical program in terms of the problematic and interests defined by its authorship's larger purposes and proposed message. The samples of the Bavli I have reviewed constitute either composites of sustained, essentially syllogistic discourse, in which case they form the whole and comprehensive statement of a system, or increments of exegetical accumulation, in which case they constitute restatements, with minor improvements, of a continuous tradition. In my view, the reader is going to review sustained, directed, purposive syllogistic discourse, not wandering and essentially agglutinative collections of observations on this and that, made we know not when, for a purpose we cannot say, to an audience we can scarcely imagine, so as to deliver a message that, all together and in the aggregate, we cannot begin to recapitulate.

True, the authorship of the Bavli drew upon a sizable corpus of materials of indeterminate character and substance, which we assuredly do classify as traditions handed on from their predecessors. Hence the authorship of the Bavli made use of both sources, completed documents, and also traditions, transmitted sayings and stories, ordinarily of modest proportions, not subjected to ultimate redaction. But the authorship of the Bavli did whatever it wished with these materials to carry out its own program and to make its own prevailing statement. These received materials, undeniably formulated and transmitted in a process of tradition, have been so reworked and revised by the penultimate and ultimate authorship that their original character does not define the syntax of argument and the processes of syllogistic discourse, except by way of supplying facts for someone else's case. Whether or not we can still discern traces of received statements, even in wordings that point to an origin other than with an authorship, is beside the point. Proof of my case does not derive from the failure or success of scholars to identify the passages of the Bavli that antedate the penultimate or ultimate work of composition.

Many claim that the Bavli supposedly draws upon and reshapes available ideas and reworks them into a definitive statement, hence turns sources into a tradition. To test that claim I have devised a simple experiment. If the authorship at hand resorts to prior writings and presents us with what is at its foundations a systematic and comprehensive summary and restatement of them, then the Bavli will take up an honorable position at the end of a long process of tradition. But if we find that the authorship of the Bavli follows an essentially independent and fresh program of its own, then the Bavli will prove to have inaugurated a tradition but not to have received and transmitted one. It will follow that, for the Judaism of the Dual Torah, holy Scripture, authoritative sources whether preserved orally or in writing, as such play no categorical role whatsoever. The Bavli will then constitute an independent and fresh statement of its own authorship, not a restatement of what its authorship has received from prior generations, and assuredly not a statement of a cumulative and incremental tradition. The Bavli, rather, will come forth as a statement that in time to come, beyond its redaction, would become traditional, but for reasons not related to its own literary let alone theological and legal traits. That set of choices explains the interest and importance of determining the relationship between the Bavli and the extant sources of the Judaism of the Dual Torah that reached closure prior to the Bavli. In fact, the Bavli is mostly the work of its own authorship, acting independently on its singular program of Mishnah exegesis and amplification, alongside its distinctive program of Scripture exegesis and amplification, both programs demonstrably unique to that authorship alone so far as extant sources and documents indicate for our sample. In the Bavli we look in vain for large tractates or even sizable units of discourse that refer to, or depend upon, the plan and program of prior documents.

What earlier authorships wished to investigate in the Mishnah, the points they wished to prove by reference to verses of Scripture important in our tractate – these have little or nothing in common with the points of special concern systematically worked out by the authorship of the Bavli. The Bavli's authorship at ca. 600 approaches Mishnah exegesis with a program distinct from that of the Yerushalmi's authorship of ca. 400, and the Bavli's authorship reads a critical verse of Scripture within a set of considerations entirely separate from those of interest to the authorships of Leviticus Rabbah and Pesiqta deRab Kahana of ca. 450 and 500. Any notion that the Bavli's authorship has taken as its principal task the restatement of received ideas on the Mishnah topics and Scripture verses at hand derives no support to speak of from the sample we shall examine.

That finding, alas, will contradict familiar and much cherished convictions concerning the character of the Bavli, and of Judaism, that is to say, the larger canonical corpus of which it forms a principal representative. Reaching the world of commonly held opinions in the the song, Tradition, that conviction leads us to expect the principal document of Judaism to say pretty much what had been said before, and, many would add, beginning at Sinai. That corpus is held to form a continuous statement, beginning in an earlier writing, standing behind, generating, and therefore continuing in a later one. Consequently, the corpus is called "traditional" in the sense that one document leads to the next, and all of the documents come to their climax and conclusion in the final one of late antiquity. To the documents of the Torah – oral and written – is imputed not only the status of tradition in the sense just now defined but also a relationship of continuity which we may call imputed canonicity, so that, we are told, we may freely cite a passage from one document alongside a counterpart from another, treating them as part of a single – hence, continuous – statement, and, in theological terms, one might say, a canonical one, though our issue is not to be confused with canonical research. And that claim for the Bavli and the literature prior to it of traditionality bears with it not merely theological, but literary implications about the nature of the documents and the correct way of reading them. Because of those implications as to literature we can test the claim at hand and ask whether it indeed so describes the documents as to find substantiation in literary facts.

That is why my particular concern is the Bavli's relationship to prior treatments of a given subject, with special interest in how the authorship of the Bavli has made use of what it had in hand, and how in its sorting out of available materials it has defined the task of making a full and authoritative statement. In assessing the stance of the Bavli, in making its final statement, vis-à-vis prior writings on a given topic, I can uncover the rules that guide an authorship in its work of summary and systematization: of systemic statement of the whole, all together and all at once, on a given subject. I can conceive of no better way of uncovering how people make a statement we now realize was canonical from the beginning, than situating those people in the setting of what had gone before. So far as traditionality constitutes a literary question concerning rules of how one writes a canonical document, giving the signals to the community that one's writing constitutes a final, authoritative statement, through inductive inquiry into relationships I should be able to answer that question and describe those rules: Why this not that? That interest requires me to collect answers to questions deriving from these comparative inquiries:

1.   The topical program of prior writings on the subject as compared to the topical program of the Bavli on the same subject, with attention to questions such as these: Does the Bavli follow the response to the Mishnah characteristic of the authorship of the Tosefta? The Sifra (or Sifré to Numbers or Sifré to Deuteronomy, where relevant)? Does the Bavli follow the response to relevant passages of Scripture that have caught the attention of compilers of Midrash exegeses in Genesis Rabbah, Leviticus Rabbah, Pesiqta deRab Kahana, and other documents generally thought to have come to closure prior to the Bavli?

2.   The Bavli's use or neglect of the available treatments ("sources") in the prior literature: If the Bavli does make use of available materials, does it impose its own issues upon those materials or does it reproduce those materials as they occur elsewhere? Has the authorship of the Bavli carried forward issues important in prior writings, or has it simply announced and effected its own program of inquiry into the topic at hand?

3.   The traits of the Bavli's statement: Are they derivative and summary at the end, or essentially fresh and imputed retrospectively? In consequence of the detailed examination of the Bavli's authorship's use of and response to available sources, how may we characterize the statement of the Bavli as a whole in comparison to prior statements? And, since that statement is canonical by the definition of the entire history of Judaism, we ask about the upshot: the shape and character of a canonical statement on a given subject.

Let us ask now about whether the Bavli has proposed to continue the received program of the Yerushalmi. Let me now specify the operative question and the criteria for answering it: Does the Bavli carry forward the exegetical program of the Yerushalmi? Or does the authorship of the Bavli invent its own altogether singular and distinctive topical exegetical program for the same chapter of the Mishnah? A comparison of the two documents will allow us to settle at the outset a number of important questions. These concern the relationships of connection between the Bavli and prior writings.

Asking the question takes longer than answering it. In fact the comparison yields one-sided evidence that the Bavli is autonomous, singular, distinctive. Its authorship delivers its message in a way that is its own and works out an exegetical program, on precisely the same chapter of the Mishnah, that is particular to itself, not dictated by the prior Talmud's treatment of the same materials. It therefore is in substantial measure distinct from the other Talmud. The Bavli is far more than a secondary development of the Yerushalmi. That is the fact because the Bavli and the Yerushalmi stand autonomous of one another. The authorship of the Bavli in its own way works out a singular and independent program of exegesis and amplification of the Mishnah. Word-for-word correspondences are few and, on the whole, peripheral. Where materials are shared, moreover, they derive from either the Mishnah or the Tosefta or some antecedent convention of exegesis. But in all instances of shared language or conventional hermeneutics the framers of the Bavli worked things out on their own. They in no way accepted the Yerushalmi as a model for how they said things let alone for the bulk of what they said. What is shared, moreover, derives principally from the Mishnah. It comes, secondarily, from some sort of conventional program (partly encapsulated, also, in the Tosefta). The Tosefta has not dictated to the Bavli's authorship a topical or logical program, it has merely contributed occasional passages for systematic analysis, much as the Mishnah has contributed a much larger volume of passages for systematic analysis. In any event the Bavli's authors developed inherited intellectual conventions in a strikingly independent way. That fact leads us to see the Bavli's authorship's composition as an essentially autonomous statement, standing on its own, borrowing from prior compilations pretty much what suited its purpose – that alone. The Bavli meets the Yerushalmi in the Mishnah. The two also come together, in markedly diminished measure, in the Tosefta and, still less, in some shared phrases deriving from post-Mishnaic authorities (for example, those of the third-century masters Yohanan and Simeon b. Laqish). So in one specific way the two documents not only intersect but prove at one with one another and therefore continuous.

When the two documents do intersect, they are connected not only to a common source but mainly or solely through that source. Where they go over the same problems, it is because the shared source presented these problems to the authors of both documents. The rhetoric and literary program of the Bavli owed remarkably little to those of its predecessor. The comparisons of actual texts yield decisive evidence for several propositions. First, there is remarkably little verbatim correspondence. The Bavli's authors scarcely ever made use of extensive constructions and only rarely of brief formulations also found in the Yerushalmi. So far as our modest sample suggests, they never did so when it came to detailed expository arguments and analyses. Where there is verbatim sharing, it is a Mishnah paragraph or Tosefta passage that is held in common, on the one side, or a prior, severely abbreviated lemma of an earlier Amoraic authority, on the other. Where the two sets of authors deal with such a shared lemma, however, each group does exactly what it wishes, imputing words to the prior authority (as if the said authority had actually spoken those words) simply not known to the other group.

Second and more important, what the framers of the Bavli wished to do with a saying of an earlier Amoraic authority in no way responded to the policy or program of the Yerushalmi's authors. Quite to the contrary, where both sets of authors shared sayings of Yohanan and Simeon b. Laqish, we noted that each set went its own way. In no aspect did the Yerushalmi's interest in these shared sayings affect the Bavli's treatment of them. The point in common was that prior authorities explained the same passage of the Mishnah. From that simple starting point, the Bavli's authors went in a direction not imagined by the Yerushalmi's. The power and intellectual force of the Bavli's authors in that context vastly overshadowed the capacities of the Yerushalmi's. The Yerushalmi and the Bavli are alike in their devotion to the exegesis and amplification of the Mishnah. Viewed as literary constructions, they share, in addition, a basic exegetical program, which flows from the Mishnah and in fundamental ways is defined by the inner logic and cogency of the Mishnah. In relationship to the Yerushalmi, therefore the Bavli's framers pursued their own interests in their own way. They reveal independence of mind and originality of taste. It must follow that the Bavli is sufficiently unlike the Yerushalmi to be judged as an autonomous document, disconnected from and unlike its predecessor in all the ways that matter.

Let me now set forth some further facts on the relationship of the Bavli to prior documents:

1. The topical program of prior writings on the subject as compared to the topical program of the Bavli on the same subject, with attention to questions such as these: Does the Bavli follow the response to the Mishnah characteristic of the authorship of the Tosefta? Not systematically, only episodically. As to the Sifra, Sifré to Numbers, or Sifré to Deuteronomy, these documents have little in common with ours. Does the Bavli follow the response to relevant passages of Scripture that have caught the attention of compilers of Midrash exegeses in Genesis Rabbah, Leviticus Rabbah, Pesiqta deRab Kahana, and other documents generally thought to have come to closure prior to the Bavli? Quite to the contrary, apart from the Yerushalmi and other authorships within the Bavli itself, our authorship turns out to define unique and uncommon points of interest in verses treated both in the Bavli and in some other document.

2. The Bavli's use or neglect of the available treatments ("sources") in the prior literature: If the Bavli does make use of available materials, does it impose its own issues upon those materials or does it reproduce those materials as they occur elsewhere? The answer to these questions

for the present sample is negative. The Bavli does not make extensive use of available materials. Most of what we find in the Bavli, as a matter of fact, turns out to be unique to the Bavli. Where there are materials that occur both here and in other documents, they provide mere facts, not a point of generative discourse. Has the authorship of the Bavli carried forward issues important in prior writings, or has it simply announced and effected its own program of inquiry into the topic at hand? Our authorship has made its own statement in its own way.

3. The traits of the Bavli's canonical statement: Are they derivative and summary at the end, or essentially fresh and imputed retrospectively? In consequence of the detailed examination of the Bavli's authorship's use of and response to available sources, for the sample at hand we may characterize the statement of the Bavli as a whole in comparison to prior statements as original, fresh, and self-defined. And, since that statement is canonical by the definition of the entire history of Judaism, we ask about the upshot: the shape and character of a canonical statement on a given subject. The answer, for the vast sample I have considered in my research, yields a negative finding: the canonical statement does not aim at drawing together available materials and restating a long-term and (assessed in terms of the extant writings) broadly circulated consensus. Data that constitute evidence for documentary traditionality do not appear to the naked eye – or even to a vision educated to discern literary traits and concerns. Quite to the contrary, the plain truth is that our document does not cite or quote or attempt to summarize and recast available materials, reaching a later authorship out of an earlier and ongoing process of tradition. True, individual sayings may have circulated and may have undergone a process of continuous tradition. But the Bavli as we have it, the work of its penultimate and ultimate authorship, makes its own statement in its own way on its own agenda. It gives us not a tradition out of a remote past but a system of its own, composed, quite obviously, in substantial measure from received materials and in accord with received conventions, but, in all and in essence, a singular, autonomous, and, by its nature, unprecedented statement: a system.

Were we therefore to enter into conversation with the penultimate and ultimate authorship of the Bavli, the first thing we should want to know is simple: What have you made up? And what have you simply repeated out of a long continuing heritage of formulation and transmission? And why should we believe you? The authorship then would be hard put to demonstrate in detail that its fundamental work of literary selection and ordering, its basic choices on sustained and logical discourse, its essential statement upon the topics it has selected – that anything important in their document derives from long generations past.

Should they say, "Look at the treatment of the Mishnah," we should answer, "But did you continue the Yerushalmi's program or did you make up your own?" And in the total candor we rightly impute to that remarkable authorship, the Bavli's compositors would say, "It is our own – demonstrably so."

And if we were to say, "To what completed documents have you resorted for a ready-made program?" our *soi-disant* traditionalists would direct our attention to Tosefta, their obvious (and sole) candidate. And, if they were to do so, we should open the Tosefta's treatment of, or counterpart to, a given chapter of the Mishnah and look in vain for a systematic, orderly, and encompassing discourse, dictated by the order and plan of the Tosefta, out of which our authorship has composed a sizable and sustained statement.

True, we readily recognize that the Tosefta's materials play their role. But seeing the Tosefta in its terms, noting how slight a portion of a given Tosefta chapter the Mishnah's authorship has found accessible and urgent, we should dismiss out of hand any claim that the Bavli's fundamental structure and plan encompasses systematic and orderly exposition of the Tosefta's structure and plan for a given Mishnah chapter. The opposite is the case. Tosefta makes its contribution unsystematically and episodically, where and when the authorship of the Bavli, for its reasons (not always obvious to us) has permitted the Tosefta to do so. That is hardly the mark of traditionality, subservience to a received text, such as the counterpart treatment of the Mishnah by the Bavli's authorship – a treatment that is orderly, routine, complete, and systematic – indicates.

And when, finally, we ask our authorship to state its policy in regard to Scripture and inquire whether or not a sustained and ongoing tradition of exegesis of Scripture has framed discourse, the reply will prove quite simple. "We looked for what we wanted to seek, and we found it."

These four loci at which boundaries may have merged, and intersections turned into commonalities, therefore mark walled and sealed borders. A received heritage of sayings and stories may have joined our authorship to its teachers and their teachers – but not to that larger community of sustained learning that stands behind the entirety of the writings received as authoritative, or even a sizable proportion of those writings. The presence, in the ultimate statement of the Bavli, of sayings imputed to prior figures – back to Scripture, back to Sinai – testifies only to the workings of a canon of taste and judgment to begin with defined and accepted as definitive by those who defined it: the authorship at hand itself. The availability, to our authorship, of a systematic exegesis of the same Mishnah chapter has not made self-evident to our authorship the work of continuation and completion of a prior approach. Quite to the contrary, we deal with an authorship of amazingly independent mind, working independently and in an essentially original way on materials on which others have handed on a quite persuasive and cogent statement. Tosefta on the one side, Scripture and a heritage of conventional reading thereof on the other – neither has defined the program of our document or determined the terms in which it would make its statement, though both, in a subordinated position and in a paltry limited measure, are given some sort of a say. The Bavli is connected to a variety of prior writings but continuous with none of them.

The Judaism of the Dual Torah knows not traditions to be recited and reviewed but merely sources, to be honored always but to be used only when pertinent to a quite independent program of thought. That is to say, to go over the first definition of tradition with which I commenced, the components of the Torah of that Judaism do not contribute equally and jointly to a single comprehensive statement, handed on from generation to generation and from book to book, all of them sources forming a tradition that constitutes the Torah. Each has a particular message and make a distinctive statement. Obviously, all fit together into a common statement, the Torah or Judaism. That fundamental theological conviction defines Judaism and cannot – and should not – give way before the mere testimony of literary evidence. But it is the fact that whatever traits join the whole of the rabbinic corpus together into the single Torah of Moses our Rabbi, revealed by God to Moses at Sinai, they are not literary traits of tradition. In literary terms, the various rabbinic documents commonly (and, from a theological perspective, quite correctly) are commonly represented as not merely autonomous and individual statements, or even connected here and there through shared passages, but in fact as continuous and interrelated developments, one out of its predecessor, in a long line of canonical writings (to Sinai). The Talmud of Babylonia, or Bavli, takes pride of place – in this picture of "the rabbinic tradition" – as the final and complete statement of that incremental, linear tradition, and so is ubiquitously described as "the tradition," par excellence. Vis-à-vis its sources, the Bavli represents an essentially autonomous, fresh, and original statement of its own. Its authorship does not take over, rework, and repeat what it has received out of prior writings but makes its own statement, on its own program, in its own terms, and for its own purposes.

Part One
THE LANGUAGES OF THE BAVLI

1

What We Learn from the Bavli's Multilingual Character

The Babylonian Talmud follows a single set of rules on the choice of languages that must serve in saying what the writers wish to say. In this way, the authors of the document carefully delineate their sources from themselves. The importance of separating one's own statements from those of one's predecessors is a mark of not the traditional but the systemic; the traditionalist looks for authority in received writings, the system builder seeks reliable information. The careful boundaries drawn between the writer and received authority characteristic of the rabbinic writers is defined by William Scott Green in these words, "In rabbinic Judaism the writing and discourse of scripture had to be inherently separable from, and could be neither merged nor confused with, the commentary upon them....The rabbinic tendency to identify antecedent materials is not limited to scripture....The adjectives 'allusive' and 'intertextual' are analytically useless for a critical description of rabbinic hermeneutics....Rabbinic literature displays its sources."[1]

Not only by routinely and ubiquitously using such language as "as it is said," or "as it is written," did the authorities of the Talmud of Babylonia separate their statements from those of Scripture. Also by their choice of the very language in which they would express what they wished to say on their own account they differentiated themselves from their antecedents. When it came to citations from prior, nonscriptural authorities, they used one formation of the Hebrew language, specifically, Middle, or Mishnaic, Hebrew; when it came to the conduct

---

[1]See his "Writing with Scripture: The Rabbinic Uses of the Hebrew Bible," in Jacob Neusner with William Scott Green, *Writing with Scripture. The Authority and Uses of the Hebrew Bible in the Torah of Formative Judaism* (Minneapolis, 1989: Fortress Press), p. 17.

of their own analytical process, they used one formation of the Aramaic language, Eastern or Talmudic Aramaic. They never alluded to authoritative facts, they always cited them in so many words; but the indication of citation – in a writing in which the modern sigla of quotation marks and footnotes were simply unavailable – came to expression in the choice of language. Green's rejection of "allusive" and "intertextual" as adjectives for the characterization of rabbinic hermeneutics is here enriched by the demonstration that the Talmud of Babylonia not only was not intertextual, but was, as we shall see, uniformly and wholly intratextual.

In point of fact, the Talmud of Babylonia or Bavli is in one language, not two, and that language is Aramaic. The infrastructure of the document, its entire repertoire of editorial conventions and sigla, are in Aramaic. When a saying is assigned to a named authority, the saying may be in Hebrew or in Aramaic, and the same named authority may be given sayings in both languages – even within the same sentence. But the editorial and conceptual infrastructure of the document comes to expression only in Aramaic, and when no name is attached to a statement, that statement is always in Aramaic, unless it forms part of a larger, autonomous Hebrew composition, cited by, or parachuted down into, "the Talmud." Rightly have the Talmudic masters in the Yeshiva world hypostatized the Talmud in such language as, "the Gemara says...," because the Talmud speaks in a single voice, forms a unitary discourse, beginning, middle, and end, and constitutes one wholly coherent and cogent document, everywhere asking questions drawn from a single determinate and limited repertoire of intellectual initiatives – and always framing those questions, pursuing those inquiries, in Aramaic.

And yet, as everybody knows, the Talmud also is full of Hebrew. So we must ask where and why framers of this writing utilize the Hebrew language, and when we may expect to find that they speak – rather, "the Talmud speaks" – in Aramaic. Specifically, what signal is given, what purpose is served by the bi- or multilingualism of the Talmud what do we know without further ado, when we are given a composition or a component of a composition in Hebrew, and what is the implicit meaning of making a statement in Aramaic? The answer is that the choice of language signals a taxonomic meaning, and in this monograph I show how language serves as a medium for the classification of discourse, hence, *language as taxonomy*. In a writing that utilizes two languages,[2] the choice of one over the other conformed to rules of

---

[2]Really, four, biblical and Middle or Mishnaic Hebrew, Eastern Aramaic in the Talmud of Babylonia, Palestinian Aramaic in the Talmud of the Land of

communication and marked what was said as one type of statement rather than another. If we know which language is used, we also know where we stand in the expression of thought, and the very language in which a statement is made therefore forms part of the method of thought and even the message of discourse of the document.

Specifically, two languages, Hebrew and Aramaic, serve a single piece of writing, the Talmud of Babylonia, a.k.a, the Bavli. Authors of compositions, framers of composites, and, it surely was assumed, those who would hear or read the document later on, all took for granted knowledge of both languages. The linguistic differences were not merely matters of word choice, for example, a Hebrew phrase or technical term introduced into an Aramaic sentence, or a Hebrew sentence of a legal, formulary character parachuted down into an Aramaic paragraph, though both phenomena prove common. Rather, one type of discussion, serving one purpose, would appear in Aramaic, and another, quite different type of statement, serving (in this context) a quite different purpose, would appear in Hebrew. The pattern is consistent throughout, which allows us, by simple observation and induction, to conclude that quite simple rules instructed the writer of a composition for the Talmud of Babylonia which language to use for a given purpose. Using Aramaic ordinarily signalled one type of writing, using Hebrew, another; Aramaic rarely, if ever, is used for the purpose served by Hebrew, and Hebrew, by Aramaic.

The rules at hand govern uniformly, without distinction on the location of a speaker or the "historical" position, earlier, middle, or later, in the unfolding of the writing. Therefore my insistence that we account for difference by appeal to rules of classification, rather than historical sequence ("biography") let alone authentic reproduction of things actually said ("ipsissima verba") will prove well justified. Since the same figures, assumed to have lived between ca. 200 and ca. 500, are quoted in

---

Israel. But in these pages I am interested only in gross taxonomic traits, hence merely "Hebrew" and "Aramaic." In point of fact, the preservation of citations of the Hebrew Scriptures in biblical Hebrew, rather than their translation into Aramaic, and the formulation of a given part of the document in Eastern rather than Palestinian Aramaic, such as was used in the Talmud of the Land of Israel, also represent important decisions on the part of writers. But my interest here is limited to the gross taxonomic function served by the principal language groups, rather than their subdivisions as well. A study of the relationship between the Talmud of the Land of Israel and the Talmud of Babylonia, particular of how the latter receives and reworks what it receives from the former, will pay attention to the two kinds of Aramaic that were available to our writers. That is not my problem here.

both Hebrew and Aramaic, "historical"[3] explanations ("Hebrew, early; Aramaic, late") by themselves turn out impertinent, irrelevant to the data.

Now let me explain what I mean by claiming that the choice of language serves a taxonomic purpose. A document that utilizes two or more languages but is addressed to a single audience conveys to its readers information not only through what is said but also through the language in which a message is set forth. In the Talmud of Babylonia the choice of language carried in particular a message, one of classification. A reader or listener[4] who read or heard Aramaic immediately knew what kind of discourse was under way, and when Hebrew was used, the reader or listener forthwith understood the status and purpose of the discourse that was then subject to representation. The selection of one language over another gave the signal that sayings, and, more to the point, whole paragraphs and even long and sustained passages, in one language were to be classified in one way, sayings or entire compositions in another, in a different way. And that taxonomic function served by the choice of language bore no relationship to the circumstance of time, place, personality, let alone the original words that were said; the same named speakers are given statements in two languages, depending upon the purpose served by a given statement within the unfolding of discourse.

---

[3]Such explanations really are not historical at all, since they take for granted that the authority to whom a saying is attributed really said what is assigned to him, and that unproven premise yields not history but merely a gullible paraphrase of the data themselves. One rather primitive conception of historical explanation claims that third-century figures commonly speak Hebrew, fifth, Aramaic. But we shall find third-century figures, Rab, Samuel, Judah, fluent in Aramaic as well as in Hebrew, and where fifth-century figures, Ashi, Rabina, Mar Zutra, wish to make a statement of a certain classification, they make it in Hebrew, not Aramaic. So if we are to believe that attributions tell us what a given historical figure really said at the time at which (we think) he lived, then the temporal distinctions proposed to account for language "preference" collapse of their own weight, and another type of distinction, one that does not appeal to rather dubious facts alleged in the form of attributions of sayings to named authorities, demands attention and sustained demonstration, such as I give here.

[4]The distinction is a valid one but forms no part of the argument of this chapter. It is clear that a great many things were memorized within the process of formulating and transmitting the Bavli; it is equally clear that, at a given point, things were written down. I am not sure where or why what was formulated orally was written down. My impression is that the document was written down very early in the process of its composition, and that people who formulated composites drew upon materials that came to them through the memories of official memorizers. But that problem of the literary history of the Bavli is not under study in these pages.

In the Talmud of Babylonia what is said in Hebrew is represented as authoritative and formulates a normative thought or rule. What is said in Aramaic is analytical and commonly signals an argument and formulates a process of inquiry and criticism. That is how language serves a taxonomic purpose: Hebrew is the language of the result, Aramaic, of the way by which the result is achieved; Hebrew is the formulation of the decision, Aramaic, of the work of deliberation. Each language serves to classify what is said in that language, and we always know where we stand, in a given process of thought and the exposition of thought, by reference to the language that is used at that particular place in the sustained discourse to which we are witness. That fixed rule, utilizing language for the purpose of classifying what is said in that language, characterizes only one document in the canon of Judaism, and that is, the Talmud.[5] All other canonical documents are monolingual, ordinarily in Hebrew,[6] so that, where Aramaic occurs, it is generally a brief allusion to something deemed external to what the author wishes to say in his own behalf, for example, a citation of everyday speech, invariably assumed to be in Aramaic.

Now to make the matter quite concrete: the Talmud of Babylonia contains passages written in two kinds of Hebrew, biblical and Mishnaic (or Middle), and also Aramaic of various classifications. When someone sat down to produce a composition for inclusion in that document, how did he know which language to use? If that writer had received from earlier generations a piece of writing, such as the Hebrew Scriptures ("Old Testament," "Written Torah") or the Mishnah, or a teaching formulated in the name of a prior authority or school, what rules told that writer which language to use for what purpose? When I speak of "a language," I mean not word choice or fixed formulations that may flow from one language to another, for example, an Aramaism in a Hebrew sentence or a Hebrew formula in an Aramaic one. By language I mean the governing framework in which words and sentences find cogency and make sense: convey meaning. "Language" – Hebrew or Aramaic – here refers to the basic sentences and paragraphs in which a whole

---

[5]I refer of course to the Talmud of Babylonia, but the same utilization of language for classification can be shown to characterize the Talmud of the Land of Israel; but that forms a separate arena for inquiry and has to be dealt with in its own terms. I have not done that work.

[6]Obviously within the canon of the Judaism of the Dual Torah some of the translations of the Hebrew Scriptures into Aramaic, or Targumim, are canonical; others are not. The standing of other Aramaic writings, such as Sefer Harazim or Megillat Taanit, remains to be worked out. But if they are canonical within the Judaism of the Dual Torah, then they too are monolingual. That fact makes all the more striking the bilingual character of the Bavli (and Yerushalmi).

thought is expressed. These invariably obey the rules of syntax and grammar, follow the rhetorical rules, of one language and not some other. If Aramaic is the paramount language, then even though Hebrew occurs, it will always bear marks that it is being quoted for a purpose dictated by the discourse that is in Aramaic: Hebrew will be illustrative, Aramaic, determinative. If the language of a passage is Hebrew, then the occurrence of an Aramaic phrase, for example, a sentence that is represented as a quotation of what someone says in everyday parlance, will not affect the grammar and syntax (not to mention the word choices) of the whole. Ordinarily, therefore, the smallest rhetorical signals will wholly conform to the conventions of one language, and when the other language occurs, it is by way of quotation, on the one side, or utilization of technical terms, on the other. For example, a sentence wholly written in Aramaic may quote a verse of Scripture in biblical Hebrew, or a sentence of the Mishnah in Middle Hebrew. But the structure of that sentence will be in Aramaic. That is not an example of bi- or multilingual writing at all, any more than using *terminus technicus,* rather than technical term, would have made the penultimate sentence a mixture of Latin and American. It is a sentence in American, using a Latin word.

There are very few mysteries, as a matter of fact, in the ways in which discourse is advanced through the choice of one or another of the languages that come into play here. Where we find Hebrew, the language of quotation, it will commonly signal one of three facts, which, through the very choice of language, our author wishes to tell us:

1. A passage is from the Hebrew Scriptures.
2. A passage is from the Mishnah or the Tosefta (or from a corpus of sayings out of which the Tosefta as we have it was selected; for our purposes that is a distinction that makes no difference).
3. A statement is authoritative and forms a normative formulation, a rule to be generalized and obeyed even where not from the Mishnah or Scripture, but from a named or anonymous authority of the time of the document itself.

While biblical Hebrew differs from Middle or Mishnaic Hebrew, the use, in the Bavli, of either kind of Hebrew invariably is the same. It is to set forth a normative statement. The fact that sayings of sages will be (re)formulated into the same Hebrew as the Mishnah's conveys the further claim, of course, that those sayings enjoy the same standing and authority as what is in Scripture or the Mishnah, and that allegation clearly is signaled by the choice of Hebrew for, for example, something said by Samuel, Rab, or Yohanan. That the issue is one of authority and standing of what is said is furthermore demonstrated by a rhetorical

signal, which assigns to the authority of a professional memorizer of
traditions, or Tannaite master, a given formulation. Whenever we find
that signal in any of its variations, all of them formed out of the same
Hebrew letters, T and N, with a Y or an A (aleph), *what follows invariably
is in (Middle) Hebrew.*

And that is the fact, whether the authority to whom the saying then
is assigned is a figure known, also, in the pages of the Mishnah, or a
named figure who flourished long after the closure of the Mishnah, such
as Rab, Samuel, or Yohanan. As a matter of fact, authorities of our
document generally supposed to have flourished fairly late in the
formative history of the writing, such as Ashi or Kahana, will not
uncommonly instruct the Tannaite colleague of their own time and place
to formulate matters in one way rather than in some other, and when
that is done, what follows, once more, always is marked TNY and always
is in Middle Hebrew. The upshot is that Hebrew is used to signal that a
thought forms a normative statement.

These remarks have now to be made concrete, and, for that purpose,
I give three samples of how a single passage conforms to the simple rules
that I have announced. The Mishnah paragraph is given in boldface
type, Aramaic in italics, Hebrew in regular type. And the rest follows.
The first is the simplest. The point of the composition, towards which
the author is aiming, is in Aramaic. The sustaining voice, asking,
answering, probing, speaks in Aramaic. The facts that are under
discussion are in Hebrew; these facts are identified as to source, for
example, Mishnah, Tosefta, Scripture, being set off, as Green insists, from
the document's authors' utilization of them; our authors do not allude to
a shared corpus of facts or truths, though they obviously take for granted
the omnipresence of such a corpus; they explicitly and articulately cite
items out of that corpus, and, as we shall now see, when they shift
language, it serves the purpose of quotation marks or footnotes (media
for signification not available to the authors who either formulated and
transmitted their composition or composite orally, or who wrote things
down, or who found some intermediary medium for the fixed
preservation of their thought, and the distinctions make no difference so
far as the taxonomic power of language is concerned). My example
derives from Bavli Bekhorot 4:1-2:

IV.1   A   **[If] a blemish appeared in it during its first year, it is permitted to
           keep it for the whole twelve months. [If a blemish appeared in it]
           after its first year, it is permitted to keep it only for thirty days:**
       B   *The question was raised: What is the sense of this passage? When it says,*
           **[If] a blemish appeared in it during its first year, it is permitted to
           keep it for the whole twelve months,** *does it mean,* **and an
           additional thirty days as well? Or perhaps the sense is, [If] a**

blemish appeared in it during its first year, it is permitted to keep it for the whole twelve months – *but no longer, and* [If a blemish appeared in it] after its first year, it is permitted to keep it only for thirty days?

C. *Come and take note, for it has been taught on Tannaite authority:*

D. At this time [after the destruction of the Temple] a firstling, so long as it is not fit to show to a sage [that is, before there is a blemish on it, to be shown to the sage for a decision on whether it is transient or permanent], may be kept two or three years. Once it is fit to be shown to a sage, if a blemish appeared on it during the first year, he may keep it the entire twelve months. If it was after its first year, he is not allowed to keep it even a single day, even a single hour, but on grounds of restoring what is lost to the owner, rabbis have said that he is permitted to keep the animal for thirty days [T. Bekh. 3:2A-C].

E. *And still the question is to be raised: Does this mean,* thirty days after the first year, *or does it mean* thirty days before its first year is over?

F. *Come and take note:* If a blemish appeared on the beast on the fifteenth day within its first year, we complete it for fifteen days after its first year.

G. *That proves the matter.*

H. *It further supports the position of R. Eleazar, for R. Eleazar has said,* "They assign to the animal thirty days from the moment at which the blemish appeared on the beast."

I. *There are those who say,* said R. Eleazar, "How do we know in the case of a firstling that if a blemish appeared in its first year, we assign to it thirty days after its year? 'You shall eat it before the Lord your God year by year' (Deut. 15:20) [but not in the year in which its blemish has appeared]. Now what is the span of days that is reckoned as a year? You have to say it is thirty days."

J. *An objection was raised:* If a blemish appeared on the beast on the fifteenth day within its first year, we complete it for fifteen days after its first year. *That indicates, then, that we complete the thirty days, but we do not give it thirty full days after the first year, and that would appear to refute the position of R. Eleazar!*

K. *It does indeed refute his position.*

The reason the example of how the rule that I have defined does its work is blatant and – at this stage – merely formal. Where a received document is cited, here, the Mishnah, it is in Hebrew. The language of citation is in Aramaic, so A, B, C, D alternative within that fixed, formal rule. A poor framing of the rule that is implicit then is that we quote in Hebrew, but talk in Aramaic.

But of course recourse to such formalities hardly supplies the key. For the question is asked properly only when we inquire, what guidance do we gain – automatically and implicitly – when we find words framed in Aramaic, and what does the use of Hebrew tell us? The answer cannot concern only the pedantry involved in knowing what comes from where. Who (other than a mere scholar) would care? The document as a whole is a sustained labor of applied reason and practical logic; it makes important points not only discretely but through the formation of the whole. Its authorship over and over again pursues a single intellectual program, which means that, at every detail, the intellectuals who produced this remarkable document wished to make the same point(s), just as their predecessors did in the treatment of the myriad of details treated in the Mishnah.

In point of fact, the composition means to pursue a problem, which is formulated at B. And the operative language used in the formulation of the problem is Aramaic, pure and simple. We note at E that fixed formulas in Hebrew are preserved, but Hebrew is not the language of the sentence, any more than, in an American legal brief, the occurrence of a phrase or sentence in Latin signals that the author is writing in Latin; these are conventions of rhetoric or technical terms, nothing more. The continuity and coherence derive from what is said in Aramaic, and that is the case throughout. What we are given in Hebrew then are the facts, the received and established data. When Aramaic appears, it is the voice of the framer of the passage. Since, as a matter of fact, that voice is monotonous and ubiquitous, we realize that it is "the Talmud" that speaks Aramaic, or, in less mythic language, Aramaic is the language of the Talmud, and the use of Hebrew serves a purpose dictated by the document and bears significance within the norms of thought that the framers of the document have defined.

As I suggested in the setting of my first example, one may well argue that using Hebrew in citations of Scripture or the Mishnah or related materials is simply a medium for preserving what is cited in the original, not part of the system of signals that the authors at hand utilized for the purpose of communicating with their readers. Admittedly, since the rabbinic literature in general is highly differentiated, so that what derives from a received, canonical writing such as the Written Torah or Scripture is always differentiated from what is assigned to a later figure, for example, by saying "as it is written" or "as it is said," and what derives from the Mishnah likewise is marked off in a similarly intratextualist and profoundly anti-intertextualist manner, that is hardly a source of surprise. But Hebrew is used, the very same Hebrew of the Mishnah, when a statement is made that is not Mishnaic or derived from an associated source or authority. A master generally assumed to have lived in the fifth or sixth century will instruct the Tannaite memorizer of his household or school or court to state matters in one way rather than in some other. His instructions always will be presented in Hebrew: say "this," not "that," and both "this" and "that" are in Hebrew. The use of Hebrew therefore forms part of the conventional substrate of the document, conveying a claim and a meaning, and what it signals is not merely "quoting from the original source," though that is, as a matter of fact, part of the message of facticity, the classification of a statement as a datum, that the use of Hebrew is meant to convey.

What about Aramaic? That, too, signals not where or when a saying was formulated but the classification of the saying. Where we find Aramaic, the language of sustained discourse, of continuity, cogency, and coherence, it will commonly tell us, through the very choice of language:

1. A passage formulates an analytical or critical problem and is engaged in solving it.
2. A passage is particular and episodic, for example, commonly case reports about things decided in courts of the time of the document set forth in Aramaic, or stories about things authorities have done, told in Aramaic; these invariably are asked to exemplify a point beyond themselves.

These two purposes for which Aramaic is used on the surface do not entirely cohere. The first is abstract, the second, concrete; the first pursues a problem of theory and calls upon evidence in the service of the sustained process of applied reason and practical logic; the second signals the presence of thought that is singular and concrete. So if we find a passage in Aramaic, we may stand in two quite unrelated points in the unfolding re-presentation of thought.

But, in point of fact, the second way in which Aramaic may be used invariably finds its place within the framework of a discussion formulated as a sustained process of critical analysis, so the choice of Aramaic for what is episodic turns out not surprising, when we realize that the episode is presented specifically so as to be transformed from an anecdote into a medium of demonstration and proof. The case forms part of an argument; evidence flows into argument; and all argument then is in the same language, the Aramaic that forms the language of the document when the framers of the document speak for themselves and within the process of their own thought. When they shift to Hebrew, it will signal either the upshot of analysis, or *mutatis mutandis*, the precipitating occasion for analysis.

That, in the Talmud of Babylonia, language serves a taxonomic purpose, should not be taken for granted, since simply choosing a given language in a bi- or multilingual document does not invariably serve the purpose of classification. A variety of signals can be given through the use of one language, as against some other, in a bi- or multilingual writing. For instance, if everybody spoke Aramaic but an ancient text, in Hebrew, is cited, and then some figure from that same period is given further statements, the choice of the Hebrew of that early document may serve to endow with the authority of antiquity the statement given in that language. (That never happens in the Bavli, but it does happen, for example, in the Dead Sea Scrolls.) Along these same lines, the antiquity of a passage that utilizes a language no longer spoken; the authority of a passage that is written in a language different from the one that predominates; the different choices characteristic of authorities whose words are preserved at hand – all of these represent signals that may be conveyed by shifting from one to another language in writing addressed to a single set of readers or listeners.

The upshot is that if a document forms a conglomerate of diverse sources, originally written in a variety of languages, then the framer who utilizes passages chosen from those sources will tell us, by preserving the sources in their original language, not only that he assumes we can read and understand those other languages, but that he wants us to know that his writing is authentic to those sources. The range of possible interpretations for the use of more than a single language in a piece of writing hardly runs its course with these few proposals. I mean only to point out that the utilization of more than a single language in a piece of writing may bear a variety of messages, and that the possible conventions dictating the choice of language are many.

Among them, two stand out. One possibility of accounting for the presence of more than a single language directs our attention to the sources that have contributed to the writing. If these sources are in several languages, and if the author of our writing has chosen to preserve his sources in the original, then the multilingual character of his writing attests to the diversity of his sources and his theory of how he wanted his writing to be received. But then, we must ask ourselves, why has he used the Hebrew of his principal source when formulating the words of authorities who do not occur in that source, for example, figures of a clearly later period? The issue of preserving what was originally said in the language in which it was said cannot exhaust the repertoire of explanations. A second possibility of account for the use of more than a single language – not ruled out by the first – is that the use of more than a single language formed an integral part of the author's (or authors') medium for communicating their message. Sentences in one language then bore one set of meanings, those in another, a different set; or sentences in one language functioned in one way within the larger framework of discourse, those in another language then fulfilled a quite different function. And that other convention, it is clear, is the one that, in my view, dictated when one language would be used, when the other. One language in general would stand for fact, another, for analysis of fact. Using one language therefore established one frame of reference, the other, a different, and complementary frame of reference.

The reason that this second theory is not eliminated by the first is that a language used for the re-presentation of givens may well derive from a source that supplies those data. But the second theory does eliminate the first, since if rules intrinsic to the mode and intentionality of discourse govern, then these same rules will tell authors how all the materials that they use, whether early or late, are to be set forth: *which language*. And then any appeal to a long process of agglutination and conglomeration, in which the original words were preserved in the original language, will contradict the fact that, at any point in that allegedly long, historical process, precisely the same rules will have dictated precisely the same choices as to the use of one language or another. If the rules for choosing one language for one purpose and another for a different purpose prove to emerge from an inductive study, then, we shall find it difficult to concur that, over a long period, a great variety of writers found themselves bound to these same rules in the formulation of their thoughts into words to be preserved and handed on. The difficulty will derive from the particularity of the rules to the document that yields them: this writing follows these rules, and no other (extant) writing follows those same rules. On the face of it that fact will point away from the first, and toward the second, possibility just now set forth.[7]

The upshot is that the linguistic traits of the Bavli demonstrate a pervasive unity and uniformity of discourse. We see the recurrence of a few fixed forms and formulas, a few rules govern throughout, and, over all, the rather monotonous and even tedious character of the writing at hand attests to its authorship's adherence to a few rules characteristic of this writing and determinative of its traits, beginning to end. The document exhibits remarkable integrity; the limits of the document clearly are delineated, and when other documents are introduced in evidence, they, too, are marked in the manner in which, in this period and within the technical limitations operative then, people were able to cite or place in quotations or footnote materials borrowed from other sources. This is a writing that does not (merely) allude or hint at something found somewhere else, it articulately cites, it explicitly quotes. Within the limits of the Bavli, the document defines its own infrastructure in both rhetoric and logic.

---

[7]Theories that take at face value the veracity of attributions, assuming that a given authority really said what is assigned to him, and that we know exactly when he lived, rest on gullibility and need not be seriously entertained. But a taxonomic theory is required in any event, even within such theories, by the fact that Hebrew serves the same authority who speaks, also, in Aramaic, and hence we want to know how he knew which language to use, if he really said what he is supposed to have said.

What we see in the Bavli is that *context* – this setting, this specific, documentary discourse – in fact is determinative and probative of meaning. The linguistic rules that everywhere are followed will show us how carefully the authors of our document have distinguished between themselves and all other writings, that is, have presented a writing that is intra- and not intertextual at its foundations. That language choice follows rules shows us that the document at hand possesses integrity. That is in three definitive dimensions. First, the Bavli's discrete components follow a cogent outline and an intelligible principle of organization. Second, its discrete components conform, in their large aggregates, to a limited and discernible rhetorical plan. Third, the discrete components also contribute to the demonstration of propositions that recur through the document, indeed that the authorship of the document clearly wishes to make. And fourth, that means that the document takes priority over its details, and that the initial discourse of the document takes place within the documentary setting, viewed whole and within a broad perspective of balance, order, and proportion – there, and not solely, or primarily, within the smallest whole units of discourse of which the document is made up, of which the authorship has made use in proving its broader propositions. As I said at the outset, the framers of the Bavli invariably differentiate their own voice from the voices of those whom they introduce as sources of fact and evidence. Obviously, Scripture is invariably identified as such, and this is in two aspects. First of all, when a verse of Scripture is cited, it is labeled as such with the language of "as it is said...," or "as it is written," or with circumlocutions of various sorts. Second, Scripture's language is always distinct from that of the Mishnah and of the sages in general. So there is no possibility of describing the relationship of the document – the Bavli – and Scripture as "intertextual." It is to the contrary, intratextual: each document is preserved in all its autonomy. But the intratextuality of the Bavli emerges with still greater clarity in the care with which different languages are utilized for distinct purposes: citation of a source of facts in Mishnaic Hebrew, discussion of the facts for the purposes of proposition and argument in Aramaic. Since that is the case not merely in general but consistently throughout, the taxonomic power of language shows us how our authorship has wished carefully to preserve the distinctions between not only Scripture and the Bavli, but also the Mishnah and related authoritative materials of undisputed fact and the Bavli.

To conclude: what this fact proves is that the Talmud of Babylonia is an accessible document, a systematic piece of writing, not agglutinative but crafted. The fact is that its authors followed rules, which we can discern and employ in our reading of this writing. The rule of linguistic preference is that where Hebrew is used, it is ordinarily for the purpose of setting forth facts, deriving from authoritative writings, on the one side, or authoritative figures, on the other. Where Aramaic is used, it is ordinarily for the purpose of analyzing facts, though it may serve, also, to set forth cases that invariably are subordinated to the analytical task. The simple fact that in the pages of the Bavli the same figures "speak" in both Hebrew and Aramaic proves that at stake is not merely "how people said things," let alone *ipsissima verba*; if Yohanan in the Land of Israel or Samuel and Rab in Babylonia are sometimes represented as speaking in Hebrew and other times in Aramaic, the function served by using the two languages, respectively, must form the point of inquiry into how and why these languages are used where and when they make their appearance. The choice of language clearly conveys part of the message that the authorship means to set forth, signalling to the reader precisely what is happening at any given point. Along these same lines, a story, told in Aramaic, yields a formulation of a general rule or conclusion, presented in (Middle) Hebrew. Once more, the function of the language that is chosen, within the same sustained unit of thought, clearly is to make one thought in one way, another thought in a different way.

To revert to our starting point: one fundamental problem is whether a document of this kind derives from a long agglutinative process, as the sediment of the ages accumulates into a hard tradition, or whether heirs of diverse materials reshape and restate the whole in a single formulation of their own. What is at stake in solving that problem is knowledge of how foundation documents emerge: over time, through tradition, or all at once, through the intellection of some few persons working together in one specific context? If the former, then in the formative history of the writing, we trace what we may rightly call tradition – a historical study. If the later, then in the analytical deconstruction and reconstitution of the tradition the framers set before us a single cogent vision, formulated into words at some one moment, a system, whole and complete – a philosophical study. The uniformity of language rules strongly points to a systemic, not a traditional document. The Bavli forms a coherent document. We have now to ask, does it speak in a single voice?

Part Two
LITERATURES: THE BAVLI'S TYPES OF WRITING, THEIR PLAN AND PROGRAM

2

The Bavli's One Voice

The Talmud of Babylonia is a commentary to the Mishnah. Let me start by giving a simple example of what characterizes the initial phase of nearly every sustained composite of the Bavli: a commentary to the Mishnah. This is what I mean by Mishnah commentary:

Mishnah-Tractate Baba Qamma 3:1

A. He who leaves a jug in the public domain,

B. and someone else came along and stumbled on it and broke it –

C. [the one who broke it] is exempt.

D. And if [the one who broke it] was injured by it, the owner of the barrel is liable [to pay damages for] his injury.

I.1   A. *How come the framer of the passage refers, to begin with, to a jug but then concludes with reference to a* **barrel?** *And so, too, we have learned in another passage in the Mishnah:* **This one comes along with his barrel, and that one comes along with his beam – [if] the jar of this one was broken by the beam of that one, [the owner of the beam] is exempt.** *How come the framer of the passage refers, to begin with, to a* **barrel** *but then concludes with reference to a jug? And so, too, we have learned in the Mishnah:* **This one is coming along with his barrel of wine, and that one is coming along with his jug of honey – the jug of honey cracked, and this one poured out his wine and saved the honey in his jar – he has a claim only for his wages [M. B.Q. 10:4A-E].** *How come the framer of the passage refers, to begin with, to a* **barrel** *but then concludes with reference to a* **jug?**

B. Said R. Hisda, "Well, as a matter of fact, there really is no difference between a jar and a barrel.'

C. *So what is the practical difference between the usages?*

D. It has to do with buying and selling.

E. *How can we imagine such a case? If it is in a place in which a jug is not called a barrel, nor a barrel a jug, for in such a case, the two terms are kept distinct!*

F. *The distinction is required for a place in which most of the people call a jug a jug and a barrel a barrel, but some call a barrel a jug and some call a jug*

*a barrel. What might you then have supposed? That we follow the
majority usage? [27B] So we are informed that that is not the case, for in
disputes over monetary transactions, we do not follow the majority usage.*

All that we have here is an investigation of the linguistic properties
of the Mishnah paragraph that is cited. The framer of the anonymous
writing notes that a variety of other passages seem to vary word choices
in a somewhat odd way. The point of insistence – the document is
carefully drafted, the writers do not forget what they were talking about,
so when they change words in the middle of a stream of thought, it is
purposeful – constitutes an exegetical point, pure and simple.

We therefore have very good reason to suppose that the text as we
have it speaks about the limited context of the period of the actual
framing of the text's principal building blocks. These building blocks
give evidence of having been put together in a moment of deliberation,
in accordance with a plan of exposition, and in response to a finite
problem of logical analysis. The units of discourse in no way appear to
have taken shape slowly, over a long period of time, in a process
governed by the order in which sayings were framed, now and here,
then and there, later and anywhere else (so to speak). Before us is the
result of considered redaction, not protracted accretion; mindful
construction, not sedimentary accretion. And, as I stated at the outset,
the traits of the bulk of the Talmud of the Land of Israel may be
explained in one of only two ways. One way is this: the very heirs of the
Mishnah, in the opening generation, ca. C.E. 200-250, whether in the
Land of Israel or Babylonia, agreed upon conventions not merely of
speech and rhetorical formulation, but also of thought and modes of
analysis. They further imposed these conventions on all subsequent
generations, wherever they lived, whenever they did their work.
Accordingly, at the outset the decision was made to do the work
precisely in the way in which, four hundred years later – the same span
of time that separates us from the founding of New England, twice the
span of time that has passed since our country became an independent
nation! – the work turns out to have been done.

The alternative view is that, some time late in the formation of
diverse materials in response to the Mishnah (and to various other
considerations), some people got together and made a decision to rework
whatever was in hand into a single, stunningly cogent document, the
Talmud as we know it in the bulk of its units of discourse. Whether this
work took a day or a half-century, it was the work of sages who knew
precisely what they wished to do and who did it over and over again.
This second view is the one I take. The Talmud exhibits a viewpoint. It
is portrayed in what I have called "the Talmud's one voice." In claiming
that we deal not only with uniform rhetoric, but with a single cogent

viewpoint, we must take full account of the contrary claim of the Talmud's framers themselves. This claim they lay down through the constant citations of sayings in the names of specific authorities. It must follow that differentiation by chronology – the periods in which the several sages cited actually flourished – is possible. To be sure, the original purpose of citing named authorities was not to set forth chronological lines, but to establish the authority behind a given view of the law. But the history of viewpoints should be possible. True, if we could show, on the basis of evidence external to the Talmud itself, that the Talmud's own claim in attributing statements to specific people is subject to verification or falsification, such a history can be undertaken; but it will not lead us into a deeper understanding of the document before us, not at all. All it will tell us is what this one thought then, and what that one thought later on; the document before us has put these things together in its way, for its purposes, and knowing that Rabbi X really said what is assigned to him in no way tells us the something we otherwise do not know about that way and those purposes. In any case, the organizing principle of discourse (even in anthologies) never derives from the order in which authorities lived. And that is the main point. The logical requirements of the analysis at hand determine the limits of applied and practical reason framed by the sustained discourses of which the Talmud is composed.[1]

Let us now consider in detail the eleven tractates' proportions of types of composites, to see the foundation for these generalizations.

---

[1]Units of discourse organized not in accordance with the requirements of cogent and dialectical argument exhibit one of two qualities. (1) They present an anthology of sayings on a single topic, without reworking these sayings into a coherent argument. (2) They present a sequence of related, short-term statements, zigzagging from point to point without evidence of an overall plan or purpose: this, then that. Stories, tales, and fables, by contrast, do exhibit the traits of unity and purpose so striking in the generality of units of discourse devoted to analysis of law. So the point of differentiation is not subject matter – law as against lore. Rather, it is the literary and conceptual history of the unit of discourse at hand. Now it may well be the case that sayings not reworked into the structure of a larger argument really do derive from the authority to whom they are ascribed. But if the discrete opinions at hand then do not provide us with a logical and analytical proposition, they also do not give us much else that is very interesting. They constitute isolated data, lacking all pattern, making no clear point. The fact that Rabbi X held opinion A, while Rabbi Y maintained position Q, is without sense, unless A and Q together say more than they tell us separately. This they do not, as a review of the odd bits of opinion on what constitutes a danger to health will make amply clear.

TEMURAH	NUMBER	PERCENT
1. Exegesis of the Mishnah	58	75%
2. Exegesis of the Mishnah's Law	8	10%
3. Speculation and Abstract Thought on Law	8	10%
4. Scripture	3	4%
5. Free-standing Composites	Not calculated	
6. Miscellanies	0	0%
	77	

SUKKAH	NUMBER	PERCENT
1. Exegesis of the Mishnah	141	89%
2. Exegesis of the Mishnah's Law	8	5%
3. Speculation and Abstract Thought on Law	4	2%
4. Scripture	1	0%
5. Free-standing Composites	0	0%
6. Miscellanies	5	3%
	159	

KERITOT	NUMBER	PERCENT
1. Exegesis of the Mishnah	80	94%
2. Exegesis of the Mishnah's Law	4	4%
3. Speculation and Abstract Thought on Law	0	0%
4. Scripture	1	1%
5. Free-standing Composites	0	0%
6. Miscellanies	0	0%
	85	

ARAKHIN	NUMBER	PERCENT
1. Exegesis of the Mishnah	127	91%
2. Exegesis of the Mishnah's Law	8	6%
3. Speculation and Abstract Thought on Law	2	1.5%
4. Scripture	0	0%
5. Free-standing Composites	2	1.5%
6. Miscellanies	0	0%
	139	

The importance of the free-standing composites is not reflected by the count, since both items are enormous and the first of the two serves as the prologue to the tractate as a whole.

NIDDAH

		NUMBER	PERCENT
1.	Exegesis of the Mishnah	290	97%
2.	Exegesis of the Mishnah's Law	6	2%
3.	Speculation and Abstract Thought on Law	0	0%
4.	Scripture	0	0%
5.	Free-standing Composites	3	1%
6.	Miscellanies	0	0%
		299	

ABODAH ZARAH

		NUMBER	PERCENT
1.	Exegesis of the Mishnah	244	85%
2.	Exegesis of the Mishnah's Law	3	1%
3.	Speculation and Abstract Thought on Law	0	0%
4.	Scripture	28	10%
5.	Free-standing Composites	12	4%
6.	Miscellanies	0	0%
		287	

SOTAH

		NUMBER	PERCENT
1.	Exegesis of the Mishnah	193	91%
2.	Exegesis of the Mishnah's Law	0	0%
3.	Speculation and Abstract Thought on Law	0	0%
4.	Scripture	10	5%
5.	Free-standing Composites	8	4%
6.	Miscellanies	1	0.5%
		212	

BAVA MESIA

		NUMBER	PERCENT
1.	Exegesis of the Mishnah	334	86%
2.	Exegesis of the Mishnah's Law	42	11%
3.	Speculation and Abstract Thought on Law	0	0%
4.	Scripture	2	0.5%
5.	Free-standing Composites	10	3%
6.	Miscellanies	0	0%
		388	

BEKHOROT		NUMBER	PERCENT
1.	Exegesis of the Mishnah	281	98%
2.	Exegesis of the Mishnah's Law	2	1%
3.	Speculation and Abstract Thought on Law	0	0%
4.	Scripture	0	0%
5.	Free-standing Composites	2	1%
6.	Miscellanies	0	0%
		285	

BERAKHOT		NUMBER	PERCENT
1.	Exegesis of the Mishnah	330	59%
2.	Exegesis of the Mishnah's Law	3	0.5%
3.	Speculation and Abstract Thought on Law	0	0%
4.	Scripture	34	6%
5.	Free-standing Composites	187	34%
6.	Miscellanies	2	0.4%
		556	

SANHEDRIN		NUMBER	PERCENT
1.	Exegesis of the Mishnah	313	45%
2.	Exegesis of the Mishnah's Law	6	0.8%
3.	Speculation and Abstract Thought on Law	6	0.8%
4.	Scripture	163	23%
5.	Free-standing Composites	214	30%
6.	Miscellanies	0	0%
		702	

Seen in the aggregate, the proportions of the eleven tractates devoted solely to Mishnah exegesis average 83 percent. If we omit reference to the two clearly anomalous tractates, Berakhot and Sanhedrin, the proportion of Mishnah exegesis rises to 89.5 percent. If, then, we combine exegesis of the Mishnah and exegesis of the broader implications of the Mishnah's law – and in the process of classification, it was not always easy to keep these items apart in a consistent way – we see a still more striking result. More than 86 percent of the whole of our tractates is devoted to the exegesis of the Mishnah and the amplification of the implications of its law; without the anomalous tractates, the proportion is close to 94 to 95 percent.

We dismiss as a taxon that did not serve any useful purpose the one that was supposed to identify "speculation and abstract thought on law." As a matter of fact, nearly all speculative or abstract thought on law, measured by the number of composites devoted to that purpose, treats the Mishnah's concrete laws; nearly all speculation is precipitated by an inquiry into the premises of those laws. There is virtually no abstract thought on law that does not aim at the clarification of the Mishnah's laws in particular. That result is as stunning as the foregoing.

Composites devoted to Scripture, not the Mishnah, are calculated in two ways. In the first nine tractates, I counted each composite as one entry, just as, overall, I counted each composite devoted to the Mishnah as one entry. On the surface such a mode of counting understated the proportions of the anomalous tractates that are devoted to Scripture exegesis, or to topics drawn from Scripture. Overall, we should expect to find something on the order of 4 percent of a given tractate made up of Scripture composites. If we eliminate the two anomalous tractates, the anticipated proportion would be 2 percent. Free-standing composites, formed in general around themes, rather than passages of the Mishnah or sequences of verses of Scripture or topics provided by Scripture, average 10 percent for eight tractates (omitted: Temurah, Sukkah, Keritot, where I found none), and, without the anomalous ones, 1.5 to 3 percent. The latter figure seems to me more probable than the former.

It is now the fact that the Talmud speaks through one voice, that voice of logic that with vast assurance reaches into our own minds and by asking the logical and urgent next question tells us what we should be thinking. Fixing our attention upon the Mishnah, the Talmud's rhetoric seduces us into joining its analytical inquiry, always raising precisely the question that should trouble us (and that would trouble us if we knew all of the pertinent details as well as the Talmud does). As I have now demonstrated beyond a shadow of a doubt, the Bavli speaks about the Mishnah in essentially a single voice, about fundamentally few things. Its mode of speech as much as of thought is uniform throughout. Diverse topics produce slight differentiation in modes of analysis. The same sorts of questions phrased in the same rhetoric – a moving, or dialectical, argument, composed of questions and answers – turn out to pertain equally well to every subject and problem. The Talmud's discourse forms a closed system, in which people say the same thing about everything. The fact that the Talmud speaks in a single voice supplies striking evidence [1] that the Talmud does speak in particular for the age in which its units of discourse took shape, and [2] that that work was done toward the end of that long period of Mishnah reception that began at the end of the second century and came to an end at the conclusion of the sixth century.

The ubiquitous character of this single and continuous voice of the Talmud argues for one of two points of origin. First, powerful and prevailing conventions may have been formed in the earliest stages of the reception and study of the Mishnah, then carried on thereafter without variation or revision. Or, second, the framing of sayings into uniform and large-scale constructions of discourse – composites – may have been accomplished only toward the end of the period marked by the formation of the Talmud's units of discourse and their conglomeration into the Talmud as we know it. In the former case, we posit that the mode of reasoned analysis of the Mishnah and the repertoire of issues to be addressed to any passage of the Mishnah were defined early on, then persisted for four or five hundred years – the span of time that separates us from Columbus. The consequent, conventional mode of speech yielded that nearly total uniformity of discourse characteristic of numerous units of discourse of the Talmud at which the interpretation of a law of the Mishnah is subject to discussion. In the latter case we surmise that a vast corpus of sayings, some by themselves, some parts of larger conglomerates, was inherited at some point toward the end of the two hundred years under discussion. This corpus of miscellanies was then subjected to intense consideration as a whole, shaped and reworded into the single, cogent and rhetorically consistent Talmudic discourse before us.

As between these two possibilities, the sustained and relentless inquiry I have shown to characterize the Bavli's rules of discourse set forth in the works listed above makes the latter by far the more likely. The reason is simple. I cannot find among the units of discourse in the Talmud evidence of differentiation among the generations of names or schools. There is no interest, for instance, in the chronological sequence in which sayings took shape and in which discussions may be supposed to have been carried on. That is to say, the Talmudic unit of discourse approaches the explanation of a passage of the Mishnah without systematic attention to the layers in which ideas were set forth, the schools among which discussion must have been divided, the sequence in which statements about a Mishnah law were made. That fact points to formation at the end, not agglutination in successive layers of intellectual sediment. In a given unit of discourse, the focus, the organizing principle, the generative interest – these are defined solely by the issue at hand. The argument moves from point to point, directed by the inner logic of argument itself. A single plane of discourse is established. All things are leveled out, so that the line of logic runs straight and true. Accordingly, a single conception of the framing and formation of the unit of discourse stands prior to the spelling out of issues. More fundamental still, what people in general wanted was not to create topical anthologies – to put together instances of what this one said about that issue – but to exhibit the logic of that issue, viewed under the aspect of eternity. Under sustained inquiry we always find a theoretical issue, freed of all temporal considerations and the contingencies of politics and circumstance.

Once these elemental literary facts make their full impression, everything else falls into place as well. Arguments did not unfold over a long period of time, as one generation made its points, to be followed by the additions and revisions of another generation, in a process of gradual increment and agglutination running on for two hundred years. That theory of the formation of literature cannot account for the unity, stunning force and dynamism, of the Talmud's dialectical arguments. To the contrary, someone (or small group) at the end determined to reconstruct, so as to expose, the naked logic of a problem. For this purpose, oftentimes, it was found useful to cite sayings or positions in hand from earlier times. But these inherited materials underwent a process of reshaping, and, more aptly, refocusing. Whatever the original words – and we need not doubt that at times we have them – the point of everything in hand was defined and determined by the people who made it all up at the end. The whole shows a plan and program. Theirs are the minds behind the whole. In the nature of things, they did their work at the end, not at the outset. There are two possibilities. The first is that our document emerges out of a gradual increment of a sedimentary process. Or it emerges as the creation of single-minded geniuses of applied logic and sustained analytical inquiry. But there is no intermediate possibility.[2]

It follows that the whole is the work of the one who decided to make up the discussion on the atemporal logic of the point at issue. Otherwise the discussion would be not continuous but disjointed, full of seams and margins, marks of the existence of prior conglomerations of materials that have now been sewn together. What we have are not patchwork quilts, but woven fabric. Along these same lines, we may find discussions in which opinions of Palestinians, such as Yohanan and Simeon b. Laqish, will be joined together side by side with opinions of Babylonians, such as Rab and Samuel. The whole, once again, will unfold in a smooth way, so that the issues at hand define the sole focus

---

[2]One qualification is required. I do not mean to say that the principles of chronology were wholly ignored. Rather, they simply were not determinative of the structure of argument. So I do not suggest that the framers of the Talmud would likely have an early authority argue with a later one about what is assigned only to the later one. That I cannot and do not expect to instantiate. I do not think we shall find such slovenly work in the Talmud. These sages were painstaking and sensible. But no attention ever is devoted in particular to the temporal sequence in which various things are said. Everything is worked together into a single, temporally seamless discourse. Discussion will always focus upon the logical point at hand. The sequence of authorities is not temporal but logical: which problem has to be addressed first, and which is logically next in sequence.

of discourse.   The logic of those issues will be fully exposed. Considerations of the origin of a saying in one country or the other will play no role whatsoever in the rhetoric or literary forms of argument. There will be no possibility of differentiation among opinions on the basis of where, when, by whom, or how they are formulated, only on the basis of what, in fact, is said. The upshot is that we may fairly ask about the message of the method of those who followed this one and single, prevailing method: a fixed set of rules on choice of language, a fixed repertoire of problems, a fixed received text governing the whole – the Bavli as we have it.

On the page of the Bavli, the role of individuals is both ubiquitous – numerous statements are joined to specific names – and also unimportant.[3]   The paramount voice is that of "the Talmud."   The rhetoric of the Talmud may be described very simply: a preference for questions and answers, a willingness then to test the answers and to expand through secondary and tertiary amplification, achieved through further questions and answers. The whole gives the appearance of the script for a conversation to be reconstructed, or an argument of logical possibilities to be reenacted, in one's own mind. In this setting we of course shall be struck by the uniformity of the rhetoric, even though we need not make much of the close patterning of language. The voice of "the Talmud," moreover, authoritatively defines the mode of analysis. The inquiry is consistent and predictable; one argument differs from another not in supposition but only in detail.   When individuals' positions occur, it is because what they have to say serves the purposes of "the Talmud" and its uniform inquiry. The inquiry is into the logic and the rational potentialities of a passage. To these dimensions of thought, the details of place, time, and even of an individual's

---

[3]To be sure one has to ask about the role of individuals. Many maintain that sayings assigned to particular names circulated for a long time and only at the very end of a process of transmission were they given their place in a conglomerate or composite. This is a principal fact that leads them to see the document as a compilation and not a composition. While named authorities and sayings assigned to them do occur, the dialectic of argument is conducted outside the contributions of the specified sages. Sages' statements serve the purposes of the anonymous voice, rather than defining and governing the flow of argument. So the anonymous voice, "the Talmud," predominates even when individuals' sayings are utilized. Selecting and arranging whatever was in hand is the work of one hand, one voice.   The materials are organized so as to facilitate explanations of the law's inner structure and potentiality, not to present a mere repertoire of ideas and opinions of interest for their own sake. The upshot is a sustained argument, not an anthology of relevant sayings. Such a cogent and ongoing argument is more likely the work of a single mind than of a committee, let alone of writers who lived over a period of ten or fifteen decades.

philosophy, are secondary. All details are turned toward a common core of discourse. This, I maintain, is possible only because the document as whole takes shape in accord with an overriding program of inquiry and comes to expression in conformity with a single plan of rhetorical expression. To state the proposition simply: it did not just *grow*, but rather, someone *made* it up.

The Talmudic argument is not indifferent to the chronology of authorities. But the sequence in which things may be supposed to have been said – an early-third century figure's saying before a later fourth-century figure's saying – in no way explains the construction of protracted dialectical arguments. The argument as a whole, its direction and purpose, always govern the selection, formation, and ordering of the parts of the argument and their relationships to one another. The dialectic is determinative. Chronology, if never violated, is always subordinated. Once that fact is clear, it will become further apparent that "arguments" – analytical units of discourse – took shape at the end, with the whole in mind, as part of a plan and a program. That is to say, the components of the argument, even when associated with the names of specific authorities who lived at different times, were not added piece by piece, in order of historical appearance. They were put together whole and complete, all at one time, when the dialectical discourse was made up. By examining a few units of discourse, we shall clearly see the unimportance of the sequence in which people lived, hence of the order in which sayings (presumably) became available. The upshot is that chronological sequence, while not likely to be ignored, never determines the layout of a unit of discourse. We can never definitively settle the issue of whether a unit of discourse came into being through a long process of accumulation and agglutination, or was shaped at one point – then, at the end of the time in which named authorities flourished – with everything in hand and a particular purpose in mind. But the more likely of the two possibilities is clearly the latter. It seems to me likely that the purposes of dialectical argument determined not only which available sayings were selected for inclusion, but also the order and purpose in accordance with which sayings were laid out.

It follows that the whole – the composites of discourse as we know them, the sequence of composites as we have them – was put together at the end. At that point everything was in hand, so available for arrangement in accordance with a principle other than chronology, and in a rhetoric common to all sayings. That other principle will then have determined the arrangement, drawing in its wake resort to a single monotonous voice: "the Talmud." The principle is logical exposition, that is to say, the analysis and dissection of a problem into its conceptual components. The dialectic of argument is framed not by considerations of the chronological sequence in which sayings were said but by attention to the requirements of reasonable exposition of the problem. That is what governs.

3

The Bavli's Miscellaneous Character: The Composition and the Composites

The Bavli not only presents a commentary to the Mishnah. It also contains ample secondary expansion of that commentary. But, as any student of the document quickly learns, the Bavli proceeds to move off in directions not indicated by the requirement of Mishnah commentary and amplification. Indeed, it is not seldom difficult to understand why the framers of the passage lay matters out as they do, since they seem to wander and to lose their way, forgetting whence they started or where they are going. However, as I shall now show in a very simple and graphic way, when we understand a technical problem that the framers of the Bavli confronted, we can fully explain the run-on, meandering, and occasionally even tedious character of their writing. It is the simple fact that the framers of the Bavli quite reasonably wished to annotate their statements, adding information important in context but not pertinent to the argument at hand. When we wish to do that kind of secondary expansion and explanation, we use footnotes to present one kind of information, appendices, another. Footnotes, specifically, provide sources, add brief, pertinent explanation; appendices present sizable free-standing statements, relevant to a given subject but not required in the context of the treatment of that subject. Now, as a matter of fact, the possibilities of footnotes and appendices did not exist in the time of the Bavli's composition. As a result, the framers of the document inserted into the text materials we should today treat as footnotes or appendices. But when we identify that type of addition and set it off from the main body of the text, the Bavli emerges as a quite cogent and economical statement, not at all run-on. In order to distinguish what is primary from what is secondary, I simply indent, and re-indent, what follows, and, when I do, readers immediately see how footnotes and appendices, set off from the text that conveys the message of a given statement, fit in to the larger flow of argument and analysis. In what follows I provide a protracted example of how a composition bears the burden of its own footnotes and appendices, therefore appearing to be more of a composite than it actually is.

Babylonian Tractate Abodah Zarah 1:1

A.   [2A] **Before the festivals of gentiles for three days it is forbidden to do business with them.**

B.   **(1) To lend anything to them or to borrow anything from them.**

C.   **(2) To lend money to them or to borrow money from them.**

D.   **(3) To repay them or to be repaid by them.**

E.   **R. Judah says, "They accept repayment from them, because it is distressing to him."**

F.   **They said to him, "Even though it is distressing to him now, he will be happy about it later."**

I.1   A.   [2A] Rab and Samuel [in dealing with the reading of the keyword of the Mishnah, translated festival, the letters of which are 'aleph daled, rather than 'ayin daled, which means, calamity]:

B.   *One repeated the formulation of the Mishnah as, "their festivals."*

C.   *And the other repeated the formulation of the Mishnah as "their calamities."*

D.   *The one who repeated the formulation of the Mishnah as "their festivals" made no mistake, and the one who repeated the formulation of the Mishnah as "their calamities" made no mistake.*

E.   *For it is written, "For the day of their calamity is at hand" (Deut. 32:15).*

F.   *The one who repeated the formulation of the Mishnah as "their festivals" made no mistake, for it is written, "Let them bring their testimonies that they may be justified" (Isa. 43:9).*

G.   *And as to the position of him who repeats the formulation of the Mishnah as "their festivals," on what account does he not repeat the formulation of the Mishnah to yield, "their calamities"?*

H.   *He will say to you, "'Calamity' is preferable [as the word choice when speaking of idolatry]."*

I.   *And as to the position of him who repeats the formulation of the Mishnah as "their calamities," on what account does he not repeat the formulation of the Mishnah to yield "their festivals"?*

J.   *He will say to you, "What causes the calamity that befalls them if not their testimony, so testimony is preferable!"*

K.   *And as to the verse, "Let them bring their testimonies that they may be justified" (Isa. 43:9), is this written with reference to gentiles? Lo, it is written in regard to Israel.*

L.   For said R. Joshua b. Levi, "All of the religious duties that Israelites carry out in this world come and give testimony in their behalf in the world to come: 'Let them bring their witnesses that they may be justified' (Isa. 43:9), that is, Israel; 'and let them hear and say, It is truth' (Isa. 43:9) – this refers to gentiles."

M   Rather, said R. Huna b. R. Joshua, "He who formulates the Mishnah to refer to their calamities derives the reading from this verse: 'They that fashion a graven image are all of them vanity, and their delectable things shall not profit, and their own witnesses see not nor know' (Isa. 44:9)."

The composite begins with a very long, but coherent, exposition of a single theme, which is, God's judgment of the nations. No. 2 holds together rather well, once we realize that it is heavily footnoted. I further indent the footnoted materials of that glossed composition.

I.2   A.   R. Hanina bar Pappa, and some say, R. Simlai, gave the following exposition [of the verse,"They that fashion a graven image are all of them vanity, and their delectable things shall not profit, and their own witnesses see not nor know" (Isa. 44:9)]: "In the age to come the Holy One, blessed be He, will bring a scroll of the Torah and hold it in his bosom and say, 'Let him who has kept himself busy with it come and take his reward.' Then all the gentiles will crowd together: 'All of the nations are gathered together' (Isa. 43:9). The Holy One, blessed be He, will say to them, 'Do not crowd together before me in a mob. But let each nation enter together with [2B] its scribes, 'and let the peoples be gathered together' (Isa. 43:9), and the word 'people' means 'kingdom': 'and one kingdom shall be stronger than the other' (Gen. 25:23)."

     B.   *But can there be a mob scene before the Holy One, blessed be He? Rather, it is so that from their perspective they not form a mob, so that they will be able to hear what he says to them.*

     C.   [Resuming the narrative of A:] "The kingdom of Rome comes in first."

     D.   *How come? Because they are the most important. How do we know on the basis of Scripture they are the most important? Because it is written,* "And he shall devour the whole earth and shall tread it down and break it into pieces" (Gen. 25:23), *and said R. Yohanan,* "This Rome is answerable, for its definition [of matters] has gone forth to the entire world [Mishcon: 'this refers to Rome, whose power is known to the whole world']."

     E.   *And how do we know that the one who is most important comes in first? It is in accord with that which R. Hisda said.*

     F.   For said R. Hisda, "When the king and the community [await judgment], the king enters in first for judgment: 'That he maintain the cause of his servant [Solomon] and [then] the cause of his people Israel' (1 Kgs. 8:59)."

     G.   *And how come? If you wish, I shall say it is not appropriate to keep the king sitting outside. And if you wish, I shall say that [the king is allowed to plea his case] before the anger of the Holy One is aroused."*

     H.   [Resuming the narrative of C:] "The Holy One, blessed be He, will say to them, 'How have you defined your chief occupation?'

I.   "They will say before him, 'Lord of the world, a vast number of marketplaces have we set up, a vast number of bathhouses we have made, a vast amount of silver and gold have we accumulated. And all of these things we have done only in behalf of Israel, so that they may define as their chief occupation the study of the Torah.'

J.   "The Holy One, blessed be He, will say to them, 'You complete idiots! Whatever you have done has been for your own convenience. You have set up a vast number of marketplaces to be sure, but that was so as to set up whorehouses in them. The bathhouses were for your own pleasure. Silver and gold belong to me anyhow: "Mine is the silver and mine is the gold, says the Lord of hosts" (Hag. 2:8). Are there any among you who have been telling of "this," and "this" is only the Torah: "And this is the Torah that Moses set before the children of Israel' (Deut. 4:44)." So they will make their exit, humiliated.

K.   "When the kingdom of Rome has made its exit, the kingdom of Persia enters afterward."

L.   *How come? Because they are second in importance. And how do we know it on the basis of Scripture? Because it is written, "And behold, another beast, a second, like a bear" (Dan. 7:5), and in this connection R. Joseph repeated as a Tannaite formulation, "This refers to the Persians, who eat and drink like a bear, are obese like a bear, are shaggy like a bear, and are restless like a bear."*

M.   "The Holy One, blessed be He, will say to them, 'How have you defined your chief occupation?'

N.   "They will say before him, 'Lord of the world, we have thrown up a vast number of bridges, we have conquered a vast number of towns, we have made a vast number of wars, and all of them we did only for Israel, so that they may define as their chief occupation the study of the Torah.'

O.   "The Holy One, blessed be He, will say to them, 'Whatever you have done has been for your own convenience. You have thrown up a vast number of bridges, to collect tolls, you have conquered a vast number of towns, to collect the corvée, and, as to making a vast number of wars, I am the one who makes wars: "The Lord is a man of war" (Ex. 19:17). Are there any among you who have been telling of "this," and "this" is only the Torah: "And this is the Torah that Moses set before the children of Israel" (Deut. 4:44).' So they will make their exit, humiliated.

P.   *But if the kingdom of Persia has seen that such a claim issued by the kingdom of Rome did no good whatsoever, how come they go in at all?*

Q.   *They will say to themselves, "These are the ones who destroyed the house of the sanctuary, but we are the ones who built it."*

R.   "And so it will go with each and every nation."

S.   *But if each one of them has seen that such a claim issued by the others did no good whatsoever, how come they go in at all?*

T.	*They will say to themselves, "Those two subjugated Israel, but we never subjugated Israel."*
U.	*And how come the two conquering nations are singled out as important and the others are not?*
V.	*It is because the rule of these will continue until the Messiah comes.*
W.	"They will say to him, 'Lord of the world, in point of fact, did you actually give it to us and we did not accept it?'"
X.	*But how can they present such an argument, since it is written,* "The Lord came from Sinai and rose from Seir to them, he shined forth from Mount Paran" (Deut. 33:2), *and further,* "God comes from Teman" (Hab. 3:3). *Now what in the world did he want in Seir, and what was he looking for in Paran?* Said R. Yohanan, "This teaches that the Holy One, blessed be He, made the rounds of each and every nation and language and none accepted it, until he came to Israel, and they accepted it."
Y.	*Rather, this is what they say,* "Did we accept it but then not carry it out?"
Z.	*But to this the rejoinder must be,* "Why did you not accept it anyhow!"
AA.	Rather, "this is what they say before him, 'Lord of the world, Did you hold a mountain over us like a cask and then we refused to accept it as you did to Israel, as it is written, "And they stood beneath the mountain" (Ex. 19:17).'"
BB.	And [in connection with the verse, "And they stood beneath the mountain" (Ex. 19:17),] said R. Dimi bar Hama, "This teaches that the Holy One, blessed be He, held the mountain over Israel like a cask and said to them, 'If you accept the Torah, well and good, and if not, then there is where your grave will be.'"
CC.	"Then the Holy One, blessed be He, will say to them, 'Let us make known what happened first: "Let them announce to us former things" (Isa. 43:9). As to the seven religious duties that you did accept, where have you actually carried them out?'"
DD.	*And how do we know on the basis of Scripture that they did not carry them out?* R. Joseph formulated as a Tannaite statement, "'He stands and shakes the earth, he sees and makes the nations tremble' (Hab. 3:6): what did he see? He saw the seven religious duties that the children of Noah accepted upon themselves as obligations but never actually carried them out. Since they did not carry out those obligations, he went and remitted their obligation."
EE.	*But then they benefited – so it pays to sin!*
FF.	Said Mar b. Rabina, [3A] "What this really proves is that even when they carry out those religious duties, they get no reward on that account."
GG.	*And they don't, don't they? But has it not been taught on Tannaite authority:* R. Meir would say, "How on the basis of Scripture do we know that, even if it is a gentile, if he goes and takes up the study of the Torah as his occupation, he

is equivalent to the high priest? Scripture states, 'You shall therefore keep my statues and my ordinances, which, if a human being does them, one shall gain life through them' (Lev. 18:5). What is written is not 'priests' or 'Levites' or 'Israelites,' but rather, 'a human being.' So you have learned the fact that, even if it is a gentile, if he goes and takes up the study of the Torah as his occupation, he is equivalent to the high priest."

HH. Rather, what you learn from this [DD] is that they will not receive that reward that is coming to those who are commanded to do them and who carry them out, but rather, the reward that they receive will be like that coming to the one who is not commanded to do them and who carries them out anyhow.

II. For said R. Hanina, "Greater is the one who is commanded and who carries out the religious obligations than the one who is not commanded but nonetheless carries out religious obligations."

JJ. [Reverting to AA:] "This is what the gentiles say before him, 'Lord of the world, Israel, who accepted it – where in the world have they actually carried it out?'

KK. "The Holy One, blessed be He, will say to them, 'I shall bear witness concerning them, that they have carried out the whole of the Torah!'

LL. "They will say before him, 'Lord of the world, is there a father who is permitted to give testimony concerning his son? For it is written, "Israel is my son, my firstborn" (Ex. 4:22).'

MM. "The Holy One, blessed be He, will say to them, 'The heaven and the earth will give testimony in their behalf that they have carried out the entirety of the Torah.'

NN. "They will say before him, 'Lord of the world, The heaven and earth have a selfish interest in the testimony that they give: 'If not for my covenant with day and with night, I should not have appointed the ordinances of heaven and earth' (Jer. 33:25).'"

OO. *For said R. Simeon b. Laqish, "What is the meaning of the verse of Scripture, 'And there was evening, and there was morning, the sixth day' (Gen. 1:31)? This teaches that the Holy One, blessed be He, made a stipulation with all of the works of creation, saying to them, 'If Israel accepts my Torah, well and good, but if not, I shall return you to chaos and void.' That is in line with what is written: 'You did cause sentence to be heard from heaven, the earth trembled and was still' (Ps. 76:9). If 'trembling' then where is the stillness, and if stillness, then where is the trembling? Rather, to begin with, trembling, but at the end, stillness."*

PP. [Reverting to MM-NN:] "The Holy One, blessed be He, will say to them, 'Some of them may well come and give testimony concerning Israel that they have observed the entirety of the Torah. Let Nimrod come and give testimony in behalf of

Abraham that he never worshipped idols. Let Laban come and give testimony in behalf of Jacob, that he never was suspect of thievery. Let the wife of Potiphar come and give testimony in behalf of Joseph, that he was never suspect of 'sin.' Let Nebuchadnezzar come and give testimony in behalf of Hananiah, Mishael, and Azariah, that they never bowed down to the idol. Let Darius come and give testimony in behalf of Daniel, that he did not neglect even the optional prayers. Let Bildad the Shuhite and Zophar the Naamatite and Eliphaz the Temanite and Elihu son of Barachel the Buzite come and testify in behalf of Israel that they have observed the entirety of the Torah: "Let the nations bring their own witnesses, that they may be justified" (Isa. 43:9).'

QQ. "They will say before him, 'Lord of the world, Give it to us to begin with, and let us carry it out.'

RR. "The Holy One, blessed be He, will say to them, 'World class idiots! He who took the trouble to prepare on the eve of the Sabbath [Friday] will eat on the Sabbath, but he who took no trouble on the even of the Sabbath – what in the world is he going to eat on the Sabbath! Still, [I'll give you another chance.] I have a rather simple religious duty, which is called "the tabernacle." Go and do that one.'"

SS. *But can you say any such thing? Lo, R. Joshua b. Levi has said, "What is the meaning of the verse of Scripture, 'The ordinances that I command you this day to do them' (Deut. 7:11)? Today is the day to do them, but not tomorrow; they are not to be done tomorrow; today is the day to do them, but not the day on which to receive a reward for doing them."*

TT. Rather, it is that the Holy One, blessed be He, does not exercise tyranny over his creatures.

UU. *And why does he refer to it as a simple religious duty? Because it does not involve enormous expense [to carry out that religious duty].*

VV. "Forthwith every one of them will take up the task and go and make a tabernacle on his roof. But then the Holy, One, blessed be He, will come and make the sun blaze over them as at the summer solstice, and every one of them will knock down his tabernacle and go his way: 'Let us break their bands asunder and cast away their cords from us' (Ps. 23:3)."

WW. But lo, you have just said, "it is that the Holy One, blessed be He, does not exercise tyranny over his creatures"!

XX. *It is because the Israelites, too – sometimes [3B] the summer solstice goes on to the festival of Tabernacles, and therefore they are bothered by the heat!*

YY. But has not Raba stated, "One who is bothered [by the heat] is exempt from the obligation of dwelling in the tabernacle"?

ZZ. *Granting that one may be exempt from the duty, is he going to go and tear the thing down?*

AAA. [Continuing from VV:] "Then the Holy One, blessed be He, goes into session and laughs at them: 'He who sits in heaven laughs' (Ps. 2:4)."

BBB. Said R. Isaac, "Laughter before the Holy One, blessed be He, takes place only on that day alone."

CCC. *There are those who repeat as a Tannaite version this statement of R. Isaac in respect to that which has been taught on Tannaite authority:*

DDD. R. Yosé says, "In the coming age gentiles will come and convert."

EEE. *But will they be accepted? Has it not been taught on Tannaite authority:* Converts will not be accepted in the days of the Messiah, just as they did not accept proselytes either in the time of David or in the time of Solomon?

FFF. Rather, "they will make themselves converts, and they will put on phylacteries on their heads and arms and fringes on their garments and a mezuzah on their doors. But when they witness the war of Gog and Magog, he will say to them, 'How come you have come?' They will say, '"Against the Lord and against his Messiah."' For so it is said, 'Why are the nations in an uproar and why do the peoples mutter in vain' (Ps. 2:1). Then each one of them will rid himself of his religious duty and go his way: 'Let us break their bands asunder' (Ps. 2:3). Then the Holy One, blessed be He, goes into session and laughs at them: 'He who sits in heaven laughs' (Ps. 2:4)."

GGG. Said R. Isaac, "Laughter before the Holy One, blessed be He, takes place only on that day alone."

HHH. But is this really so? And has not R. Judah said Rab said, "The day is made up of twelve hours. In the first three the Holy One, blessed be He, goes into session and engages in study of the Torah; in the second he goes into session and judges the entire world. When he realizes that the world is liable to annihilation, he arises from the throne of justice and takes up a seat on the throne of mercy. In the third period he goes into session and nourishes the whole world from the horned buffalo to the brood of vermin. During the fourth quarter he laughs [and plays] with leviathan: 'There is leviathan, whom you have formed to play with' (Ps. 104:26)." [This proves that God does laugh more than on that one day alone.]

III. Said R. Nahman bar Isaac, "With his creatures he laughs [everyday], but at his creatures he laughs only on that day alone."

I.3   A. Said R. Aha to R. Nahman bar Isaac, "From the day on which the house of the sanctuary was destroyed, the Holy One blessed be He has had no laughter.

      B. *"And how on the basis of Scripture do we know that he has had none? If we say that it is because it is written, 'And on that day did the Lord, the god of hosts, call to weeping and lamentation' (Isa. 22:12), that verse refers* to that day in particular. *Shall we then say that that fact derives from the verse, 'If I forget you, Jerusalem, let my right hand forget her cunning, let my tongue cleave to the roof of my mouth if I do not remember you'* (Ps. 137:5-6)? *That refers to forgetfulness, not laughter. Rather, the fact derives from this verse: 'I have long held my peace, I have been still, I have kept in, now I will cry'* (Isa. 42:14)."

I.4   A.   [Referring to the statement that during the fourth quarter he laughs [and plays] with leviathan,] *[nowadays] what does he do in the fourth quarter of the day?*

B.   He sits and teaches Torah to kindergarten students: "Whom shall one teach knowledge, and whom shall one make understand the message? Those who are weaned from the milk? (Isa. 28:19).

C.   *And to begin with [prior to the destruction of the Temple, which ended his spending his time playing with leviathan], who taught them?*

D.   *If you wish, I shall say it was Metatron, and if you wish, I shall say that he did both [but now does only one].*

E.   And at night what does he do?

F.   *If you wish, I shall say that it is the sort of thing he does by day;*

G.   *and if you wish, I shall say,* he rides his light cherub and floats through eighteen thousand worlds: "The chariots of God are myriads, even thousands and thousands [*shinan*] (Ps. 68:17). Read the letters translated as thousands, *shinan,* as though they were written, *she-enan,* meaning, that are not [thus: "the chariots are twice ten thousand less two thousand, eighteen thousand (Mishcon)].

H   *And if you wish, I shall say,* he sits and listens to the song of the Living Creatures [*hayyot*]: "By the day the Lord will command his loving kindness and in the night his song shall be with me" (Ps. 42:9).

If we regard the deeply indented materials as footnotes and appendices, attached for thematic reasons, then we can see Nos. 1-4 as an entirely coherent statement, a composite to be sure, but in no way a miscellany. Having examined that set and seen the clear connections between one composition and the next, on the one side, and the coherent character of the whole (with its footnotes and appendix), on the other, we are now ready to look at the miscellany that follows and to ask ourselves how each entry is linked to what is juxtaposed to it, fore and aft. If I had to find a rational explanation for putting No. 5 in at all, it is because it addresses the theme of study of Torah, to which No. 4 has made reference.

I.5   A   Said R. Levi, "Whoever stops studying the words of the Torah and instead takes up words of mere chatter they feed glowing coals of juniper: 'They pluck saltwort with wormwood and the roots of juniper are their food' (Job 30:4)."

      B   Said R. Simeon b. Laqish, "For whoever engages in study of the Torah by night – the Holy One, blessed be He, draws out the thread of grace by day: 'By day the Lord will command his loving kindness, and in the night his song shall be with me' (Ps. 42:9). Why is it that 'By day the Lord will command his loving kindness'? Because 'in the night his song shall be with me.'"

      C   *Some say,* said R. Simeon b. Laqish, "For whoever engages in study of the Torah in this world, which is like the night, the Holy One, blessed be He, draws out the thread of grace in the world to come, which is like the day: 'By day the Lord will command his loving kindness, and in the night his song shall be with me' (Ps. 42:9). [Supply: Why is it that 'By day the Lord will command his loving kindness'? Because 'in the night his song shall be with me.']"

The sustaining character of study of the Torah, No. 5, explains the relevance of the composition of No. 6.

I.6   A   Said R. Judah said Samuel, "*What is the meaning of the verse of Scripture,* 'And you make man as the fish of the sea and as the creeping things, that have no ruler over them' (Hab. 1:14)? Why are human beings compared to fish of the sea? To tell you, just as fish in the sea, when they come up on dry land, forthwith begin to die, so with human beings, when they take their leave of teachings of the Torah and religious deeds, forthwith they begin to die.

      B   "Another matter: Just as the fish of the sea, as soon as dried by the sun, die, so human beings, when struck by the sun, die."

      C   *If you want, this refers to this world, and if you want, this refers to the world to come.*

      D   *If you want, this refers to this world, in line with that which R. Hanina [said],* for said R. Hanina, "Everything is in the hands of Heaven except cold and heat: 'colds and heat boils are in the way of the froward, he who keeps his soul holds himself far from them' (Prov. 22:5)."

      E   *And if you want, this refers to the world to come, in accord with that which was stated by R. Simeon b. Laqish.* For said R. Simeon b. Laqish, "In the world to come, there is no Gehenna, but rather, the Holy One, blessed be He, brings the sun out of its sheath and he heats the wicked but heals the righteous through it. The wicked are brought to judgment by [4A] it': For behold, the day comes, it burns as a furnace, and all the proud and all who do wicked things shall be stubble, and the day that comes shall set them ablaze, says the Lord of hosts, that it shall leave them neither root nor branch' (Mal. 3:19).

F.	"'It shall leave them neither root' – in this world; 'nor branch' – in the world to come.
G.	"'But heals the righteous through it': 'But to you that fear my name shall the sun of righteousness arise with healing in its wings' (Mal. 3:20). They will revel in it: 'And you shall go forth and gambol as calves of the stall' (Mal. 3:20)."
H	[Continuing C, above:] "Another matter: just with as the fish of the sea, whoever is bigger than his fellow swallows his fellow, so in the case of human beings, were it not for fear of the government, whoever is bigger than his fellow would swallow his fellow."
I.	*That is in line with what we have learned in the Mishnah:* **R. Hananiah, Prefect of the Priests, says, "Pray for the welfare of the government. For if it were not for fear of it, one man would swallow his fellow alive" [M. Abot 3:2A-B].**

The foregoing has mentioned the theme of Gehenna and the world to come, and we shall now pursue that theme, now the contrast between Gehenna and the world to come, the gentiles and Israel, God's anger and God's grace. No. 7 contrasts the time of judgment and the time of God's war against his enemies; No. 8 then deals with the anger of God with the gentiles; Nos. 9, 10 with God's destruction.

I.7	A.	R. Hinena bar Pappa contrasted verses of Scripture: "It is written, 'As to the Almighty, we do not find him exercising plenteous power' (Job 37:23), but by contrast, 'Great is our Lord and of abundant power' (Ps. 147:5), and further, 'Your right hand, Lord, is glorious in power' (Ex. 15:6).
	B.	"But there is no contradiction between the first and second and third statements, for the former speaks of the time of judgment [when justice is tempered with mercy, so God does not do what he could] and the latter two statements refer to a time of war [of God against his enemies]."
I.8	A.	R. Hama bar Hanina contrasted verses of Scripture: "It is written, 'Fury is not in me' (Isa. 27:4) but also 'The Lord revenges and is furious' (Nah. 1:2).
	B.	*"But there is no contradiction between the first and second statements,* for the former speaks of Israel, the latter of the gentiles."
	C.	R. Hinena bar Pappa said, "'Fury is not in me' (Isa. 54:9), for I have already taken an oath: 'Would that I had not so vowed, then as the briars and thorns in flame would I with one step burn it altogether' (Isa. 54:9)."
I.9	A.	*That is in line with what R. Alexandri said,* "What is the meaning of the verse, 'And it shall come to pass on that day that I will seek to destroy all the nations' (Zech. 12:9) –
	B.	"'Seek' – seek permission from whom?
	C.	"Said the Holy One, blessed be He, 'I shall seek in the records that deal with them, to see whether there is a cause of merit, on

account of which I shall redeem them, but if not, I shall destroy them.'"

I.10   A   *That is in line with what Raba said, "What is the meaning of the verse, 'Howbeit he will not stretch out a hand for a ruinous neap though they cry in his destruction' (Job 30:24)?*

       B   "Said the Holy One, blessed be He, to Israel, 'When I judge Israel, I shall not judge them as I do the gentiles, for it is written, "I will overturn, overturn, overturn it" (Ezek. 21:32), rather, I shall exact punishment from them as a hen pecks.'

       C   "Another matter: 'Even if the Israelites do not carry out a religious duty before me more than a hen pecking at a rubbish heap, I shall join together [all the little pecks] into a great sum: "although they pick little they are saved" (Job 30:24) [following Mishcon's rendering].'

       D   "Another matter: 'As a reward for their crying out to me, I shall help them' (Job 30:24) [following Mishcon's rendering]."

The sequence of compositions on the same theme, God's judgment, this world and the world to come, suffering in this world so as to enjoy the world to come, Israel's suffering in this world and its enjoyment of the world to come, goes on through Nos. 11, 12, 13, 14. Then we shall have a set on God's anger. The movement is imperceptible, since No. 15 simply refers to God's anger in the context of judgment. But forthwith, at No. 16, we move into the theme of divine anger, and that sets us off in a slightly different direction from the one that we have followed up to now.

I.11   A   *That is in line with what R. Abba said, "What is the meaning of the verse, 'Though I would redeem them, yet they have spoken lies against me' (Hos. 7:23)? 'I said that I would redeem them through [inflicting a penalty] on their property in this world, so that they might have the merit of enjoying the world to come, "yet they have spoken lies against me" (Hos. 7:23).'"*

I.12   A   *That is in line with what R. Pappi in the name of Raba said, "What is the meaning of the verse, 'Though I have trained [and] strengthened their arms, yet they imagine mischief against me' (Hos. 7:15)?*

       B   "'Said the Holy One, blessed be He, I thought that I would punish them with suffering in this world, so that their arm might be strengthened in the world to come, "yet they have spoken lies against me" (Hos. 7:23).'"

I.13   A   *R. Abbahu praised R. Safra to the* minim *[in context: Christian authorities of Caesarea], saying that he was a highly accomplished authority. They therefore remitted his taxes for thirteen years.*

       B   *One day they came upon him and said to him, "It is written, 'You only have I known among all the families of the earth; therefore I will visit upon you all your iniquities' (Amos 3:2). If one is angry, does he vent it on someone he loves?"*

C.   *He fell silent and said nothing at all. They wrapped a scarf around his neck and tortured him. R. Abbahu came along and found them. He said to them, "Why are you torturing him?"*

D.   *They said to him, "Didn't you tell us that he is a* highly accomplished authority, *but he does not know how to explain this verse!"*

E.   *He said to them, "True enough, I told you that he was a master of Tannaite statements, but did I say anything at all to you about his knowledge of Scripture?"*

F.   *They said to him, "So how come you know?"*

G.   *He said to them, "Since we, for our part, spend a lot of time with you, we have taken the task of studying it thoroughly, while others [in Babylonia, Safra's place of origin] do not study [Scripture] that carefully."*

H.   *They said to him, "So tell us."*

I.   He said to them, "I shall tell you a parable. To what is the matter comparable? To the case of a man who lent money to two people, one a friend, the other an enemy. From the friend he collects the money little by little, from the enemy he collects all at once."

I.14   A.   *Said R. Abba bar Kahana, "What is the meaning of the following verse of Scripture: 'Far be it from you to do after this manner, to* slay the righteous with the wicked' (Gen. 18:25).

B.   "Said Abraham before the Holy One, blessed be He, 'Lord of the world! It is a profanation to act in such a way [a play on the Hebrew letters, shared by the words 'far be it' and 'profanation'], 'to slay the righteous with the wicked' (Gen. 18:25)."

C.   But is it not [so that God might do just that]? And is it not written, "And I will cut off from you the righteous and the wicked" (Ezek. 21:8)?

D.   That speaks of one who is not completely righteous, but not of one who is completely righteous.

E.   And will he not do so to one who is completely righteous? And is it not written, "And begin the slaughter with my sanctuary" (Ezek. 9:6), in which connection R. Joseph repeated as a Tannaite version, "Read not 'with my sanctuary' but rather, 'with those who are holy to me,' namely, the ones who carried out the Torah beginning to end."

F.   *There, too,* since they had the power to protest against the wickedness of the others and did not do so, they were not regarded as completely righteous at all.

I.15   A.   *R. Pappa contrasted verses of Scripture: "It is written, 'God is angry every day' (Ps. 7:12) but also 'who could stand before his anger' (Nah. 1:6).*

B.   *"But there is no contradiction between the first and second statements, for the former speaks of the individual, the latter of the community."*

The reference to God's anger, No. 16, marks an imperceptible movement to a new theme, namely Balaam, the prophet of the gentiles. Balaam then forms the unifying theme for Nos. 17-19. Because I regard these as footnote entries, I indent them.

I.16	A.	*Our rabbis have taught on Tannaite authority:*
	B.	"God is angry every day" (Ps. 7:12), and how long is his anger? It is for a moment. And how long is a moment? The portion 1/53,848th of an hour is a moment.
	C.	And no creature can determine that moment, except for Balaam that wicked man, of whom it is written, **[5A]** "who knew the knowledge of the Most High" (Num. 24:16).
	D.	How can it be that a man who did not know the mind of his animal could have known the mind of the Most High?
I.17	A.	*And what is the meaning of the statement that* he did not know the mind of his animal?
	B.	*When they saw him riding on his ass, they said to him, "How come you're not riding on a horse?"*
	C.	*He said to them, "I sent it to the meadow."*
	D.	Forthwith: "The ass said, Am I not your ass" (Num. 22:30).
	E.	*He said to it, "Just as a beast of burden in general."*
	F.	*She said to him, "Upon whom you have ridden"* (Num. 22:30).
	G.	*He said to it, "Only from time to time."*
	H.	*She said to him, "Ever since I was yours* (Num. 22:30). And not only so, but I serve you for riding by day and fucking by night."
	I.	For here the word "I was wont" is used, and the same letters bear the meaning of bed mate: "...and she served him as a bed mate" (1 Kgs. 1:2).
I.18	A.	*And what is the meaning of the statement that* he could have known the mind of the Most High?
	B.	For he knew precisely that moment at which the Holy One, blessed be He, was angry.
	C.	*That is in line with what the prophet had said to them,* "O my people, remember now what Balak king of Moab consulted and what Balaam son of Beor answered him from Shittim to Gilgal, that you may know the righteousness of the Lord" (Mic. 6:5).
I.19	A.	["O my people, remember now what Balak king of Moab consulted and what Balaam son of Beor answered him from Shittim to Gilgal, that you may know the righteousness of the Lord" (Mic. 6:5)]:
	B.	Said R. Eleazar, "Said the Holy one blessed be He to Israel, 'My people, see how many acts of righteousness I carried out with you, for I did not grow angry with you during all those [perilous] days, for if I had grown angry with you, there would not have remained from Israel a remnant or a survivor.'
	C.	"And that is in line with what Balaam says: 'How can I curse seeing that God does not curse, and how can I be wrathful, seeing that the Lord has not been wrathful' (Num. 23:8)."

We now realize that Nos. 17-19 form a protracted footnote to No.16, for No. 20 will return us to the theme broken off at No. 16, namely, God's anger. The composite that follows, Nos. 20-23, is held together by that theme.

I.20 A   And how long is his wrath? It is for a moment. And how long is a moment? The portion 1/53,848th of an hour is a moment.

      B.   And how long is a moment?

      C.   Said Amemar – others say, Rabina – "So long as it takes to say the word 'moment.'"

      D.   *And how on the basis of Scripture do we know that his wrath lasts for only a moment?*

      E.   *As it is written,* "For his anger is for a moment, his favor is for a lifetime" (Ps. 30:6).

      F.   *If you prefer:* "Hide yourself for a brief moment, until the wrath be past" (Isa. 26:20).

I.21 A.   *When is he angry?*

      B.   *Said Abbayye, "In the first three hours of the day, when the comb of the cock is white."*

      C.   *Isn't it white all the rest of the day?*

      D.   *At other times it has red streaks, but then it has none.*

I.22 A   *R. Joshua b. Levi – a certain min would bother him about verses of Scripture. Once he took a chicken and put it between the legs of the bed and watched it. He reasoned, "When that hour comes, I shall curse him."*

      B.   *But when that hour came, he was dozing. He said, "What you learn from this experience is that it is not correct to act in such a way: 'His tender mercies are over all his works' (Ps. 145:9), 'Neither is it good for the righteous to inflict punishment' (Prov. 17:26)."*

I.23 A   *It was taught as a Tannaite version in the name of R. Meir,* "[That time at which God gets angry comes] when the kings put on their crowns on their heads and prostrate themselves to the sun. Forthwith the Holy One, blessed be He, grows angry."

Once again we are at a borderline between one set and another, and once more, the movement is subtle. We have just now referred to times at which God is angry, and times at which he is merciful. God is particularly angry, No. 23, when the kings put their crowns on their heads and worship the sun; No. 24 completes this composite, a different but related distinction between the time to pray and the time not to pray.

I.24 A   *Said R. Joseph, "A person should not recite the Prayer of the Additional Service for the first day of the New Year [the Day of Judgment] during the first three hours of the day or in private, lest, since that is the time of judgment, his deeds may be examined, and his prayer rejected."*

      B.   *If so, then the prayer of the community also should not be recited at that time?*

      C.   *The merit [accruing to the community as a whole] is greater.*

D.   *If so, then that of the Morning Service also should not be recited in private?*

E.   *Since at that time the community also will be engaged in reciting the Morning Prayer, the individual's recitation of the Prayer will not be rejected.*

F.   *But have you not said,* "In the first three hours the Holy One, blessed be He, goes into session and engages in study of the Torah; in the second he goes into session and judges the entire world"?

G.   *Reverse the order.*

H   *Or, if you prefer, actually do not reverse the order.* For when God is occupied with study of the Torah, called by Scripture "truth" as in "buy the truth and do not sell it" (Prov. 23:23), the Holy One, blessed be He, in any event will not violate the strict rule of justice. But when engaged in judgment, which is not called "truth" by Scripture, the Holy One, blessed be He, may step across the line of strict justice [towards mercy].

No. 25 is going to direct our attention way back to 2.RR. What we have, then, is a massive appendix to that reference, once that was formed in its own terms and is coherent around its own theme. That theme is the religious deeds and duties carried out by Israel, and how these will be rewarded not now but in the world to come. No. 26 introduces David's sin in the context of this discussion, explicitly referring back to No. 25. Then, Nos. 26-27, we pursue a composite devoted to David.

I.25   A.   Reverting to the body of the prior text:

        B.   *R. Joshua b. Levi has said,* "What is the meaning of the verse of Scripture, 'The ordinances that I command you this day to do them' (Deut. 7:11)? Today is the day to do them, but not tomorrow; they are not to be done tomorrow; today is the day to do them, but today is not the day on which to receive a reward for doing them":

        C.   Said R. Joshua b. Levi, "All the religious duties that Israelites do in this world come and give evidence in their behalf in the world to come: 'Let them bring their witnesses that they may be justified, let them hear and say it is truth.'"

        D.   "Let them bring their witnesses that they may be justified": This is Israel.

        E.   "let them hear and say it is truth": This refers to the gentiles.

        F.   And said R. Joshua b. Levi, "All the religious duties that Israelites do in this world come and flap about the faces of gentiles in the world to come: 'Keep them and do them, for this, your wisdom and understanding, will be in the eyes of the peoples' (Deut. 4:6).

        G   "What is stated here is not 'in the presence of the peoples' but 'in the eyes of the peoples,' which teaches you that they will come and flap about the faces of gentiles in the world to come."

        H   And said R. Joshua b. Levi, "The Israelites made the golden calf only to give an opening to penitents: 'O that they had such a heart as this always, to fear me and keep my commandments' (Deut. 5:26)."

I.26 A. That is in line with what R. Yohanan said in the name of R. Simeon b. Yohai: "David was really not so unfit as to do such a deed [as he did with Beth Sheva]: 'My heart is slain within me' (Ps. 109:22) [Mishcon: David's inclinations had been completely conquered by himself]. And the Israelites were hardly the kind of people to commit such an act: 'O that they had such a heart as this always, to fear me and keep my commandments' (Deut. 5:26). So why did they do it?

B. "[5A] It was to show you that if an individual has sinned, they say to him, 'Go to the individual [such as David, and follow his example], and if the community as a whole has sinned, they say to them, 'Go to the community [such as Israel].'

C. *And it was necessary to give both examples. For had we been given the rule governing the individual, that might have been supposed to be because his personal sins were not broadly known, but in the case of the community, the sins of which will be broadly known, I might have said that that is not the case.*

D. *And if we had been given the rule governing the community, that might have been supposed to be the case because they enjoy greater mercy, but an individual, who has not got such powerful zekhut, might have been thought not subject to the rule.*

E. *So both cases had to be made explicit.*

I.27 A. *That is in line with what R. Samuel bar Nahmani said R. Jonathan said, "What is the meaning of the verse of Scripture, 'The saying of David, son of Jesse, and the saying of the man raised on high' (2 Sam. 23:1)?*

B. "It means, 'The saying of David, son of Jesse, the man who raised up the yoke of repentance.'"

No. 28 brings us back to the general theme of doing a good deed in this world and enjoying the result in the world to come. That theme spills over into No. 29.

I.28 A. Said R. Samuel bar Nahmani said R. Jonathan, "Whoever does a religious duty in this world – that deed goes before him to the world to come, as it is said, 'And your righteousness shall go before you' (Isa. 58:8).

B. "And whoever commits a transgression in this world – that act turns aside from him and goes before him on the Day of Judgment, as it is said, 'The paths of their way are turned aside, they go up into the waste and perish' (Job 6:18)."

C. R. Eliezer says, "It attaches to him like a dog, as it is said, 'He did not listen to her to lie by her or to be with her' (Gen. 39:10).

D. "'To lie by her' in this world.

E. "'Or to be with her' in the world to come."

I.29 A. Said R. Simeon b. Laqish, "Come and let us express our gratitude to our ancestors, for if it were not for their having sinned, we for our part should never have been able to come into the world: 'I said you are gods and all of you sons of the

Most High' (Ps. 82:6). Now that you have ruined things by what you have done: 'you shall indeed die like mortals' (Ps. 82:6).''

B. *Does that statement then bear the implication, therefore, that if they had not sinned, they would not have propagated? But has it not been written,* "And you, be fruitful and multiply" (Gen. 9:7)?

C. *That applies up to Sinai.*

D. *But in connection with Sinai it also is written,* "Go say to them, Go back to your tents" (Ex. 19:15), meaning, to marital relationships. *And is it not also written,* "that it might be well with them and with their children" (Deut. 5:26)?

E. That speaks only to those who were actually present at Mount Sinai.

F. *But has not R. Simeon b. Laqish stated,* "What is the meaning of that which is written: 'This is the book of the generations of Adam' (Gen. 5:1)? Now did the first Adam have a book? The statement, rather, teaches that the Holy One, blessed be He, showed to the first Adam each generation and its authoritative expositors, each generations and its sages, each generation and those that administered its affairs. When he came to the generation of R. Aqiba, he rejoiced in the master's Torah but he was saddened by the master's death.

G. "He said, 'How precious are your thoughts to me, O God' (Ps. 139:17).''

H. And said R. Yosé, "The son of David will come only when all of the souls that are stored up in the body will be used up: 'For I will not contend for ever, neither will I be always angry, for the spirit should fall before me and the spirits which I have made' (Isa. 57:16).'' [Mishcon: In the face of the foregoing teachings, how could it be stated that had it not been for the sin of the golden calf, we should not have come into the world?]

I. *Do not, therefore, imagine that the sense of the statement is,* we should have not come into the world [if our ancestors had not sinned], *but rather,* it would have been as though we had not come into the world.

J. *Does that then bear the implication that, if they had not sinned, they would never have died? But have not the passages been written that deal with the deceased childless brother's widow and the chapters about inheritances [which take for granted that people die]?*

K. These passages are written conditionally [meaning, if people sin and so die, then the rules take effect, but it is not necessary that they take effect unless that stipulation is fulfilled].

L. *And are there then any verses of Scripture that are stated conditionally?*

M. *Indeed so, for said R. Simeon b. Laqish,* "What is the meaning of that which has been written, 'And it was evening and it was morning, the sixth day' (Gen. 1:31)? This teaches that the Holy One, blessed be He, made a stipulation with the works of creation and said, 'If the Israelites accept the Torah, well and good, but if not, I shall send you back to the condition of formlessness and void.''

N   *An objection was raised:* "O that they had such a heart as this always, to fear me and keep my commandments, that it may be well with them and their children" (Deut. 5:26): it is not possible to maintain that the meaning here is that he would take away the angel of death from them, for the decree had already been made. It means that the Israelites accepted the Torah only so that no nation or tongue would rule over them: "that it might be well with them and their children after them." [Mishcon: How could R. Simeon b. Laqish hold that but for the golden calf worship Israel would have enjoyed physical deathlessness?]

O   *[R. Simeon b. Laqish] made his statement in accord with the position of this Tannaite authority, for it has been taught on Tannaite authority:*

P.   R. Yosé says, "The Israelites accepted the Torah only so that the angel of death should not have power over them: 'I said you are gods and all of you sons of the Most High. Now that you have ruined things by what you have done 'you shall indeed die like mortals' (Ps. 82:6)."

Q   *But to R. Yosé also must be addressed the question, has it not been written,* "O that they had such a heart as this always, to fear me and keep my commandments, that it may be well with them and their children" (Deut. 5:26)? *Goodness is what is promised, but there still will be death!*

R.   *R. Yosé will say to you,* "If there is no death, what *greater goodness can there ever be?"*

S.   *And the other Tannaite authority – how does he read the phrase,* "You shall indeed die"?

T.   *The sense of* "death" *here is* "poverty," *for a master has said,* "Four classifications of persons are equivalent to corpses, and these are they: the poor man, the blind man, the person afflicted with the skin disease [of Lev. 13], and the person who has no children.

U.   "The poor man, as it is written: 'For all the men are dead who sought your life' (Ex. 4:19). *Now who were they? This refers to Dathan and Abiram, and they were certainly not then dead,* they had only lost all their money.

V.   "The blind man, as it is written: 'He has made me dwell in darkness as those that have been long dead' (Lam. 3:6).

W.   "The person afflicted with the skin disease, as it is written: 'Let her, I pray you, not be as one who is dead' (Num. 12:12).

X.   "And the person who has no children, as it is written: 'Give me children or else I die' (Gen. 30:1)."

A new composite of compositions now commences. No. 30 begins with reference to Israel's sin. The connection to No. 29, so far as I can see, is simple. We have dealt with Israel's good deeds in this world, which yield the world to come. No. 29 also has referred to the penalties for sin and how these are appropriate. Now we turn to Israel's bad deeds. The composite on Israel's sins will continue through Nos. 30-33.

I.30   A.   *Our rabbis have taught on Tannaite authority:*

       B.   "If you walk in my statutes" (Lev. 26:3) – the word "if" is used in the sense of supplication, as in the verse, O that my people would hearken to me, that Israel would walk in my ways....I should soon subdue their enemies" (Ps. 81:14-15); "O that you had listened to my commandments, then my peace would have been as a river, your seed also would have been as the sand" (Isa. 48:18).

I.31   A.   *Our rabbis have taught on Tannaite authority:*

       B.   "O that they had such a heart as this always, to fear me and keep my commandments, that it may be well with them and their children" (Deut. 5:26).

       C.   Said Moses to the Israelites, "You are a bunch of ingrates, children of ingrates. When the Holy One, blessed be He, said to you, 'O that they had such a heart as this always, to fear me and keep my commandments, that it may be well with them and their children' (Deut. 5:26), they should have said, 'You give it.'

       D.   "They were ingrates, since it is written, 'Our soul loathes [5B] this light bread' (Num. 21:5).

       E.   "...the children of ingrates: 'The woman whom you gave to be with me, she gave me of the fruit of the tree and I ate it' (Gen. 3:12).

       F.   "So our rabbi, Moses, gave an indication of that fact to the Israelites only after forty years: 'And I have led you forty years in the wilderness...but the Lord has not give you a heart to know and eyes to see and ears to hear unto this day' (Deut. 29:3, 4)."

I.32   A.   ["And I have led you forty years in the wilderness...but the Lord has not given you a heart to know and eyes to see and ears to hear unto this day" (Deut. 29:3, 4):]

       B.   Said Raba, "This proves that a person will fully grasp the mind of his master only after forty years have passed."

I.33   A.   *Said R. Yohanan in the name of R. Benaah, "What is the meaning of the verse of Scripture,* 'Happy are you who sow beside all waters, that send forth the feet of the ox and the ass' (Isa. 32:20)? 'Happy are you, O Israel, when you are devoted to the Torah and to doing deeds of grace, then their inclination to do evil is handed over to them, and they are not handed over into the power of their inclination to do evil.

       B.   "For it is said, 'Happy are you who sow beside all waters.' For what does the word 'sowing' mean, if not 'doing deeds of grace,' in line with the use of the word in this verse: 'Sow for yourselves in righteousness, reap according to mercy' (Hos. 10:12), and what is the meaning of 'water' if not Torah: 'Oh you who are thirsty, come to the water' (Isa. 55:1)."

       C.   As to the phrase, "that send forth the feet of the ox and the ass":

       D.   it has been taught by the Tannaite authority of the household of Elijah:

E.   "A person should always place upon himself the work of studying the Torah as an ox accepts the yoke, and as an ass, its burden."

That completes the miscellany. It certainly plays no role in Mishnah exegesis. It also sets forth no proposition, in a way in which compositions of Mishnah exegesis, and even composites thereof, commonly do. Rather, we have a set of compositions of a rather diverse quality, which are grouped by common themes; the points that they make jointly are at best commonplaces. The grouping of the compositions into subcomposites is fairly easy to explain, and their further agglutination into the large-scale composite before us lays within the range of reasonable explanation. We have something more than a random scrapbook of this and that. The survey just now concluded leaves us with an impression somewhat different from what we expected at the outset. First of all, identifying the supplementary entries – footnotes, appendices – shows us that a fair amount of the miscellany in fact is made up of secondary expansions of a quite coherent text. Within the technical limitations of our authorship, who, after all, had no way of signifying footnotes and appendices, the framers of the whole had no choice but to gloss. Second, the rather sizable sequence of free-standing compositions in the aggregate is made up of conglomerates, the cogency of which we are able to explain. Third, the order of the conglomerates is not entirely beyond reason, since if we were to state the propositions not proved but illustrated by what is before us, we would have these simple statements:

1.   Study of the Torah on the part of a human being elicits in God a counterpart response, one of grace.
2.   Israel lives through study of the Torah.
3.   God favors Israel, by reason of Israel's study of the Torah, and is angry with the gentiles.
4.   Israel's good deeds in this world will be rewarded not now but in the world to come.

We then end with what is labelled as an appendix to materials introduced earlier. Now while we can hardly claim that the enormous composite made up of Nos. 2 through 33 is a sustained and well-crafted whole, we also cannot settle for the characterization of the set as a mere miscellany. It is made up of clearly identifiable composites, each of them comprising already made up compositions. Where there is a movement from one to the next, there is ordinarily a clear connection, for example, a reference to a subtheme now given principal place as a main theme; an allusion to a person, now formed into the focus of a set of compositions. What holds the parts together, one to the next, is a connection of a formal, generally a thematic, character. What holds the whole together is a sequence of unfolding themes. It would claim far too much to allege that we have a demonstration of a single proposition, for example, God hates and is angry with idolators and loves and rewards Israel. But it would be obtuse not to observe that that theme, remarkably coherent with the Mishnah tractate overall and with the opening paragraph of the Mishnah in particular, is present and is treated.

Let me now summarize the whole. I.1 begins with a systematic inquiry into the correct reading of the Mishnah's word choices. The dispute is fully articulated in balance, beginning to end. No. 2 then forms a footnote to No. 1. No. 3 then provides a footnote to the leitmotif of No. 2, the conception of God's not laughing. and No. 4 returns us to the exposition of No. 2, at III. Nos. 5, 6 are tacked on – a Torah study anthology – because they continue the general theme of Torah study every day, which formed the main motif of No. 2 – the gentiles did not accept the Torah, study it, or carry it out. So that theme accounts for the accumulation of sayings on Torah study in general, a kind of appendix on the theme. Then – so far as I can see, because of the reference to God's power – No. 7 begins with a complement to 6.I. The compositions, Nos. 7, 8, then are strung together because of a point that is deemed to link each to its predecessor. No. 7 is linked to the foregoing because of the theme of God's power; but it also intersects with 2.III and complements that reference; the entire sequence beyond No. 2 then in one way or another relates to either No. 2, theme or proposition, or to an item that is tacked on to No. 2 as a complement. Thus No. 8 is joined to No. 7 because of the shared method of contrasting verses. Then No. 9 is tacked on because it continues the proposition of No. 8. No. 10 continues the foregoing. No. 11 is tacked on to No. 10 for the reason made explicit: it continues what has gone before. The same is so for No. 12. No. 13 continues the theme, but not the form or the proposition, of the prior compositions, namely, punishment little by little, for example, in this world, in exchange for a great reward later on. The established theme then is divine punishment and how it is inflicted: gently to Israel, harshly to the gentiles; the preferred form is the contrast among two verses. That overall principle of conglomeration – form and theme – explains the inclusion of Nos. 14, 15+16, which is tacked on to 15. But then the introduction of Balaam, taken as the prototype for the min, accounts for the inclusion of a variety of further sayings on the same theme, specifically, No. 17, a gloss on the foregoing; No. 18, a continuation of the foregoing process of glossing, No. 19, an amplification on the now dominant theme; No. 20, a reversion to No. 16; No. 21, a story on the theme of how difficult it is to define precisely the matter dealt with in the foregoing. Nos. 21, 22, 23 complete the discussion of that particular time at which God is angry, a brief moment but one that is marked by a just cause. No. 23 then introduces the theme of choosing the right time – that is not the moment of divine wrath – for prayer. This seems to me a rather miscellaneous item, and it marks the conclusion of the systematic expansion begun much earlier. That that is the fact is shown by the character of No. 24, which cites 2.HHH, and by No. 25, which explicitly reverts to 2.RR, which justifies my insistence that the entire corpus of materials that follow No. 2 simply amplify and augment No. 2, and that is done in a very systematic way. Some of the sets, as we have seen, were formed into conglomerates prior to insertion here, but once we recognize that all of the sets serve the single task at hand, we see the coherence of what on the surface appears to be run-on and miscellaneous. In my *Rules of Composition*, Chapter Two, I show in a graphic way how these materials serve No. 2, some as footnotes, some as appendices, and some as footnotes or appendices to footnotes or appendices. No. 26 is a fine case in point. It complements 25.H, and is tacked on for that reason. Then No. 27 complements No. 26's statements concerning David. Bearing a formal tie to No. 27, with the same authority, No. 28 fits in also because it reverts to the theme of No. 25, the power of the religious duties that one carries out. No. 29 continues the theme of No. 28, that is, death and the day of judgment. Simeon's statement defines the center of gravity of the passage, which obviously was complete prior to its inclusion here. The reason it has been added is its general congruence to the discussions of sin, penitence, death, and forgiveness. No. 30 is attached to No. 31, and No. 31 is tacked on because it refers to the prooftext in the prior composition. No. 32 takes up the prooftext of No. 31. No. 33 writes a solid conclusion to the whole, addressing as it does the basic theme that Israel's actions define their fate, and that study of the Torah is what determines everything else. That is a thematic conclusion to a composite largely devoted, one way or another, to that one theme.

What then leads us to see Nos. 2 through 33 as a miscellany? It is the contrast between that composite and the amazingly coherent character of the Talmud's Mishnah commentary. And since the Talmud is made up mostly of Mishnah commentary, what holds together its thematic sets, and what accounts for their relationship to the Mishnah, are considerations that are easy to miss. But in the case of what is before us, we can readily see both what holds the several composites together, what links one composite to the next, and what defines the relationship of the entire group of composites to the Mishnah paragraph that stands at the head. The upshot may be easily stated. The miscellanies really are not at all miscellaneous. They form an integral part of the Talmud's program of Mishnah commentary. But they are made up of materials that, on their own, do not address the language or propositions of the Mishnah, only its (implicit) themes. As a result, they do not exhibit the literary cogency that makes the bulk of the Talmud so remarkably coherent. Viewed in their own terms, however, the materials we have examined answer the question the Mishnah paragraph raises and respond to its topical program: gentiles observe holy days in the service of idols. Israel should have nothing to do with such things. God loves Israel, who study the Torah, forgives their sins, and in the world to come will give them their lasting, and just reward. In light of the propositions of the Mishnah, we can hardly have asked for a more appropriate set of compositions than those selected and arranged in the massive "miscellany" at hand.

4

The Bavli's Massive Miscellanies:
The Problem of Agglutinative
Discourse in the Talmud of Babylonia

It is very simple to define agglutinative discourse in the context of the Bavli. The Talmud of Babylonia makes use of two distinct principles for the formation of large-scale composites of distinct compositions, and the framers of the document very rarely set forth a composition on its own, standing without clear ties to a larger context. Ordinarily, they brought together distinct and free-standing compositions in the service of Mishnah exegesis and amplification of law originating in a Mishnah paragraph under analysis. For that purpose they would then draw upon already written compositions, which would be adduced as cases, statements of principles, fully exposed analyses, inclusive of debate and argument, in the service of that analysis. So all of the compositions in a given composite would serve the governing analytical or propositional purpose of the framer of the composite. Where a composition appears to shade over into a direction of its own, that very quickly is seen to serve as a footnote or even an appendix to the composite at hand. Now to spell out what is at stake in this simple definition.

To understand what I mean by a "miscellany" in the context of the Bavli, let me now set forth the traits of the document that, over all, classify the writing as anything but miscellaneous. Then the problem of the literary formations treated in these pages will become entirely clear. For until I have established that most of the Bavli follows easily discerned rules of composition and the formation of composites, and that these rules dictate the character of the document as a whole – a commentary to the Mishnah – my claim to identify and differentiate writing of a quite different character will not be fully understood. Since I propose not only to identify this other kind of writing, but also to define and explain the rules that dictate the making of those composites of the Bavli that serve a different purpose from Mishnah commentary, I had best begin with the norms of the document, and only then to turn to what is different from the normal but also, in its way, governed by reasons we can uncover.

The writers of the Talmud spoke in a single voice. Whatever its writers wished to say, they said in a single way. Viewed as a whole, the Talmud of Babylonia covers thirty-seven of the Mishnah's sixty-three tractates, and, in discussing these thirty-seven Mishnah tractates, the authorship of the Talmud speaks in a single way. A fixed rhetorical pattern and a limited program of logical inquiry governs throughout. Whatever authors wish to say, they say within a severely restricted repertoire of rhetorical choices, and the intellectual initiatives they are free to explore everywhere dictate one set of questions and problems and not any other. The document's "voice," then, comprises that monotonous and repetitious language, which conveys a recurrent and single melody. In the ancient and great centers of learning in which the Talmud of Babylonia is studied today, masters and their disciples – studying out loud and in dialogue with one another and with the text – commonly and correctly say, "the Talmud says...," (Yiddish: *zogt die gemara*; Hebrew: *hattalmud omeret*), meaning, the anonymous, uniform, ubiquitous voice of the document, speaking in the name of no one in particular and within an indeterminate context of space and time, makes a given statement or point. Through years of encounter with the document, within the conventions of centuries of study in continuing circles of learning, by reference to "the Talmud says," the masters express the result of innumerable observations of coherence, uniformity, and cogency. I represent their usage when I speak of "the Talmud's one voice."

Why do I claim that the document may be read as a single coherent statement? The reason is that the document as a whole is cogent, doing some few things over and over again; it conforms to a few simple rules of rhetoric, including choice of languages for discrete purposes, and that fact attests to the coherent viewpoint of the authorship at the end – the people who put it all together as we have it – because it speaks, over all, in a single way, in a uniform voice. It is not merely an encyclopaedia of information, but a sustained, remarkably protracted, uniform inquiry into the logical traits of passages of the Mishnah or of Scripture. Most of the Talmud deals with the exegesis and amplification of the Mishnah's rules or of passages of Scripture. Wherever we turn, that labor of exegesis and amplification, without differentiation in topics or tractates, conforms to a few simple rules in inquiry, repeatedly phrased, implicitly or explicitly, in a few simple rhetorical forms or patterns.

The Bavli's one voice governs throughout, about a considerably repertoire of topics speaking within a single restricted rhetorical vocabulary. "The Bavli's one voice" refers to a remarkably limited set of intellectual initiatives, only this and that, initiatives that moreover always adhere to a single sequence or order: this first, then that – but never the other thing. I can identify the Bavli's authorships' rules of composition. These are not many. Not only so, but the order of types of compositions (written in accord with a determinate set of rules) itself follows a fixed pattern, so that a composition written in obedience to a given rule as to form will always appear in the same point in a sequence of compositions that are written in obedience to two or more rules: type A first, type B next, in fixed sequence. The Talmud's one voice then represents the outcome of the work of the following:

1.   An author preparing a composition for inclusion in the Bavli would conform to one of a very few rules of thought and expression; and, more to the point,
2.   A framer of a cogent composite, often encompassing a set of compositions, for presentation as the Bavli would follow a fixed order in selecting and arranging the types of consequential forms that authors had made available for his use.

With a clear and specific account of the facts yielding that anticipated result, I shall be well justified in asking about the message of the rhetorical and logical method of the Bavli. The Talmud of Babylonia is made up of large-scale composites – completed units of discourse, with a beginning, middle, and end, which supply all of the data a reader (or listener) requires to understand the point that the framer of that composite wishes to make. A composite commonly draws upon available information, made available in part by prior and completed composites, for example, Scripture, the Mishnah, the Tosefta, and in part by compositions worked out entirely within their own limits, which we might compare with a paragraph of a chapter; or a free-standing composition of a few lines. By "rules of composition" I mean the laws that dictated to the framers of a cogent and coherent composites – such as I allege comprise the whole of the Talmud of Babylonia – precisely how to put together whatever they wished to say, together with the supporting evidence as well as argument, in the composition that they proposed to write. Here, then, "rules of composition" govern how people formed composites that comprise the Bavli: how they are classified, how they are ordered.

So it is the simple fact that the Bavli throughout speaks in a single and singular voice. It is single because it is a voice that expresses the same limited set of notes everywhere. It is singular because these notes are arranged in one and the same way throughout. The Bavli's one voice, sounding through all tractates, is the voice of exegetes of the Mishnah. The document is organized around the Mishnah, and that is not a merely formal, but a substantive order. At every point, if the framers have chosen a passage of Mishnah exegesis, that passage will stand at the head of all further discussion. Every turning point brings the editors back to the Mishnah, always read in its own order and sequence. The Bavli's speaks in a single way about some few things, and that is the upshot of my sustained inquiry. It follows that well-crafted and orderly rules governed the character of the sustained discourse that the writing in the Bavli sets forth. All framers of composites and editors of sequences of composites found guidance in the same limited repertoire of rules of analytical rhetoric: some few questions or procedures, directed always toward one and the same prior writing. Not only so, but a fixed order of discourse dictated that a composition of one sort, A, always come prior to a composite of another type, B. A simple logic instructed framers of composites, who sometimes also were authors of compositions, and who sometimes drew upon available compositions in the making of their cogent composites. We have now to see the Bavli as entirely of a piece, cogent and coherent, made up of well-composed large-scale constructions. It is coherent not only in its rules of the use of Hebrew and Aramaic, it is even more coherent in its rhetorical laws.

The Bavli's one voice utilizes only a few, well-modulated tones: a scale of not many notes. As we saw, when we classify more than three thousand composites, spread over eleven tractates, we find that nearly 90 percent of the whole comprises Mishnah commentary of various kinds; not only so, but the variety of the types of Mishnah commentary is limited, as a review of the representation of Temurah in detail, and of the ten tractates of our sample in brief characterization, has shown. Cogent composites are further devoted to Scripture or to topics of a moral or theological character not closely tied to the exegesis of verses of Scripture; these form in the aggregate approximately 10 percent of the whole number of composites, but, of tractates to begin with not concerned with scriptural or theological topics (in our sample these are Sanhedrin and Berakhot), they make up scarcely 3 percent of the whole. So the Bavli has one voice, and it is the voice of a person or persons who propose to speak about one document and to do so in some few ways. Let me spell out precisely what I mean.

We are able to classify all composites in three principal categories: [1] exegesis and amplification of the law of the Mishnah; [2] exegesis and exposition of verses of, or topics in, Scripture; [3] free-standing composites devoted to topics other than those defined by the Mishnah or Scripture. That means that my initial proposal of a taxonomic system left no lacunae. Second, with the classification in place, we see that much more than four-fifths of all composites of the Bavli address the Mishnah and systematically expound that document. These composites are subject to subclassification in two ways: Mishnah exegesis and speculation and abstract theorizing about the implications of the Mishnah's statements. The former type of composite, further, is to be classified in a few and simple taxa, for example, composites organized around [1] clarification of the statements of the Mishnah; [2] identification of the authority behind an anonymous statement in the Mishnah; [3] scriptural foundation for the Mishnah's rules; [4] citation and not seldom systematic exposition of the Tosefta's amplification of the Mishnah. That means that most of the Bavli is a systematic exposition of the Mishnah.

Third, the other fifth (or less) of a given tractate will comprise composites that take shape around [1] Scripture or [2] themes or topics of a generally theological or moral character. Distinguishing the latter from the former, of course, is merely formal; very often a scriptural topic will be set forth in a theological or moral framework, and very seldom does a composite on a topic omit all reference to the amplification of a verse or topic of Scripture. The proportion of a given tractate devoted to other-than-Mishnah exegesis and amplification is generally not more than 10 percent. 'My figure, as we shall note presently, is distorted by the special problems of tractates Sanhedrin and Berakhot, and, in the former, Chapter Eleven in particular.

These two tractates prove anomalous for the categories I have invented, because both of them contain important components that are devoted, to begin with, to scriptural or theological topics. And it is these anomalies that called my attention to the necessity of a closer look at what I here call "miscellanies." To take the cases before us in particular, Tractate Sanhedrin Chapter Eleven, lists various scriptural figures in catalogues of those who do, or do not, inherit the world to come; it further specifies certain doctrines that define the norms of the community of Israel that inherits the world to come. It will therefore prove quite natural that numerous composites will attend to scriptural or theological topics. Tractate Berakhot addresses matters of prayer and other forms of virtue, with the same consequence. In the analysis that follows, therefore, I calculate the averages of proportions of various types of composites both with and without these anomalous tractates. The upshot is that a rather inconsequential proportion of most tractates, and a small proportion of the whole, of the Bavli, is devoted to the systematic exposition of either verses of Scripture or topics of a theological or moral character. But even though the miscellanies prove anomalous within the Bavli, we are going to see that, in their own setting, viewed in relationship to one another, there are quite clear rules that govern throughout. Someone who had in hand a variety of compositions that were candidates for a composite of a miscellaneous character knew precisely what to choose for his work and exactly how to string together these composites. The one thing that he knew to begin with is that these composites would not serve the purpose of Mishnah commentary. I cannot point to a single miscellaneous composite that intersects with the Mishnah's propositions in any detailed way, and where the composite shares a topic with the Mishnah, the topical congruence plays no role in the framing of said composite. So, up front, we must recognize that the miscellany addresses a problem other than the exegesis and amplification of the Mishnah. The people who made it up then obeyed one rule that is clear at the outset: their "miscellany" would not address the Mishnah in any way at all. But then, if that rule of formation is sound, then the miscellanies look considerably less miscellaneous than they did at the outset.

When I speak of the Bavli's one voice, as now is clear, I mean to say it everywhere speaks uniformly, consistently, and predictably. The voice is the voice of a book. The message is one deriving from a community, the collectivity of sages for whom and to whom the book speaks. The document seems, in the main, to intend to provide notes, an abbreviated script which anyone may use to reconstruct and reenact formal discussions of problems: about this, one says that. Curt and often arcane, these notes can be translated only with immense bodies of inserted explanation. All of this script of information is public and undifferentiated, not individual and idiosyncratic. We must assume people took for granted that, out of the signs of speech, it would be possible for anyone to reconstruct speech, doing so in accurate and fully conventional ways. So the literary traits of the document presuppose a uniform code of communication: a single voice.

So it is time to ask the purpose of that composition: what the authors, authorships, or framers of the document wished to say through the writing that they have given us. If there is a single governing method, then what can we expect to learn about the single, repeated message? The evidence before us indicates that the purpose of the Talmud is to clarify and amplify selected passages of the Mishnah. We may say very simply that the Mishnah is about life, and the Talmud is about the Mishnah. That is to say, while the Mishnah records rules governing the conduct of the holy life of Israel, the holy people, the Talmud concerns itself with the details of the Mishnah. The one is descriptive and free-standing, the other analytical and contingent. Where there no Mishnah, there would be no Talmud. But what is the message of the method, which is to insist upon the Mishnah's near monopoly over serious discourse? To begin with, the very character of the Talmud tells us the sages' view of the Mishnah. The Mishnah presented itself to them as constitutive, the text of ultimate concern. So, in our instance, the Mishnah speaks of a quarrel over a coat, the Talmud, of the Mishnah's provision of an oath as a means of settling the quarrel in a fair way: substance transformed into process. What the framers of the Bavli wished to say about the Mishnah will guide us toward the definition of the message of their method, but it will not tell us what that message was, or why it was important. A long process of close study of texts is required to guide us toward the center of matters. The upshot is simple. We may speak about "the Talmud," its voice, its purposes, its mode of constructing a view of the Israelite world. The reason is that, when we claim "the Talmud" speaks, we replicate both the main lines of chronology and the literary character of the document. These point toward the formation of the bulk of materials – its units of discourse – in a process lasting (to take a guess) about half a century, prior to the ultimate arrangement of these units of discourse around passages of the Mishnah and the closure and redaction of the whole into the document we now know. What comes next? Well, now that we know that the Bavli is a document of remarkable integrity, repeatedly insisting upon the harmony of the parts within a whole and unitary structure of belief and behavior, we want to know what the Bavli says: the one thing that is repeated in regard to many things. Dismantling ("deconstructing") its components and identifying them, perhaps even describing the kinds of compilations that the authors of those components can have had in mind in writing their compositions – these activities of literary criticism yield no insight into the religious system that guided the document's framers. But the Talmud of Babylonia recapitulates, in grand and acute detail, a religious system, and the generative problematic of that writing directs our attention not to the aesthetics of writing as literature, but to the religion of writing as a document of faith in the formation of the social order.

Recognizing the orderly character of the Bavli, we may now turn to the agglutinative composites that do not conform to the norms of rhetorical form and logical cogency that impart to the Bavli its wonderful cogency. Forthwith, let us turn to a sample of what I characterize as a miscellany. It is given in Bavli Baba Batra Chapter Five, starting at 73A, with the further page numbers signified in the text.

IV.2   A.   *Our rabbis have taught on Tannaite authority:*
      B.   **He who sells a ship has sold the wooden implements and the water tank on it.**
      C.   R. Nathan says, "He who sells a ship has sold its rowboat."

D.   **Sumkhos says, "He who has sold a ship has sold its lighter" [T. B.B. 4:1A-C].**

IV.3   A   *Said Raba, "The rowboat and the lighter are pretty much the same thing. But R. Nathan, who was a Babylonian, uses the word familiar to him, as people use that word in Babylonia when referring to the rowboat that is used at the shallows, and Sumkhos, who was from the Land of Israel, used the word that is familiar to him, as people say in the verse,* 'And your residue shall be taken away in lighters' (Amos 4:2)."

IV.4   A   *Said Rabbah, "Sailors told me, 'The wave that sinks a ship appears with a white froth of fire at the crest, and when stricken with clubs on which is incised, "I am that I am, Yah, the Lord of Hosts, Amen, Amen, Selah," it will subside [and not sink the ship].'"*

IV.5   A   *Said Rabbah, "Sailors told me, 'Between one wave and another there is a distance of three hundred parasangs, and the height of the wave is the same three hundred parasangs. Once, when we were on a voyage, a wave lifted us up so high that we could see the resting place of the smallest star, and there was a flash, as if one shot forty arrows of iron; and if it had lifted us up any higher, we would have been burned by the heat. And one wave called to the next, "Friend, have you left anything in the world that you did not wash away? I'll go and wipe it out." And the other said, "Go see the power of the master, by whose command I must not pass the sand of the shore by even so much as the breadth of a thread:* 'Fear you not me? says the Lord? Will you not tremble at my presence, who have placed the sand for the bound of the sea, an everlasting ordinance, which it cannot pass' (Jer. 5:22).""*

IV.6   A   *Said Rabbah, "I personally saw Hormin, son of Lilith, running on the parapet of the wall of Mahoza, and a rider, galloping below on horseback, could not catch up with him. Once they put a saddle for him two mules, which* **[73B]** *stood on two bridges of the Rognag, and he jumped from one to the other, backward and forward, holding two cups of wine in his hands, pouring from one to the other without spilling a drop on the ground. It was a stormy day:* 'They that go down to the sea in ships mounted up to he heaven, they went down to the deeps' (Ps. 107:27). *Now when the state heard about this, they killed him."*

IV.7   A   *Said Rabbah bar bar Hannah, "I personally saw a day-old antelope as big as Mount Tabor. How big is Mount Tabor? Four parasangs. Its neck was three parasangs long, and his head rested on a spot a parasang and a half. Its ball of shit blocked up the Jordan River."*

IV.8   A   *And said Rabbah bar bar Hannah, "I personally saw a frog as big as the Fort of Hagronia – how big is that? sixty houses! – and a snake came along and swallowed the frog; a raven came along and swallowed the snake; and perched on a tree. So you can just imagine how strong was the tree."*

      B.   *Said R. Pappa bar Samuel "If I weren't there on the spot, I would never have believed it!"*

IV.9   A   *And said Rabbah bar bar Hannah, "Once we were traveling on a ship, and we saw a fish [whale] in the nostrils of which a mud eater had entered. The water cast up the fish and threw it on the shore. Sixty towns were destroyed by it, sixty towns got their food from it, and sixty towns salted the remnants, and from one of its eyeballs three hundred kegs of oil were filled. Coming back twelve months later, we saw that they were cutting rafters from the skeleton and rebuilding the towns."*

IV.10 A   *And said Rabbah bar bar Hannah, "Once we were traveling on a ship, and we saw a fish the back of which was covered with sand out of which grass was growing. We thought it was dry land so we went up and baked and cooked on the back of the fish. When the back got hot, it rolled over, and if the ship hadn't been nearby, we would have drowned."*

IV.11 A   *And said Rabbah bar bar Hannah, "Once we were traveling on a ship, and the ship sailed between one fin of a fish and the other for three days and three nights; the fish was swimming upwards and we were floating downwards [with the wind]."*

B.   *Now, should you suppose that the ship did not sail fast enough, when R. Dimi came, he said, "It covered sixty parasangs in the time that it takes to heat a kettle of water. And when a cavalryman shot an arrow, the ship outstripped the arrow."*

C.   *R. Ashi said, "That was one of the small sea monsters, the ones that have only two fins."*

IV.12 A   *And said Rabbah bar bar Hannah, "Once we were traveling on a ship, and we saw a bird standing in the water only up to its ankles, with its head touching the sky. So we thought the water wasn't very deep, and we thought of going down to cool ourselves, but an echo called out, 'Don't go down into the water here, for a carpenter's axe dropped into this water seven years ago, and it hasn't yet reached the bottom.' And it was not only deep but also rapidly flowing."*

B.   *Said R. Ashi, "The bird was the wild cock, for it is written, 'And the wild cock is with me [with God in heaven]' (Ps. 50:11)."*

IV.13 A   *And said Rabbah bar bar Hannah, "Once we were traveling in the desert, and we saw geese whose feathers fell out because they were so fat, and streams of fat flowed under them. I said to them, 'May we have a share of your meat in the world to come?' One of them lifted a wing, the other a leg [showing me what my portion would be]. When I came before R. Eleazar,* he said to me, 'Israel will be called to account on account of these geese.'" [Slotki: The protracted suffering of the geese caused by their growing fatness is due to Israel's sins, which delay the coming of the Messiah.]

IV.14 A   *And said Rabbah bar bar Hannah, "Once we were traveling in the desert, and a Tai-Arab joined us, who could pick up sand and smell it and tell us which was the road to one place and which to another. We said to him, 'How far are we from water?' He said to us, 'Give me sand.' We gave him some, and he said to us, 'Eight parasangs.' When we gave him some sand later, he told us that we were three parasangs off. I had changed the sand, but I was not able to confuse him.*

B.   *"He said to me, 'Come on, and I'll show you the dead of the wilderness' (Num. 14:32ff.). I went with him and saw them. They looked as though they were exhilarated. [74A] They slept on their backs and the knee of one of them was raised. The Arab merchant passed under the knee, riding on a camel with a spear on high and did not touch it. I cut off one corner of the purple-blue cloak of one of them, but we could not move away. He said to me, 'If you've taken something from them, return it, for we have a tradition that if anybody takes something from them, he cannot move away.' I went and returned it and then we could move away.*

C.   *"When I came before rabbis, they said to me, 'Every Abba is an ass, and every son of Bar Hana is an idiot. What did you do that for? Was it to* find out whether the law accords with the House of Shammai or the House of Hillel? You could have counted the threads and the joints [to find out the answer to your question].'

D. "He said to me, 'Come and I will show you Mount Sinai.' I went and saw scorpions surrounding it, and they stood like white asses. I heard an echo saying, 'Woe is me that I have taken an oath, and now that I have taken the oath, who will release me from it?' When I came before rabbis, they said to me, 'Every Abba is an ass, and every son of Bar Hana is an idiot. You should have said, 'It is released for you.' But I was thinking that perhaps it was an oath in connection with the flood [which favored humanity]."

E. And rabbis?

F. If so, what need is there for the language, "woe is me"?

G. "He said to me, 'Come and I will show you those who were associated with Korah who were swallowed up (Num. 16:32ff). I saw two cracks that emitted smoke. I took a piece of clipped wool and soaked it in water, put it on the point of a spear, and pushed it in there. When I took it out, it was singed. He said to me, 'Listen closely to what you will hear.' and I heard them say, 'Moses and his Torah are truth, and we are liars.' He said to me, 'Every thirty days Gehenna causes them to turn over as one rotates meat in a pot, and this is what they say: "Moses and his Torah are truth and we are liars."'"

H. "He said to me, 'Come and I will show you where heaven and earth meet.' I took my basket and put it in a window of heaven. When I finished saying my prayers, I looked for it but did not find it. I said to him, 'Are there thieves here?' He said to me, 'It is the result of the wheel of heaven turning, wait here until tomorrow, and you will find it.'"

IV.15 A R. Yohanan told this story: "Once we were traveling along on a ship, and we saw a fish that raised its head from the sea. Its eyes were like two moons, and water streamed from its nostrils like the two rivers of Sura."

IV.16 A R. Safra told this story: "Once we were traveling along on a ship, and we saw a fish that raised its head from the sea. It had horns on which was engraven: 'I am a lesser creature of the sea. I am three hundred parasangs long, and I am going into the mouth of Leviathan.'"

B. Said R. Ashi, "That was a sea goat that searches for food and has horns."

IV.17 A R. Yohanan told this story: "Once we were traveling along on a ship, and we saw a chest in which were set jewels and pearls, surrounded by a kind of fish called a Karisa-fish. A diver went down [74B] to bring up the chest, but the fish realized it and was about to wrench his thigh. He poured on it a bottle of vinegar, and it sank. An echo came forth, saying to us, 'What in the world have you got to do with the chest of the wife of R. Hanina b. Dosa, who is going to store in it the purple-blue for the righteous in the world to come.'"

IV.18 A R. Judah the Hindu told this story: "Once we were traveling along on a ship, and we saw a jewel with a snake wrapped around it. A diver went down to bring up the jewel. The snake drew near, to swallow the ship. A raven came and bit off its head. The waters turned to blood. Another snake drew near and took the head of the snake and attached it to the body again, and it revived. The snake again came to swallow the ship. A bird again came and cut off its head. The diver seized the jewel and threw it

> into the ship. We had salted birds. We put the stone on them, and they took it up and flew away with it."

IV.19 A.   *Our rabbis have taught on Tannaite authority:*

B.   There was the case involving R. Eliezer and R. Joshua, who were traveling on a ship. R. Eliezer was sleeping, and R. Joshua was awake. R. Joshua shuddered and R. Eliezer woke up. He said to him, "What's wrong, Joshua? How come you trembled?"

C.   He said to him, "I saw a great light on the sea."

D.   He said to him, "It might have been the eye of Leviathan that you saw, for it is written, 'His eyes are like the eyelids of the morning' (Isa. 27:1)."

IV.20 A.   *Said R. Ashi, "Said to me Huna bar Nathan, 'Once we were traveling in the desert, and we had taken with us a leg of meat. We cut it open, picked out [what we are not allowed to eat] and put it on the grass. While we were going to get some wood, the leg returned to its original form, and we roasted it. When we came back after twelve months, we saw the coals still glowing. When I presented the matter to Amemar, he said to me, "The grass was an herb that can unite severed parts, and the coals were broom [which burns a long time inside, while the surface is extinguished]"'"*

IV.21 A.   "And God created the great sea monsters" (Gen. 1:21):

B.   *Here this is interpreted, "the sea gazelles."*

C.   R. Yohanan said, "This refers to Leviathan, [Slotki:] the slant serpent, and Leviathan the tortuous serpent: 'In that day the Lord with his hard and great and strong sword will punish Leviathan the slant serpent and Leviathan the tortuous serpent' (Isa. 27:1)."

IV.22 A.   Said R. Judah said Rab, "Whatever the Holy One, blessed be He, created in his world did he create male and female, and so, too, Leviathan the slant serpent and Leviathan the tortuous serpent he created male and female, and if they had mated with one another, they would have destroyed the whole world.

B.   "What did the Holy One, blessed be He, do? He castrated the male and killed the female and salted it for the righteous in the world to come: 'And he will slay the dragon that is in the sea' (Isa. 27:1).

C.   "And also Behemoth on a thousand hills (Ps. 50:10) he created male and female, and if they had mated with one another, they would have destroyed the whole world.

D.   "What did the Holy One, blessed be He, do? He castrated the male and quick-froze the female and preserved her for the righteous in the world to come: 'Lo, now his strength is in his loins' (Job 40:16) speaks of the male, 'and his force is in the stays of his body' (Job 40:16) speaks of the female."

E.   *In that other case, too, while castrating the male, why did he not simply quick-freeze the female [instead of killing it]?*

F.   *Fish is dissolute [and cooling would not have sufficed].*

G.   *Why not do it in reverse order?*

H.   *If you wish, I shall say that the female fish preserved in salt tastes better, and if you wish, I shall say, "Because it is written, 'There is Leviathan whom you have formed to sport with' (Ps. 104:26), and with the female that would not be seemly."*

I.   Here, too, in the case of the Behemoth, why not preserve the female in salt?

J.   *Salted fish tastes good, salted meat doesn't.*

IV.23 A.   And said R. Judah said Rab, "When the Holy One, blessed be He, proposed to create the world, he said to the prince of the sea, 'Open your mouth, and swallow all the water in the world.'

B.   "He said to him, 'Lord of the world, it is enough that I stay in my own territory.'

C.   "So on the spot he hit him with his foot and killed him: 'He stirs up the sea with his power and by his understanding he smites through Rahab' (Job 26:12)."

D.   *Said R. Isaac, "That bears the implication that* the name of the prince of the sea is Rahab."

E.   [Rab continues,] "And had the waters not covered him over, no creature could stand because of his stench: 'They shall not hurt nor destroy in all my holy mountain...as the waters cover the sea' (Isa. 11:9). Do not read 'they cover the sea' but 'they cover the angel of the sea.'"

IV.24 A.   And said R. Judah said Rab, "The Jordan issues from the cave of Paneas."

B.   *So, too, it has been taught on Tannaite authority:*

C.   The Jordan issues from the cave of Paneas.

D.   And it goes through the Lake of Sibkay and the Lake of Tiberias and rolls down into the great sea, and from there it rolls onward until it rushes into the mouth of Leviathan: "He is confident because the Jordan rushes forth to his mouth" (Job 40:23).

E.   *Objected Raba bar Ulla, "This verse speaks of* Behemoth on a thousand hills."

F.   Rather, said Raba bar Ulla, "When is Behemoth on a thousand hills confident? When the Jordan rushes into the mouth of Leviathan." [Slotki: So long as Leviathan is alive, Behemoth also is safe.]

IV.25 A.   *When R. Dimi came, he said R. Yohanan said, "What is the meaning of the verse,* 'For he has founded it upon the seas and established it upon the floods' (Ps. 24:2)? This refers to the seven seas and four rivers that surround the Land of Israel. And what are the seven seas? The sea of Tiberias, the sea of Sodom, the sea of Helath, the sea of Hiltha, the sea of Sibkay, the sea of Aspamia, and the Great sea. And what are the four rivers? The Jordan, the Yarmuk, the Keramyhon, and the Pigah."

IV.26 A.   *When R. Dimi came, he said R. Yohanan said, "Gabriel is destined to* organize a hunt [75A] for Leviathan: 'Can you draw out Leviathan with a fish hook, or press down his tongue with a cord' (Job 40:25). And if the Holy One, blessed be He, does not help him, he will never be able to prevail over him: 'He only that made him can make his sword approach him' (Job 40:19)."

IV.27 A.   *When R. Dimi came, he said R. Yohanan said, "When Leviathan is* hungry, he sends out fiery breath from his mouth and boils all the waters of the deep: 'He makes the deep to boil like a pot' (Job 41:23). And if he did not put his head into the Garden of Eden, no creature could endure his stench: 'he makes the sea like a spiced broth' (Job 41:23). And when he is thirsty, he makes the sea into furrows: 'He makes a path to shine after him' (Job 41:24)."

B. Said R. Aha bar Jacob, "The great deep does not recover its strength for seventy years: 'One thinks the deep to be hoary' (Job 41:24), and hoary old age takes seventy years."

IV.28 A. Rabbah said R. Yohanan said, "The Holy One, blessed be He, is destined to make a banquet for the righteous out of the meat of Leviathan: 'Companions will make a banquet of it' (Job 40:30). The meaning of 'banquet' derives from the usage of the same word in the verse, 'And he prepared for them a great banquet and they ate and drank' (2 Kgs. 6:23).

B. "'Companions' can refer only to disciples of sages, in line with this usage: 'You that dwells in the gardens, the companions hearken for your voice, cause me to hear it' (Song 8:13). The rest of the creature will be cut up and sold in the markets of Jerusalem: 'They will part him among the Canaanites' (Job 40:30), and 'Canaanites' must be merchants, in line with this usage: 'As for the Canaanite, the balances of deceit are in his hand, he loves to oppress' (Hos. 12:8). If you prefer: 'Whose merchants are princes, whose traffickers are the honorable of the earth' (Isa. 23:8)."

IV.29 A. Rabbah said R. Yohanan said, "The Holy One, blessed be He, is destined to make a tabernacle for the righteous out of the hide of Leviathan: 'Can you fill tabernacles with his skin' (Job 40:31). If someone has sufficient merit, a tabernacle is made for him; if he does not have sufficient merit, a mere shade is made for him: 'And his head with a fish covering' (Job 40:31). If someone has sufficient merit, a shade is made for him, if not, then a mere necklace is made for him: 'And necklaces about your neck' (Prov. 1:9). If someone has sufficient merit, a necklace is made for him; if not, then an amulet: 'And you will bind him for your maidens' (Job 40:29).

B. "And the rest of the beast will the Holy One, blessed be He, spread over the walls of Jerusalem, and the glow will illuminate the world from one end to the other: 'And nations shall walk at your light, and kings at the brightness of your rising' (Isa. 60:3)."

IV.30 A. "And I will make your pinnacles of rubies" (Isa. 54:12):

B. *Said R. Samuel bar Nahmani, "There is a dispute between two angels in the firmament, Gabriel and Michael, and some say, two Amoraim in the West, and who might they be? Judah and Hezekiah, sons of R. Hiyya.*

C. *"One said, 'The word translated rubies means onyx....'*

D. *"The other said, 'It means jasper.'*

E. *"Said to them the Holy One, blessed be He, 'Let it be in accord with both this opinion and that opinion.'"*

IV.31 A. "And your gates of carbuncles" (Isa. 60:3):

B. *That is in line with what was said when R. Yohanan went into session and expounded as follows: "The Holy One, blessed be He, is destined to bring jewels and pearls that are thirty cubits by thirty and will cut out openings from them ten cubits by twenty, setting them up at the gates of Jerusalem."*

C. *A certain disciple ridiculed him, "Well, jewels even the size of the egg of a dove are not available, so will jewels of such dimensions be found?"*

D. *After a while his ship went out to sea. He saw ministering angels engaged in cutting up jewels and pearls thirty cubits by thirty, on which were engravings ten by twenty. He said to him, "For whom are these?"*

E.   *They said to him, "The Holy One, blessed be He, is destined to set them up at the gates of Jerusalem."*

F.   *The man came before R. Yohanan. He said to him, "Give your exposition, my lord. It is truly fitting for you to give an exposition. For just as you said, so I myself have seen."*

G.   He said to him, "Empty headed idiot! If you had not seen, you would not have believed! So you ridicule the teachings of sages." He set his eye on him and the student turned into a heap of bones.

IV.32 A.   *An objection was raised:*

B.   "And I will lead you upright" (Lev. 26:13) –

C.   [Since the word for "upright" can be read to mean, at twice the normal height], R. Meir says, "That means, two hundred cubits, twice the height of the First Man."

D.   R. Judah says, "A hundred cubits, the height of the temple and its walls: 'We whose sons are as plants grown up in their youth, whose daughters are as corner pillars carved after the fashion of the temple' (Ps. 144:12)." [Slotki: How then in view of their increase to a hundred cubits in height, requiring correspondingly high gates, can Yohanan say that the gates were only twenty cubits in height?]

E.   *When R. Yohanan made that statement, it was with reference only to [Slotki:] ventilation windows.*

IV.33 A.   And said Rabbah said R. Yohanan, "The Holy One, blessed be He, is destined to make seven canopies for every righteous person: 'And the Lord will create over the whole habitation of Mount Zion and over her assemblies a cloud of smoke by day and the shining of a flaming fire by night, for over all the glory shall be a canopy' (Isa. 4:5). This teaches that for every one will the Holy One create a canopy in accord with the honor that is due him."

B.   Why is smoke needed for the canopy?

C.   Said R. Hanina, "It is because everyone who treats disciples of sages in a niggardly way in this world will have his eyes filled with smoke in the world to come."

D.   Why is fire needed in a canopy?

E.   Said R. Hanina, "This teaches that each one will be burned by [envy for] the canopy of the other. Woe for the shame, woe for the reproach!"

IV.34 A.   Along these same lines you may say: "And you shall put some of your honor upon him" (Num. 27:20) – but not of your honor.

B.   The elders of that generation said, "The face of Moses glows like the face of the sun, the face of Joshua like the face of the moon.

C.   "Woe for the shame, woe for the reproach!"

IV.35 A.   Said R. Hama bar Hanina, "Ten canopies did the Holy One, blessed be He, make for the First Man in the garden of Eden: 'You were in Eden, the garden of God; every precious stone was your covering, the cornelian, the topaz, the emerald, the beryl, the onyx, the jasper, the sapphire, the carbuncle, and the emerald and gold' (Ezek. 28:13)."

B.   Mar Zutra said, "Eleven: 'every precious stone.'"

C.   Said R. Yohanan, "The least of them all was gold, *since it was mentioned last.*"

IV.36 A.   *What is the meaning of* "by the work of your timbrels and holes" (Ezek. 28:13)?

B.   Said R. Judah said Rab, "Said the Holy One, blessed be He, to Hiram, king of Tyre, 'I looked at you [for your arrogance] when I created the excretory holes of human beings.'"

C.   *And some say that this is what he said to him,* "I looked at you **[75B]** when I decreed the death penalty against the First Man."

IV.37 A.   *What is the meaning of* "and over her assemblies" (Isa. 4:5)?

B.   Said Rabbah said R. Yohanan, "Jerusalem in the age to come will not be like Jerusalem in this age. To Jerusalem in this age anyone who wants to go up may go up. But to Jerusalem in the age to come only those who are deemed worthy of coming will go up."

IV.38 A.   And said Rabbah said R. Yohanan, "The righteous are destined to be called by the name of the Holy One, blessed be He: 'Every one that is called by my name, and whom I have created for my glory, I have formed him, yes, I have made him' (Isa. 43:7)."

IV.39 A.   Said R. Samuel bar Nahmani said R. Yohanan, "There are three who are called by the name of the Holy One, blessed be He, and these are they: the righteous, the Messiah, and Jerusalem.

B.   "The righteous, as we have just said.

C.   "The Messiah: 'And this is the name whereby he shall be called, the Lord is our righteousness' (Jer. 23:6).

D.   "Jerusalem: 'It shall be eighteen thousand reeds round about, and the name of the city from that day shall be, "the Lord is there"' (Ezek. 48:35). Do not read 'there' but 'its name.'"

IV.40 A.   Said R. Eleazar, "The time will come when 'holy' will be said before the name of the righteous as it is said before the name of the Holy One, blessed be He: 'And it shall come to pass that he that is left in Zion and he that remains in Jerusalem shall be called holy' (Isa. 4:3)."

IV.41 A.   And said Rabbah said R. Yohanan, "The Holy One, blessed be He, is destined to lift up Jerusalem to a height of three parasangs: 'And she shall be lifted up and be settled in her place' (Isa. 4:3). '...In her place' means 'like her place' [Slotki: Jerusalem will be lifted up to a height equal to the extent of the space it occupies]."

IV.42 A.   *So how do we know that the place that Jerusalem occupied was three parasangs?*

B.   Said Rabbah, "Said to me a certain elder, 'I myself saw the original Jerusalem, and it filled up three parasangs.'"

IV.43 A.   And lest you suppose that there will be pain in the ascension, Scripture states, "Who are these that fly as a cloud and as the doves to their cotes" (Isa. 60:8).

B.   *Said R. Pappa, "You may derive from that statement the fact that a cloud rises to a height of three parasangs."*

IV.44 A.   Said R. Hanina bar Pappa, "The Holy One, blessed be He, wanted to give Jerusalem a fixed size: 'Then said I, whither do you go? And he said to me, to measure Jerusalem, to see what is its breadth and what is its length' (Zech. 2:6).

B.   "Said the ministering angels before the Holy One, blessed be He, 'Lord of the world, you have created in your world any number of cities for the nations of the earth, and you did not fix the

measurements of their length or breadth. So are you going to fix
measurements for Jerusalem, in the midst of which are your name,
sanctuary, and the righteous?'

C   "Then: 'An angel said to him, run, speak to this young man, saying,
Jerusalem shall be inhabited without walls, for the multitude of
men and cattle therein' (Zech. 2:8)."

IV.45 A   Said R. Simeon b. Laqish, "The Holy One, blessed be He, is destined
to add to Jerusalem [Slotki:] a thousand gardens, a thousand
towers, a thousand palaces, a thousand mansions. And each one of
these will be as vast as Sepphoris in its hour of prosperity."

IV.46 A.   *It has been taught on Tannaite authority:*

B.   Said R. Yosé, "I saw Sepphoris in its hour of prosperity, and in it
were one hundred and eighty thousand markets for those who sold
pudding [alone]."

IV.47 A   "And the side chambers were one over another, three and thirty
times" (Ezek. 41:6):

B.   *What is the meaning of* three and thirty times?

C   Said R. Pappi in the name of R. Joshua of Sikni, "If there will be
three Jerusalems, each building will contain thirty dwellings piled
up on top of one another; if there will be thirty Jerusalems, then
each building will contain three apartments on top of one another."

From the viewpoint of the Bavli overall, the anomalous traits of the
conglomerate are clear: once we have left behind us the Tannaite
complement to the Mishnah, there is no clear purpose or point
established in what follows. No. 3 provides a talmud to No. 2, that is to
say, a well-crafted expansion, in this instance explaining the word
choices of the prior item. But then we have a sequence of units that have
only the most tenuous connection to the foregoing. Nos. 2-3 have spoken
of ships, and No. 4 speaks of a ship. No. 4 does not continue No. 3 (nor
does any following unit); it is parachuted down because of a shared
subject, that alone. But even the subject is not a substantial point in
common, since No. 4 wants to talk about ships that sink and how God
participates in the matter, and nothing could be further from the frame of
reference of No. 3.

What, then, are the units that do coalesce in the conglomerate that
follows? Clearly, Nos. 4, 5 talk about the supernatural in connection
with ships that founder at sea. No. 6 runs along the same lines, but its
connection to No. 5 is not much tighter than that of No. 4 to No. 3. No. 7,
however, is another matter; it shares the "I personally saw" formula, and
not only so, but what the master personally saw is a quite extraordinary
thing. So we can see how the compositions at Nos. 6, 7, 8 were formed
into a piece; obviously, there is no explanation for why one is prior,
another later, in the sequence; but there is a tight connection among the
three items. Another such set begins at No. 9: "once we were traveling
and...," which is the recurrent formula through Nos. 10-18+19. Now why
have Nos. 9-18+19 been linked to Nos. 6-8? No. 8 speaks of "I personally

saw" a frog as big as..., and the next, "Once we were traveling and we saw a fish...as big as...." So the shift is from one rhetorical formula to another, but the subject matter remains the same. That strikes me as rather deft composite making indeed. The following items, Nos. 10-12, conform to the same pattern, talking about wonders of nature that a sage saw. No. 13 then marks another shift, however, since while the wonders of nature go forward, the fat geese are not really of the same order as the amazingly huge fish; and the lesson is a different one, namely, "Israel will be called to account...." That this is the commencement of a new topic, joined with the prior form, is shown at No. 14. Here we retain the "once we were traveling" formula; but we drop the sustaining theme, big fish and the like, and instead, we pick up the new motif, which is, God's judgment of Israel, now: the dead raised by Ezekiel, No. 14; and the same story repeats the new motif, now the theme of God's judgment of Israel in connection with the oath of Sinai. What follows at No. 15 is yet another formula: "X told this story; once we were traveling...," and now we revert to the theme of the wonders of nature. Have we really lost the immediately prior theme? Not at all, for now our natural wonders turn out to concern Leviathan, and, later on, that theme is explicitly joined to the judgment of Israel: the righteous will get invited to the banquet at which Leviathan will form the main course. So Nos. 15-17 (and much that follows) turn out to link the two distinct themes that have been joined, and, we see, the movement is quite deft. We have a rhetorical device to link a variety of compositions on a given subject, we retain that rhetorical device but shift the subject, then we shift the rhetorical device but retain the same subject, and, finally, we join the two distinct subjects. The theme of Leviathan holds together Nos. 21-22+23. No. 24 is tacked on because Leviathan plays a role, and the same is to be said for No. 30. The general interest in the restoration of Israel moves from the messianic meal to Jerusalem, Nos. 31-45+46, 47. So there is a clear topical program, and while we have a variety of subunits, these are put together in a way that we can explain without stretching.

Abbreviating appropriately, let me now repeat the entire composite, this time clearly distinguishing not the rhetorical but the topical (even propositional) components. I simply set forth in a single column everything I take to form a single large-scale composite, distinct from everything fore and aft thereof.

IV.4   A   *Said Rabbah, "Sailors told me, 'The wave*
that sinks a ship appears with a white
froth of fire at the crest, and when stricken
with clubs on which is incised, "I am that
I am, Yah, the Lord of Hosts, Amen,

Amen, Selah," *it will subside [and not sink the ship].'"*

IV.5 A *Said Rabbah, "Sailors told me, 'Between one wave and another there is a distance of three hundred parasangs, and the height of the wave is the same three hundred parasangs. Once, when we were on a voyage, a wave lifted us up so high that we could see the resting place of the smallest star, and there was a flash, as if one shot forty arrows of iron; and if it had lifted us up any higher, we would have been burned by the heat. And one wave called to the next, "Friend, have you left anything in the world that you did not wash away? I'll go and wipe it out." And the other said, "Go see the power of the master, by whose command I must not pass the sand of the shore by even so much as the breadth of a thread:* 'Fear you not me? says the Lord? Will you not tremble at my presence, who have placed the sand for the bound of the sea, an everlasting ordinance, which it cannot pass' (Jer. 5:22).*"'"*

IV.6 A *Said Rabbah, "I personally saw Hormin, son of Lilith, running on the parapet of the wall of Mahoza, and a rider, galloping below on horseback, could not catch up with him. Once they put a saddle for him two mules, which* [73 B] *stood on two bridges of the Rognag, and he jumped from one to the other, backward and forward, holding two cups of wine in his hands, pouring from one to the other without spilling a drop on the ground. It was a stormy day:* 'They that go down to the sea in ships mounted up to he heaven, they went down to the deeps' (Ps. 107:27). *Now when the state heard about this, they killed him."*

IV.7 A *Said Rabbah bar bar Hannah, "I personally saw a day-old antelope as big as Mount Tabor. How big is Mount Tabor? Four parasangs. Its neck was three parasangs long, and his head rested on a spot a parasang and a half. Its ball of shit blocked up the Jordan River."*

IV.8 A *And said Rabbah bar bar Hannah, "I personally saw a frog as big as the Fort of Hagronia — how big is that? sixty houses!*

– and a snake came along and swallowed the frog; a raven came along and swallowed the snake; and perched on a tree. So you can just imagine how strong was the tree."

IV.9   A   *And said Rabbah bar bar Hannah, "Once we were traveling on a ship, and we saw a fish [whale] in the nostrils of which a mud eater had entered. The water cast up the fish and threw it on the shore. Sixty towns were destroyed by it, sixty towns got their food from it, and sixty towns salted the remnants, and from one of its eyeballs three hundred kegs of oil were filled. Coming back twelve months later, we saw that they were cutting rafters from the skeleton and rebuilding the towns."*

IV.10   A   *And said Rabbah bar bar Hannah, "Once we were traveling on a ship, and we saw a fish the back of which was covered with sand out of which grass was growing. We thought it was dry land so we went up and baked and cooked on the back of the fish. When the back got hot, it rolled over, and if the ship hadn't been nearby, we would have drowned."*

IV.11   A   *And said Rabbah bar bar Hannah, "Once we were traveling on a ship, and the ship sailed between one fin of a fish and the other for three days and three nights; the fish was swimming upwards and we were floating downwards [with the wind]."*

IV.12   A   *And said Rabbah bar bar Hannah, "Once we were traveling on a ship, and we saw a bird standing in the water only up to its ankles, with its head touching the sky. So we thought the water wasn't very deep, and we thought of going down to cool ourselves, but an echo called out, 'Don't go down into the water here, for a carpenter's axe dropped into this water seven years ago, and it hasn't yet reached the bottom.' And it was not only deep but also rapidly flowing."*

IV.13   A   *And said Rabbah bar bar Hannah, "Once we were traveling in the desert, and we saw geese whose feathers fell out because they were so fat, and streams of fat flowed under them. I said to them, 'May we have a share of your meat in the world to* come?' One of them lifted a wing, the other a leg [showing me what my portion would be]. When I came before R. Eleazar, he said to me, 'Israel will be called to account on account of these geese.'" [Slotki: The protracted suffering of the geese caused by their growing fatness is due to Israel's sins, which delay the coming of the Messiah.]

IV.14 A

And said Rabbah bar bar Hannah, "Once we were traveling in the desert, and a Tai-Arab joined us, who could pick up sand and smell it and tell us which was the road to one place and which to another. We said to him, 'How far are we from water?' He said to us, 'Give me sand.' We gave him some, and he said to us, 'Eight parasangs.' When we gave him some sand later, he told us that we were three parasangs off. I had changed the sand, but I was not able to confuse him.

IV.15 A

R. Yohanan told this story: "Once we were traveling along on a ship, and we saw a fish that raised its head from the sea. Its eyes were like two moons, and water streamed from its nostrils like the two rivers of Sura."

IV.16 A

R. Safra told this story: "Once we were traveling along on a ship, and we saw a fish that raised its head from the sea. It had horns on which was engraven: 'I am a lesser creature of the sea. I am three hundred parasangs long, and I am going into the mouth of Leviathan.'"

IV.17 A

R. Yohanan told this story: "Once we were traveling along on a ship, and we saw a chest in which were set jewels and pearls, surrounded by a kind of fish called a Karisa-fish. A diver went down [74B] to bring up the chest, but the fish realized it and was about to wrench his thigh. He poured on it a bottle of vinegar, and it sank. An echo came forth, saying to us, 'What in the world have you got to do with the chest of the wife of R. Hanina b. Dosa, who is going to store in it the purple-blue for the righteous in the world to come.'"

IV.18 A

R. Judah the Hindu told this story: "Once we were traveling along on a ship, and we *saw a jewel with a snake wrapped around it. A diver went down to bring up the jewel. The snake drew near, to swallow the ship. A raven came and bit off its head. The waters turned to blood. Another snake drew near and took the head of the snake and attached it to the body again, and it revived. The snake again came to swallow the ship. A bird again came and cut off its head. The diver seized the jewel and threw it into the ship. We had salted birds. We put the stone on them, and they took it up and flew away with it."*

IV.19 A   *Our rabbis have taught on Tannaite authority:*

B   There was the case involving R. Eliezer and R. Joshua, who were traveling on a ship. R. Eliezer was sleeping, and R. Joshua was awake. R. Joshua shuddered and R. Eliezer woke up. He said to him, "What's wrong, Joshua? How come you trembled?"

IV.20 A   *Said R. Ashi, "Said to me Huna bar Nathan, 'Once we were traveling in the desert, and we had taken with us a leg of meat. We cut it open, picked out [what we are not allowed to eat] and put it on the grass. While we were going to get some wood, the leg returned to its original form, and we roasted it. When we came back after twelve months, we saw the coals still glowing. When I presented the matter to Amemar, he said to me, "The grass was an herb that can unite severed parts, and the coals were broom [which burns a long time inside, while the surface is extinguished]."'"*

IV.21 A   "And God created the great sea monsters" (Gen. 1:21): R. Yohanan said, "This refers to Leviathan, [Slotki:] the slant serpent, and Leviathan the tortuous serpent: 'In that day the Lord with his hard and great and strong sword will punish Leviathan the slant serpent and Leviathan the tortuous serpent' (Isa. 27:1)."

IV.22 A   Said R. Judah said Rab, "Whatever the Holy One, blessed be He, created in his world did he create male and female, and so, too, Leviathan the slant serpent and Leviathan the tortuous serpent he created male and female, and if they had mated with one another, they would have destroyed the whole world.

IV.23 A   And said R. Judah said Rab, "When the Holy One, blessed be He, proposed to create the world, he said to the prince of the sea, 'Open your mouth, and swallow all the water in the world.'

IV.24 A   And said R. Judah said Rab, "The Jordan issues from the cave of Paneas."

IV.25 A   *When R. Dimi came, he said R. Yohanan said, "What is the meaning of the verse,* 'For he has founded it upon the seas and established it upon the floods' (Ps. 24:2)? This refers to the seven seas and four rivers that surround the Land of Israel. And what are the seven seas? The sea of Tiberias, the sea of Sodom, the sea of Helath, the sea of Hiltha, the sea of Sibkay, the sea of Aspamia, and the Great sea. And what are the four rivers? The Jordan, the Yarmuk, the Keramyhon, and the Pigah."

IV.26 A   *When R. Dimi came, he said R. Yohanan said,* "Gabriel is destined to organize a hunt **[75A]** for Leviathan: 'Can you draw out Leviathan with a fish hook, or press down his tongue with a cord' (Job 40:25). And if the Holy One, blessed be He, does not help him, he will never be able to prevail over him: 'He only that made him can make his sword approach him' (Job 40:19)."

IV.27 A   *When R. Dimi came, he said R. Yohanan said,* "When Leviathan is hungry, he sends out fiery breath from his mouth and boils all the waters of the deep: 'He makes the deep to boil like a pot' (Job 41:23). And if he did not put his head into the Garden of Eden, no creature could endure his stench: 'he makes the sea like a spiced broth' (Job 41:23). And when he is thirsty, he makes the sea into furrows: 'He makes a path to shine after him' (Job 41:24)."

IV.28 A Rabbah said R. Yohanan said, "The Holy One, blessed be He, is destined to make a banquet for the righteous out of the meat of Leviathan: 'Companions will make a banquet of it' (Job 40:30). The meaning of 'banquet' derives from the usage of the same word in the verse, 'And he prepared for them a great banquet and they ate and drank' (2 Kgs. 6:23).

IV.29 A Rabbah said R. Yohanan said, "The Holy One, blessed be He, is destined to make a tabernacle for the righteous out of the hide of Leviathan: 'Can you fill tabernacles with his skin' (Job 40:31). If someone has sufficient merit, a tabernacle is made for him; if he does not have sufficient merit, a mere shade is made for him: 'And his head with a fish covering' (Job 40:31). If someone has sufficient merit, a shade is made for him, if not, then a mere necklace is made for him: 'And necklaces about your neck' (Prov. 1:9). If someone has sufficient merit, a necklace is made for him; if not, then an amulet: 'And you will bind him for your maidens' (Job 40:29).

IV.30 A "And I will make your pinnacles of rubies" (Isa. 54:12):

C. *"One said, 'The word translated rubies means onyx....'*

D. *"The other said, 'It means jasper.'*

E. *"Said to them the Holy One, blessed be He, 'Let it be in accord with both this opinion and that opinion.'"*

IV.31 A "And your gates of carbuncles" (Isa. 60:3):

B. *That is in line with what was said when R. Yohanan went into session and expounded as follows: "The Holy One, blessed be He, is destined to bring jewels and pearls that are thirty cubits by thirty and will cut out openings from them ten cubits by twenty, setting them up at the gates of Jerusalem."*

IV.32 A. *An objection was raised:*

B. "And I will lead you upright" (Lev. 26:13) —

C.   [Since the word for "upright" can be read to mean, at twice the normal height], R. Meir says, "That means, two hundred cubits, twice the height of the First Man."

IV.33 A.   And said Rabbah said R. Yohanan, "The Holy One, blessed be He, is destined to make seven canopies for every righteous person: 'And the Lord will create over the whole habitation of Mount Zion and over her assemblies a cloud of smoke by day and the shining of a flaming fire by night, for over all the glory shall be a canopy' (Isa. 4:5). This teaches that for every one will the Holy One create a canopy in accord with the honor that is due him."

IV.34 A.   Along these same lines you may say: "And you shall put some of your honor upon him" (Num. 27:20) – but not of your honor.

       B.   The elders of that generation said, "The face of Moses glows like the face of the sun, the face of Joshua like the face of the moon.

IV.35 A.   Said R. Hama bar Hanina, "Ten canopies did the Holy One, blessed be He, make for the First Man in the garden of Eden: 'You were in Eden, the garden of God; every precious stone was your covering, the cornelian, the topaz, the emerald, the beryl, the onyx, the jasper, the sapphire, the carbuncle, and the emerald and gold' (Ezek. 28:13)."

IV.36 A.   *What is the meaning of* "by the work of your timbrels and holes" (Ezek. 28:13)?

       B.   Said R. Judah said Rab, "Said the Holy One, blessed be He, to Hiram, king of Tyre, 'I looked at you [for your arrogance] when I created the excretory holes of human beings.'"

       C.   *And some say that this is what he said to him,* "I looked at you [75B] when I decreed the death penalty against the First Man."

IV.37 A.   *What is the meaning of* "and over her assemblies" (Isa. 4:5)?

       B.   Said Rabbah said R. Yohanan, "Jerusalem in the age to come will not be like Jerusalem in this age. To Jerusalem in this age anyone who wants

IV.38 A   to go up may go up. But to Jerusalem in the age to come only those who are deemed worthy of coming will go up."

And said Rabbah said R. Yohanan, "The righteous are destined to be called by the name of the Holy One, blessed be He: 'Every one that is called by my name, and whom I have created for my glory, I have formed him, yes, I have made him' (Isa. 43:7)."

IV.39 A   Said R. Samuel bar Nahmani said R. Yohanan, "There are three who are called by the name of the Holy One, blessed be He, and these are they: the righteous, the Messiah, and Jerusalem.

B.   "The righteous, as we have just said.

C.   "The Messiah: 'And this is the name whereby he shall be called, the Lord is our righteousness' (Jer. 23:6).

D.   "Jerusalem: 'It shall be eighteen thousand reeds round about, and the name of the city from that day shall be, "the Lord is there"' (Ezek. 48:35). Do not read 'there' but 'its name.'"

IV.40 A   Said R. Eleazar, "The time will come when 'holy' will be said before the name of the righteous as it is said before the name of the Holy One, blessed be He: 'And it shall come to pass that he that is left in Zion and he that remains in Jerusalem shall be called holy' (Isa. 4:3)."

IV.41 A   And said Rabbah said R. Yohanan, "The Holy One, blessed be He, is destined to lift up Jerusalem to a height of three parasangs: 'And she shall be lifted up and be settled in her place' (Isa. 4:3). '...In her place' means 'like her place' [Slotki: Jerusalem will be lifted up to a height equal to the extent of the space it occupies]."

IV.42 A   *So how do we know that the place that Jerusalem occupied was three parasangs?*

B.   Said Rabbah, "Said to me a certain elder, 'I myself saw the original Jerusalem, and it filled up three parasangs.'"

IV.43 A   And lest you suppose that there will be pain in the ascension, Scripture states, "Who are these that fly as a cloud and as the doves to their cotes" (Isa. 60:8).

IV.44 A   Said R. Hanina bar Pappa, "The Holy One, blessed be He, wanted to give

Jerusalem a fixed size: 'Then said I, whither do you go? And he said to me, to measure Jerusalem, to see what is its breadth and what is its length' (Zech. 2:6).

B.   "Said the ministering angels before the Holy One, blessed be He, 'Lord of the world, you have created in your world any number of cities for the nations of the earth, and you did not fix the measurements of their length or breadth. So are you going to fix measurements for Jerusalem, in the midst of which are your name, sanctuary, and the righteous?'

IV.45 A.   Said R. Simeon b. Laqish, "The Holy One, blessed be He, is destined to add to Jerusalem [Slotki:] a thousand gardens, a thousand towers, a thousand palaces, a thousand mansions. And each one of these will be as vast as Sepphoris in its hour of prosperity."

IV.46 A.   *It has been taught on Tannaite authority:*
       B.   Said R. Yosé, "I saw Sepphoris in its hour of prosperity, and in it were one hundred and eighty thousand markets for those who sold pudding [alone]."

IV.47 A.   "And the side chambers were one over another, three and thirty times" (Ezek. 41:6):

       B.   *What is the meaning of* three and thirty times?

       C.   Said R. Pappi in the name of R. Joshua of Sikni, "If there will be three Jerusalems, each building will contain thirty dwellings piled up on top of one another; if there will be thirty Jerusalems, then each building will contain three apartments on top of one another."

There is a very clear and simple topical program before us. We treat three subjects, and the order in which they are treated is the only possible order. By that I mean, had we dealt with the third topic first, it would have had no context nor would it have supplied a context to the first and second. The same is to be said with respect to the second; if it came first, then the first sequence would have made no sense at all. So the first sequence prepares the way for the second, the second, for the third. Within each set of compositions, there are some clear points of connection and not mere intersection, let alone formal coherence through a shared topic.   Obviously, the triptych can be represented as propositional in only the most general terms.   But, equally obviously, we have much more than just this, that, and the other thing, all thrown together: a miscellany.   What we have, rather, is a different mode of agglutination of compositions into composites, and small composites into big composites, from the mode that is familiar to us throughout approximately 85 to 90 percent of the Bavli.   These conclusions now stand firm:

1.   In the miscellany before us, do we identify the first-class, cogent exposition of a proposition?   Not at all.   Is there the sustained consideration of a given problem?   No again.
2.   But is it a mere miscellany – disorganized, pointless, a scrapbook of one thing and another?   Hardly.

Well, then, if not exactly a miscellany, but also not a composite of the kind the predominates in the Bavli in its exposition of the Mishnah, then what do we have?   This brief account has raised more questions than it has settled.   The main point must not be lost.   The Bavli contains important composites that differ in their redactional, rhetorical, topical, and logical traits from its paramount composites.   Compared to the dominant type of composite, the one that serves as Mishnah commentary and amplification, these other composites exhibit a miscellaneous quality.   The real issue is whether or not before us are anomalies, and for that purpose, we shall have to ask not only whether we deal with miscellanies, viewed in their own terms, but whether or not we confront anomalies, viewed in the context of the chapters that contain them.   So let us examine three important composites and see [1] how they hold together, [2] what place they make for themselves in the context of the chapters in which they occur, and [3] how, if at all, the composites or miscellaneous type of composite proposes to expand our understanding of the Mishnah.

In addition to propositional and even analytical composites, the framers of the Bavli also formed compositions into thematic composites, and on the face of it, this second type of composite presents the appearance of a miscellany.   But far from forming a mere rubbish heap of this and that, this other type of composite proves not at all miscellaneous.   Clear, governing, and entirely predictable principles allow us to explain how one composition is joined to another.   Ordinarily, a sizable miscellany will tell us more about a subject that the Mishnah addresses or richly illustrate a principle that the Mishnah means to set forth through its cases and examples.   In that sense, the miscellaneous kind of composite is set forth as Mishnah commentary of a particular kind.   As we have seen, an agglutinative composite may be formed by appeal to a common theme, ordinarily stated by the Mishnah or at least suggested by its contents, and several closely related themes will then come under exposition in a massive miscellany. One common theme will be a passage of Scripture, systematically examined. A subordinate principle of agglutination will join composites attributed to the same authority or tradent, though it would be unusual for the compositions so joined to deal with entirely unrelated topics. So the principal point of differentiation between propositional composites and agglutinative ones is that the former analyze a problem, the latter illustrate a theme or even a proposition.

It follows that two modes of forming composites serve the framers of the Bavli, the paramount, propositional and analytical mode, and the subordinate, agglutinative sort. The one joins together a variety of distinct compositions into a propositional statement, commonly enriched with analytical initiatives, and frequently bearing a burden of footnotes and appendices. The other combines distinct compositions into a thematic composite, the proposition of which is ordinarily rather general and commonplace. A second principle of agglutinative composite making appeals to common attributions, though when two or more compositions are joined into a composite because they are assigned to the same authority or tradental chain, they very likely will also bear in common an interest in a single theme, if not in a uniform proposition in connection with that theme.

Since all of the miscellanies we have examined concern theological or exegetical subjects, none focusing upon a problem of law, we should be tempted to propose that agglutinative discourse governs the treatment of one type of subject matter, theology or exegesis, but not another, the more prominent, and generally held, normative one, of law. To demonstrate that the distinction between lore and law (*aggadah* and *halakhah*) makes no difference in whether or not compositions will be linked into composites by appeal to propositional analytical or merely agglutinative principles of formation, let me give a fine example of an agglutinative legal ("halakhic") passage, which shows beyond any doubt that there is no important point of distinction, so far as agglutinative discourse is concerned, between compositions and subcomposites of one kind and of the other. We find in both types of subject matter precisely the same literary traits of composite making. Here the compositions are joined agglutinatively, by reference to a common subject matter; but the composite that results does not make a point, for example of proposition, analysis, or argument. Rather, it serves to illustrate a theme, very much the way the massive miscellanies in tractates Berakhot and Sanhedrin illustrate a theme. We deal with Bavli Baba Batra Chapter Five.

5:11

A. Said Rabban Simeon b. Gamaliel, "Under what circumstances?
B. "In the case of liquid measures.
C. "But in the case of dry measures, it is not necessary."
D. [88B] And [a shopkeeper] is liable to let the scales go down by a handbreadth [to the buyer's advantage].
E. [If] he was measuring out for him exactly, he has to give him an overweight –
F. One part in ten for liquid measure,
G. one part in twenty for dry measure.
H. In a place in which they are accustomed to measure with small measures, one must not measure with large measures;
I. With large ones, one must not measure with small;
J. [In a place in which it is customary] to smooth down [what is in the measure], one should not heap it up;
K. To heap it up, one should not smooth it down.

III.1 A. In a place in which they are accustomed to measure with small measures, one must not measure with large measures; with large ones, one must not measure with small; in a place in which it is customary to smooth down what is in the measure, one should not heap it up; to heap it up, one should not smooth it down:

B. *Our rabbis have taught on Tannaite authority:*
C. How on the basis of Scripture do we know that in a place in which it is customary to smooth down what is in the measure, one should not heap it up; to heap it up, one should not smooth it down? Scripture says, "A perfect measure" (Deut. 25:15). [Slotki: Deviating from the usual practice the buyer or the seller may defraud or mislead others.]
D. And how do we know that if one said, "Lo, where it is customary to heap up, I will level it off, and reduce the price," or, in a place where they level, "I will heap it up, and raise the price," they do not listen to him [he may not do so]?
E. Scripture says, "A perfect and just measure you shall have" (Deut. 25:15).

III.2 A. *Our rabbis have taught on Tannaite authority:*
B. How on the basis of Scripture do we know that in a place where the practice is to allow an overweight, they do not give the exact weight, and in a place in which they give an exact weight, they do not give an overweight?
C. Scripture says, "A perfect weight" (Deut. 25:15).
D. And how on the basis of Scripture do we know that if one said in a place in which they give an overweight, "Lo, I shall give an exact weight and charge him less," or in a place in which they give an exact weight, "Lo, I shall give him an overweight and add to the price," they do not listen to him?
E. Scripture says, "A perfect weight and a just one" (Deut. 25:15).
F. Said R. Judah of Sura, "'You shall not have anything in your house' (Deut. 25:14). Why? Because of your 'diverse weights' (Deut. 25:13). But if you keep 'a perfect and just weight, you shall have'

(Deut. 25:15) things, 'if a perfect and just measure, you shall have....'"

There is no problem in explaining why No. 2 is tacked on to No. 1. The proposition is the same, so is the form. But what follows is another matter, since we are now going to entertain a different proposition altogether.

III.3   A.   *Our rabbis have taught on Tannaite authority:*
        B.   "You shall have...": this teaches that they appoint market supervisors to oversee measures, but they do not appoint market supervisors to control prices.

No. 4 will now illustrate the foregoing.

III.4   A   *The household of the patriarch appointed market supervisors to oversee measures and to control prices. Said Samuel to Qarna, "Go, repeat the Tannaite rule to them:* They appoint market supervisors to oversee measures, but they do not appoint market supervisors to control prices.
        B.   *He went out and instructed them: "*They appoint market supervisors to oversee measures and to control prices."
        C   *He said to him, "What do they call you? Qarna [horn]? Let a horn grow out of your eye." A horn grew out of his eye.*
        D.   *And as for Qarna, in accord with what authority did he reach this conclusion?*
        E.   *It was in accord with what Rammi bar Hama said R. Isaac said,* "They appoint market supervisors to oversee measures and to control prices, on account of crooks."

Now we have a miscellany, meaning, a set of compositions, each standing on its own foundation, all making clearly articulated points, none related except in a shared theme to what stands fore or aft. What we shall also observe is subsets, clearly joined to one another, but connected to the larger context only by the general theme. These subsets do not require explicit specification, being obvious on the face of it.

III.5   A.   *Our rabbis have taught on Tannaite authority:*
        B.   If somebody ordered a litra, he should measure out a litra; if he ordered a half-litra, he should measure out for him a half-litra; a quarter-litra, he should measure out a quarter.
        C.   *So what does that passage tell us?*
        D.   *It is that we provide weights in these denominations.*
III.6   A.   *Our rabbis have taught on Tannaite authority:*
        B.   If someone ordered three-quarters of a litra, he should not say to him, "Weigh out for me three-quarters of a litra one by one," but he should say to him, "Weight out a litra for me but leave out a quarter-litra with the meat" [Slotki: on the other scale].
III.7   A.   *Our rabbis have taught on Tannaite authority:*

    B.   If someone wanted to order ten litras, he should not say to him, "Weigh them out for me one by one and allow an overweight for each," but all of them are weighed together, with one overweight covering the whole order [cf. T. B.B. 5:9B-I].

III.8 A.   *Our rabbis have taught on Tannaite authority:*

    B.   [Slotki:] The hollow handle in which the tongue of the balance rests must be suspended in the air three handbreadths [removed from the roof from which the balance hangs], and it must be three handbreadths above the ground.

    C.   The beam and the rope that goes with it should be twelve handbreadths, and the balances of wool dealers and glassware dealers must be suspended two handbreadths in the air from the ceiling and two above the ground. The beams and ropes that go with them must be nine handbreadths in length. The balance of a shopkeeper and a householder must be suspended a handbreadth in the air from above and a handbreadth above the ground. The beam and ropes that go with them must be six handbreadths. A gold balance must be suspended three fingerbreadths in the air from above and three above the ground. I don't know the length of the beam and the cords.

    D.   *What kind of balance is the one mentioned first [before the specific rulings for those of the wool dealers, glassware dealers, and so on]?*

    E.   [89B] *Said R. Pappa, "The one used for heavy pieces of metal."*

III.9 A   Said R. Mani bar Patish, "Just as they have specified certain restrictions with regard to disqualifying balances for commercial purposes, so they have laid down disqualifications with regard to their constituting utensils for the purpose of receiving cultic uncleanness."

    B.   *What does he tell us that we do not learn from the following:* The cord of the scales of the storekeepers and [or] of householders – [to be susceptible to uncleanness must be in length at least] a handbreadth. A handle of the ax at its front – a handbreadth. The projection of the shaft of a pair of compasses – a handbreadth. The shaft of a stonemason's chisel – a handbreadth. A cord of the balances of wool dealers and of glass weighers – two handbreadths. The shaft of a millstone chisel – two handbreadths. The battle ax of the legions – two handbreadths. The goldsmith's hammer – two handbreadths. And of the carpenter's – three handbreadths [M. Kel. 29:5-6]! [Slotki: Since this restriction has been applied to one kind of balance, are not the other kinds of balance to be implied?]

    C.   The statement that he made is necessary to deal with the sizes of the beam and cords [that are not dealt with at the parallel].

A subset now follows, Nos. 10-13, glossed by No. 14.

III.10 A.   *Our rabbis have taught on Tannaite authority:*

    B.   They make weights out of neither tin or lead or alloy but of stone or glass.

III.11 A.   *Our rabbis have taught on Tannaite authority:*

B.   They make the strike not out of a board, because it is light, nor out of metal, because it is heavy, but out of olive, nut, sycamore, or box wood.

III.12 A.   *Our rabbis have taught on Tannaite authority:*

B.   They do not make the strike thick on one side and thin on the other.

C.   They do not make the strike with a single quick movement, because striking in that way brings loss to the seller and advantage to the buyer, nor very slowly, since this is a loss to the buyer but a benefit to the seller.

D.   In regard to all of these shady practices, said Rabban Yohanan b. Zakkai, "Woe is me if I speak, woe is me if I do not speak. If I speak, then sharpers will learn from me, and if I don't speak, then the sharpers will say, 'The disciples of sages haven't got the slightest idea what we are doing.'"

III.13 A.   *The question was raised: "So did he speak of them or didn't he?"*

B.   Said R. Samuel bar R. Isaac, "He did speak of them: 'For the ways of the Lord are right, and the just walk in them; but transgressors stumble therein' (Hos. 14:10)."

III.14 A.   *Our rabbis have taught on Tannaite authority:*

B.   "You shall do no unrighteousness in judgment, in surveying, weight, or in measure" (Lev. 19:35):

C.   "In surveying": This refers to surveying the real estate, meaning, one should not measure for one party in the dry season and another in the rainy season.

D.   "Weight": One should not keep one's weights in salt.

E.   "In measure" (Lev. 19:35): One should not make the liquid from a head.

F.   And that yields an argument a fortiori: if with reference to a mere "measure" (Lev. 19:35), which is merely one sixth of a log, the Torah demanded meticulous attention, how much the more so must one give meticulous care in measuring out a hin, half a hin, a third of a hin, a quarter of a hin, a log, a half a log, a quarter of a log, a toman, half a toman, and an uqla.

III.15 A   Said R. Judah said Rab, "It is forbidden for someone to keep in his house a measure that is either smaller or larger than the norm, even for the purpose of a piss pot."

B.   *Said R. Pappa, "But we have stated that rule only in a place where measures are not properly marked with a seal, but where they are properly sealed, they are permitted, since, if the purchaser sees no mark, he is not going to accept their use. And even in a place where measures are not properly marked with a seal, we have stated that rule only in a case in which they are not supervised [by administrative officers of the market], but if they are ordinarily supervised, we should have no objection."*

C.   *But that is not the case, for sometimes the buyer may come by at twilight and may happen to take a faulty measure. And so, too, that has been taught on Tannaite authority:* It is forbidden for someone to keep in his house a measure that is either smaller or larger than the norm, even for the purpose of a piss pot. But he may make a seah measure, a tarqab, a half-tarqab, a qab, a half-qab, a quarter-qab, a toman, [90B] and an uqla measure. How much is an uqla measure? It is a fifth of a quarter of a qab. In the case of liquid measures, one may make a hin, a half-hin, third-hin, quarter-hin, log, half-log, quarter-log, eighth-log, and eight of an eighth, which is a qortob.

D. *So why shouldn't someone also make a double-qab measure?*

E. *It might be confused with a tarqab.*

F. *Therefore people may err by as much as a third.*

G. *If so, then a qab also people should not make, since they might confuse it with a half-tarqab. Rather, as to a double-qab, this is the reason that one is not to make it, specifically, that one will confuse it with a half-tarqab.*

H. *And this proves that one may err by a quarter.*

I. *If so, a half-toman and an uqla measure are things people should not make.* [Slotki: The difference between a half-toman, a sixteenth-qab, and an uqla, a twentieth-qab, is only one-eightieth of a qab, which is a fifth of the half-toman, less than a quarter, so that these two measures could certainly be mistaken for one another.]

J. *Said R. Pappa, "With small measures people are quite expert."*

K. *What about a third of a hin and a fourth of a hin — shouldn't people be forbidden to make these?*

L. *Since these were utilized in the sanctuary, rabbis made no decree in their regard.*

M. *Well, shouldn't there be a precautionary decree with respect to the sanctuary?*

N. *The priests are meticulous in their work.*

III.16 A. Said Samuel, "They may not increase the size of the measures [whether or not people concur] by more than a sixth, nor the coins by more than a sixth, and he who makes a profit must not profit by more than a sixth."

B. What is the operative consideration for the first of these three rulings?

C. *If we say that it is because the market prices will rise, then for that same consideration, it should not be permitted to increase the size of the measures even by a sixth. And if the operative consideration is overreaching, so that the transaction should not have to be annulled, did not Raba say, "One can retract from an agreement that involves fraud in measure, weight, or number, even though it is less than the standard, a sixth, of overreaching." And if the operative consideration is that the dealer may not incur any loss, then is the whole purpose of the law to guard him from loss? Is he not entitled to make a profit? But "buy and sell at no profit, merely to be called a merchant!"*

D. *Rather, said R. Hisda, "Samuel identified a verse of Scripture and interpreted it, 'And the sheqel shall be twenty gerahs, twenty sheqels, twenty-five sheqels, ten and five sheqels shall be your maneh' (Ezek. 45:12). [90B] Now was the maneh to be two hundred forty denars?* [But it is supposed to be twenty-five sheqels or a hundred denars (Cashdan).] *But three facts are to be inferred from this statement:* [1] The maneh used in the sanctuary is worth double what the maneh is usually worth; [2] they may not increase the size of the measures [whether or not people concur] by more than a sixth, and [3] the sixth is added over and above the original [so to add a sixth, the original is divided into five parts and another part of equal value, making a sixth one, then is added to it, so the maneh consisted of 240 denars (Cashdan, *Menahot*)]."

III.17 A.   *R. Pappa bar Samuel ordained a measure of three qepizi.* They said to him, "Lo, said Samuel, 'They may not increase the size of the measures [whether or not people concur] by more than a sixth'!"

B.   *He said to them, "What I am ordaining is an entirely new measure." He sent it to Pumbedita, and they did not adopt it. He sent it to Papunia and they adopted it, naming it the Pappa measure.*

Any doubt that we are dealing with a miscellany is removed by what follows, which in no way pertains to the foregoing in any detail. And yet it is introduced for a very clear purpose, which is to make a point about a common theme and proposition: fair dealing in the market, giving and getting true value.

III.18 A.   *Our rabbis have taught on Tannaite authority:*

B.   Concerning those who store up produce, lend money on usury, falsify measures, and price gouge, Scripture says, "Saying, when will the new moon be gone, that we may sell grain, and the Sabbath, that we may set forth grain? Making the ephah small and the sheqel great and falsifying the balances of deceit" (Amos 8:5). And in their regard, Scripture states, "The Lord has sworn by the pride of Jacob, surely I will never forget any of their works" (Amos 8:7).

C.   *What would be an example of those who store up produce?*

D.   *Said R. Yohanan, "Like Shabbetai the produce hoarder."*

III.19 A.   *The father of Samuel would sell produce at the early market price when the early market price prevailed [that is, cheap, so keeping prices down through the year (Slotki)]. Samuel his son held the produce back and sold it when the late market prices prevailed, but at the early market price.*

B.   *They sent word from there, "The father is better than the son. How come? Prices that have been held down remain down."*

III.20 A.   Said Rab, "Someone may store up his own produce" [but may not hoard for trading purposes (Slotki)].

B.   *So, too, it has been taught on Tannaite authority:*

C.   [Following Tosefta's version:] They do not hoard in the Land of Israel things upon which life depends, for example, wine, oil, fine flour, and produce. But things upon which life does not depend, for instance, cummin and spice, lo, this is permitted. And they put things in storage for three years, the eve of the seventh year, the seventh year itself, and the year after the seventh year.

D.   Under what circumstances?

E.   In the case of that which one purchases in the market.

F.   But in the case of what one puts aside from what he himself has grown, even for a period of ten years it is permitted.

G.   But in a year of famine even a qab of carobs one should not put into storage, because he brings a curse on the prices [by forcing them upward through artificial demand] [T. A.Z. 4:1A-G].

III.21 A.   *Said R. Yosé b. R. Hanina to Puga his servant, "Go, store up fruit for me for the next three years: the eve of the Sabbatical Year, the Sabbatical Year, and the year after the Sabbatical Year."*

III.22 A.   *Our rabbis have taught on Tannaite authority:*

B. They do not export from the Land of Israel to Syria things upon which life depends, for example, wine, oil, and fine flour.

C. R. Judah b. Batera says, "I say that they export wine to Syria, because in doing so, one diminishes silliness [in the Land of Israel]."

D. Just as they do not export to Syria, so they do not export from one hyparchy to another.

E. And R. Judah permits doing so [91A] from one hyparchy to another [T. A.Z. 4:2].

III.23 A. *Our rabbis have taught on Tannaite authority:*

B. They are not to make a profit in the Land of Israel from the necessities of life, for instance, wine, oil, and flour.

C. They said concerning R. Eleazar b. Azariah that he would make a profit from wine and oil all his life [T. A.Z. 4:1H-J].

D. *In the matter of wine, he concurred with the view of R. Judah [b. Batera], and in the matter of oil, as it happens, in the place where R. Eleazar b. Azariah lived, oil was abundant.*

III.24 A. *Our rabbis have taught on Tannaite authority:*

B. People are not to profit from eggs twice.

C. *Said Mari bar Mari, "There was a dispute between Rab and Samuel. One says, 'Two for one' [selling for two what was bought for one], and the other said, 'Selling by a dealer to a dealer' [making two profits on the same object]."*

III.25 A. *Our rabbis have taught on Tannaite authority:*

B. They sound the alarm on account of a collapse in the market in trading goods even on the Sabbath.

C. Said R. Yohanan, "For instance, linen clothing in Babylonia and wine and oil in the Land of Israel."

D. *Said R. Joseph, "But that is the case when these are so cheap that ten go for the price of six."*

III.26 A. *Our rabbis have taught on Tannaite authority:*

B. A person is not allowed to emigrate from the Land of Israel unless wheat goes at the price of two seahs for a sela.

C. Said R. Simeon, "Under what circumstances? Only in a case in which he does not find any to buy even at that price. But if he finds some to buy at that price, even if a seah of grain goes for a sela, he should not emigrate."

D. And so did R. Simeon bar Yohai say, "Elimelech, Machlon, and Kilion were the great men of his time, and one of those who sustained the generation. But because he went abroad, he and his sons died in famine. But all the Israelites were able to survive on their own land, as it is said, 'and when they came to Bethlehem, the whole town was stirred because of them' (Ruth 1:19). This teaches that all of the town had survived, but he and his sons had died in the famine" [T. A.Z. 4:4A-H].

III.27 A "And when they came to Bethlehem, the whole town was stirred because of them, and the women said, 'Is this Naomi'" (Ruth 1:19):

B. *What is the meaning of the phrase, "Is this Naomi"?*

C. Said R. Isaac, "They said, 'Did you see what happened to Naomi, who emigrated from the Land to a foreign country?'"

III.28 A. And said R. Isaac, "The day that Ruth the Moabite emigrated from the Land to a foreign land, the wife of Boaz died. *That is in line with what people say: 'Before a person dies, his successor as master of the house is appointed.'"*

III.29 A. Said Rabbah bar R. Huna said Rab, "Isban is the same as Boaz."

B. *So what in the world does that mean?*

C. *It is in line with what Rabbah b. R. Huna further said, for* said Rabbah bar R. Huna said Rab, "Boaz made for his sons a hundred and twenty wedding banquets: 'And Isban had thirty sons and thirty daughters he sent abroad, and thirty daughters he brought from abroad for his sons, and he judged Israel seven years' (Judges 12:9). For each one of them he made two wedding feasts, one in the household of the father, the other in the household of the father-in-law. But to none of them did he invite Manoah, for he said, *'How will that barren mule ever repay my hospitality?'* And all of them died in his lifetime. That is in line with what people say, *'In your lifetime you begot sixty? What good are the sixty? Marry again and get another one, brighter than all sixty.'"*

III.30 A. Said R. Hanan bar Raba said Rab, "Elimelech and Salmon and 'such a one' (Ruth 4:1) and the father of Naomi were all sons of Nahshon b. Amminadab (Ex. 6:23, Num. 10:14)."

B. *So what in the world does that mean?*

C. It is that even one who has a substantial store of unearned merit gained from his answers, it will serve him no good when he emigrates from the Land to a foreign land."

III.31 A. And said R. Hanan bar Raba said Rab, "*The mother of Abraham was named Amathelai, daughter of Karnebo; the name of the mother of Haman was Amatehilai, daughter of Orabti; and the mnemonic will be, 'unclean to the unclean, clean to the clean.' The mother of David was Nizbeth daughter of Adael, the mother of Samson was Zlelponit, and his sister was Nasyan."*

B. *So what?*

C. For answering heretics.

III.32 A. And said R. Hanan bar Raba said Rab, "For ten years our father, Abraham, was kept in prison, three in Kuta, seven in Kardu."

B. *And R. Dimi of Nehardea repeats the matter in reverse order.*

C. *Said R. Hisda, "The lesser Kuta is the same as Ur of the Chaldees (Gen. 11:31)."*

III.33 A. And said R. Hanan bar Raba said Rab, "The day on which our father, Abraham, died, all of the principal authorities of the nations of the world formed a line and said, 'Woe is the world that has lost [91B] its leader, woe to the ship that has lost its helmsman.'"

III.34 A. "And you are exalted as head above all" (1 Chr. 29:11):

B. *Said R. Hanan bar Raba said Rab, "Even the superintendent of the water supply is appointed by Heaven."*

III.35 A. Said R. Hiyya bar Abin said R. Joshua b. Qorhah, "God forbid! Even if [Elimelech and his family] had found bran, they would never have emigrated. So why were they punished? Because they should have besought mercy for their generation but failed to do so: 'When you cry, let them that you have gathered deliver you' (Isa. 57:13)."

III.36 A   Said Rabbah bar bar Hannah said R. Yohanan, "This [prohibition against emigration] has been taught only when money is cheap [and abundant] and produce expensive, but when money is expensive [and not to be found, there being no capital], even if four seahs cost only a sela, it is permitted to emigrate."

B   *Said R. Yohanan, "I remember when four seahs of grain cost a sela and many died of starvation in Tiberias, not having an issar for bread."*

C   *And said R. Yohanan, "I remember when workmen wouldn't agree to work on the east side of town, where workers were dying because of the scent of bread [which they could not afford to buy]."*

III.37 A   *And said R. Yohanan, "I remember when a child would break open a carob pod and a line of honey would run over both his arms."*

B   *And said R. Eleazar, "I remember when a raven would grab a piece of meat and a line of oil would run down from the top of the wall to the ground."*

C   *And said R. Yohanan, "I remember when boys and girls would promenade in the market at the age of sixteen or seventeen and not sin."*

D   *And said R. Yohanan, "I remember when they would say in the house of study, 'Who agrees with them falls into their power, who trusts in them — what is his becomes theirs.'"*

III.38 A   It is written, "Mahlon and Chilion" (Ruth 1:2) and it is written "Joash and Saraph" (1 Chr. 4:22)!

B   Rab and Samuel —

C   One said, "Their names really were Mahlon and Chilion, and why were they called Joash? Because they despaired hope of redemption [the words for Joash and despair using the same letters], and Saraph? Because they become liable by the decree of the Omnipresent to be burned."

D   And the other said, "Their names really were Joash and Saraph, but they were called Mahlon and Chilion, Mahlon, because they profaned their bodies [the words for Mahlon and profane using the same letters], and Chilion, because they were condemned by the Omnipresent to destruction [the words for destruction and Chilion using the same letters]."

E   *It has been taught on Tannaite authority in accord with the view of him who said that their names really were Mahlon and Chilion. For it has been taught on Tannaite authority:* What is the meaning of the verse, "And Jokim and the men of Cozeba and Joash and Saraph, who had dominion in Moab, and Jashubilehem, and the things are ancient" (1 Chr. 4:22)?

F   "Jokim": this refers to Joshua, who kept his oath to the men of Gibeon (Josh. 9:15, 26).

G   "And the men of Cozeba": these are the men of Gibeon who lied to Joshua [the words for lie and Cozeba using the same letters] (Josh. 9:4).

H   "And Joash and Saraph": Their names really were Mahlon and Chilion, and why were they called Joash? Because they despaired hope of redemption [the words for Joash and despair using the same letters], and Saraph? Because they become liable by the decree of the Omnipresent to be burned.

I   "Who had dominion in Moab": they married wives of the women of Moab.

J.   "And Jashubilehem:" this refers to Ruth of Moab, who had returned [using letters that are shared with Jashub] and remained in Bethlehem of Judah.

K.   "And the things are ancient": these things were stated by the Ancient of Days.

III.39 A   "These were the potters and those that dwelt among plantations and hedges; there they dwelt occupied in the king's work" (1 Chr. 4:23):

B.   "These were the potters": this refers to the sons of Jonadab, son of Rahab, who kept the oath of their father (Jer. 35:6).

C.   "And those that dwelt among plantations": this speaks of Solomon, who in his rule was like a fecund plant.

D.   "And hedges": this refers to the Sanhedrin, who hedged in the breaches in Israel.

E.   "There they dwelt occupied in the kings work": this speaks of Ruth of Moab, who lived to see the rule of Solomon, her grandson's grandson: "And Solomon caused a throne to be set up for the king's mother" (1 Kgs. 2:19), in which connection R. Eleazar said, "For the mother of the dynasty."

III.40 A.   *Our rabbis have taught on Tannaite authority:*

B.   "And you shall eat of the produce, the old store" (Lev. 25:22) – without requiring preservatives.

C.   *What is the meaning of* without requiring preservatives?

D.   R. Nahman said, "Without grain worms."

E.   And R. Sheshet said, "Without blast."

F.   *It has been taught on Tannaite authority in accord with the view of R. Sheshet, and it has been taught on Tannaite authority in accord with the view of R. Nahman.*

G.   *It has been taught on Tannaite authority in accord with the view of R. Nahman:*

H.   "And you shall eat the old store" (Lev. 25:22) – might one suppose that the sense is that the Israelites will be eager for the new produce because last year's has been destroyed [by the grain worm]? Scripture says, "until her produce came in," that is, until the produce will come on its own [without an early, forced harvest (Slotki)].

I.   *It has been taught on Tannaite authority in accord with the view of R. Sheshet:*

J.   "And you shall eat of the produce, the old store" (Lev. 25:22) – might one suppose that the sense is that the Israelites will be eager for the new produce because last year's has been spoiled [Slotki: by the blast]? Scripture states, "until her produce came in," that is, until the new crop will come in the natural way.

III.41 A.   *Our rabbis have taught on Tannaite authority:*

B.   "And you shall eat old store long kept" (Lev. 26:10) – whatever is of an older vintage than its fellow is better in quality than its fellow.

C.   I know that that is so only of things that are ordinarily aged. What about things that are not ordinarily aged?

D.   Scripture is explicit: "old store long kept" (Lev. 26:10) – in all cases.

III.42 A   "And you shall bring forth the old from before the new" (Lev. 26:10) –

B.   This teaches that the storehouses will be full of last year's crop, and the threshing floors, this year's crop, and the Israelites will say, "How are we going to remove the one before the other?"

C.   *Said R. Pappa, "Everything is better when aged, except for dates, beer, and fish-hash."*

III.1, 2 provide a scriptural basis for the rule and principle of the Mishnah. The key verse of No. 2 accounts for the inclusion of No. 3, which carries in its wake No. 4. Further Tannaite thematic supplements are at Nos. 5-8. No. 8 is glossed by No. 9, and then Nos. 10-12+13, 14 continue the Tannaite supplement. Carrying forward the general theme at hand, Nos. 15-42 form a miscellany built around the general theme before us. I see no formal differences between the miscellany at hand and those we have already examined. The only difference is subject matter – but not *classification of subject matter.* Is it possible, then, to state the propositions of the subsets of the miscellany? These seem to me to state the paramount proposals:

1. People are to employ honest measures and when selling, to give accurate and honest measures: Nos. 5-17.
2. People are not to take advantage of shortages nor create shortages: Nos. 18-25.
3. If there are shortages, people are to try to remain in the Land of Israel if they possibly can: Nos. 26-28+29-36, 37-40.

One might argue that the combination of the set yields the syllogism that honesty in buying and selling the necessities of life is what makes possible Israel's possession of the Holy Land, but that does not seem to me a plausible proposal. I see here only a thematic composite, all the numbered items addressed to that single theme, perhaps, furthermore, with a number of cogent propositions joining some of the compositions as well.

The conclusion may be stated very simply. We have now formed a hypothesis that quite random compositions, each with its own focus, will be formed into a composite on the basis of one of three theories of linkage: [1] topic, [2] attribution, or [3] sequence of verses of a passage of Scripture. The agglutination of topically coherent compositions predominates. And this leads to a further theory on the miscellany. The conglomerates of random compositions formed into topical composites ordinarily serve as an amplification of a topic treated in the Mishnah, or are joined to a composite that serves in that way, so that, over all, the miscellanies are made to extend and amplify the statements of the Mishnah, as much as, though in a different way from, the commonplace propositional, analytical, and syllogistic composite.

On the basis of that hypothesis, which has to be tested against the evidence of all of the other miscellanies of the Bavli, I should be prepared to propose the further hypothesis that the Bavli contains no important or sizable sequences of compositions that are entirely unrelated to one another, that is, nothing we should classify as a mere miscellany at all. Faced with three massive miscellanies, we have come to the conclusion that what appears to be a random hodgepodge of this and that and the other thing in fact forms a considered and even crafted composite, the agglutinative principles of which we may readily discern. In fact what we have in the miscellany is nothing more than a Mishnah commentary of a peculiar sort, itself extended and spun out, as the more conventional Mishnah commentaries of the Bavli tend to be extended and spun out. The miscellany may be defined, therefore, in a very simple way: it is, specifically, a composite that has been compiled so as to present for the Mishnah a commentary intending to provide information on topics introduced by the Mishnah – that, and not much more than that. True, the miscellany is not propositional, and it is certainly not analytical. But it is very much a composite in the sense in which I have defined that literary structure in the present context: purposeful, coherent, and I think, elegant. I do not claim that the pages of tractates Berakhot and Sanhedrin may compete in power and intellect with the pages of tractate Baba Qamma where we began. I do claim that what appears by contrast to those pages to be odd, incoherent, pointless, rambling, to the contrary attests in its own way to the single and definitive program of the Bavli's framers. Whatever those framers wished to say on their own account they insisted on setting forth within the framework of that received document upon the structure of which they made everything to depend. All the more reason to admire the remarkable originality and genuinely fresh perspective – and statement – that, in the guise of a commentary, the Bavli was to make.

5

The Bavli's Essential Discourse:
The Law behind the Laws

The good student learns lessons. The great disciple draws conclusions. The framers of the Bavli, or of important materials utilized in the Bavli, comprised both excellent students and also great intellects. The fine pupils wrote the Mishnah commentary that the Bavli imposes upon the Mishnah. Great minds transformed a small part of the work of Mishnah commentary into a free-standing, autonomous inquiry into the principles of the right conduct of the social order. Elsewhere I review the good work of good minds.[1] In this chapter we encounter some of the great work of truly formidable intellects: those who not only took notes but asked their own questions, not only summarized and clarified the thought of others, but joined issue with the substance of the matter.

If they were thinking about the future reading of their writing, the framers of the document provided for two quite distinct kinds of audience for their ideas, the normal, and the exceptional. In these pages we shall see how the framers of the Bavli provided for not only good students, for whom they explained the meaning of the Mishnah's statements, but also presented for ambitious minds the challenge of drawing conclusions: rules that govern in a great many cases, the laws that explain the deepest layers of social being. The routine parts of the Bavli predominate, just as, in its audience for centuries afterward, the merely bright students of the writing would form the main body of its readers. But the great pieces of intellectual daring in the Bavli impart the flavor to the whole; they invited the reader into the processes of thought that the writers of the Bavli meant to inaugurate. And they made a place

---

[1]*The Bavli's Primary Discourse. Mishnah Commentary, its Rhetorical Paradigms and Their Theological Implications in the Talmud of Babylonia* (Atlanta, 1992: Scholars Press for South Florida Studies in the History of Judaism.)

for future intellects, at least, those capable of not merely listening but also, intelligibly and thoughtfully, finding something for themselves to say and even speaking out as well – as, for generations to come, people would. And through these great minds, wherever the Jewish people would make its life, the Bavli would govern and transform the social order of Israel through imparting the shape and structure to these formative intellects: the ones that defined thought, shaped attitude, and set forth ideas – and still do.

Even though an abstract and discursive, speculative and wide-ranging kind of writing occupies only a modest part of the Bavli overall, I maintain that it is when the framers of the Bavli test propositions of considerable weight, bearing consequences that make a substantial difference in the ordering of society, that they transform their document from a merely interesting to a truly important one.[2] For when I am told what words and phrases of the Mishnah mean, or the sources of the document, or its ad hoc and episodic principles, relating case to case, I remain entirely within the limits of the Mishnah itself. I have no occasion to move outward, from the details of the document to the main lines of order and structure that, viewed as a whole, the law that the document in detail presents turns out to set forth. And, it is clear, the framers of the Bavli read the Mishnah in such a way that it did more than teach lessons. It made possible the testing of propositions of a general intelligibility vastly transcending the details of the Mishnah itself. It provoked the drawing of conclusions. Clearly, no adequate description of the Bavli, such as this and the parallel experimental monographs are meant to make possible, is going to omit a sustained study of the essential discourse of the document: the law behind the laws, which is, the law that moves outward from the laws, toward that unknown world that the Bavli's framers turn out to have constructed, though they cannot ever have imagined it. Now we see how they did so – turning lessons into examples, drawing conclusions, forming paradigms.

By a quest for "the law behind the laws" I mean far more than a composite that surveys a variety of tractates or covers more than one or

---

[2]There is a second kind of composite building that is comparable to the discursive inquiry into principles behind many laws or yielded by many laws, such as are surveyed here. It is the composite that investigates hermeneutical or exegetical issues, not on a one-time basis or in a haphazard way, but systematically and in a comprehensive manner. One of the most interesting of these will give us a sustained argument, for two or more pages of the Bavli, on diverse ways of reading a set of verses and solving a problem of demonstration on the basis of Scripture of conflicting propositions. Whether or not the project of describing the Bavli requires a representation of this other kind of large-scale composite formation is not yet clear to me.

two topics of the law. Let me therefore provide a sizable example of a survey of linguistic usages covering many topics and tractates, which in no way proposes to identify a single principle that is shared among those laws or that generates them all. What we have in the following is a first-rate exercise in philology through the comparison and contrast of examples of a single usage. While that survey is interesting and, in context, provides lexical insight pertinent to diverse texts of the Mishnah and related compilations, it in no way attempts at generalization, abstraction, restatement of the particular in an encompassing framework, or any of those other processes that, we shall deem, characterize the essential discourses, the ones that aim at finding the law behind the laws. Here is the form, but not the substance of a survey of many things from a single perspective.

Bavli Arakhin 1:1 A-G

A. [2A] All pledge the Valuation [of others] and are subject to the pledge of Valuation [by others],

B. vow [the worth of another] and are subject to the vow [of payment of their worth by another]:

C. priests and Levites and Israelites, women and slaves.

D. A person of doubtful sexual traits and hermaphrodites vow [the worth of another] and are subject to the vow [of payment of their worth by another], pledge the Valuation [of others], but are not subject to the pledge of Valuation by others,

E. for only [a person of] clear masculine or clear feminine [traits] is subject to the pledge of Valuation [by others].

F. A deaf mute, an imbecile, and a minor are subject to the vow [of payment of their worth by another], and are subject to the pledge of Valuation by others, but do not vow the worth, and do not pledge the Valuation, of others,

G. for they do not possess understanding.

I.

A. [When the framer explicitly refers to] all, [in framing the Mishnah paragraph at hand, saying All pledge...,] what [classification of persons does he intend] to include, [seeing that in what follows, C, he lists the available classifications of persons in any event, and, further, at D-G specifies categories of persons that are excluded? Accordingly, to what purpose does he add the encompassing language, all, at the outset?]

B. It serves to encompass a male nearing puberty [who has not yet passed puberty. Such a one is subject to examination to determine whether he grasps the meaning of a vow, such as is under discussion. A child younger than the specified age, twelve years to thirteen, is assumed not to have such understanding, and one older is taken for granted to have it.]

C. [When the framer explicitly frames matters as **all] are subject to the pledge of Valuation,** what [classification of persons does he intend] to include?

D. It is to include a person who is disfigured or afflicted with a skin ailment.

E. [Why in any event should one imagine that persons of that classification would be omitted?] I might have supposed that, since it is written, "A vow... according to your Valuation" (Lev. 27:2), [with Scripture using as equivalent terms "vow" and "Valuation,"] the rule is that [only] those who possess an [intrinsic] worth [e.g., whoever would be purchased for a sum of money in the marketplace, hence excluding the disfigured persons under discussion, who are worthless] also would be subject to a vow of Valuation [at a fixed price, such as Scripture specified]. On the other hand, [I might have supposed that] whoever does not possess an [intrinsic] worth also would not be subject to a vow of Valuation. [Thus, according to this line of reasoning, I might think a person disfigured or afflicted with a skin ailment is not subject to the pledge of Valuation.]

F. Accordingly, [the formulation of the Mishnah passage at hand] tells us, [to the contrary, that a pledge of Valuation is not dependent upon the market value of the person subject to that pledge. The Valuation represents an absolute charge and is not relative to the subject's market value.]

G. [How does Scripture so signify? When the framer of Scripture refers at Lev. 27:2 to] "persons," [the meaning is that a pledge of Valuation applies] to anyone at all.

H. [When the framer of the Mishnah, further, states that *all*] vow [the worth of another], what [classification of persons does he thereby intend] to include [seeing that at C we go over the same matter, specifying those who may make such a vow]?

I. It is necessary for him [to specify *all* to indicate that *all* also applies to] those concerning whom such a vow is taken.

J. [Therefore, when the framer specifies that all] are subject to a vow, what [classification of persons does he thereby intend] to include?

K. [Here matters are not so self-evident, for] if the intention is to include a person of doubtful sexual traits and a person who exhibits the traits of both sexes, both of these classifications are explicitly stated [in the formulation of the Mishnah passage itself].

L. And if the intention is to include a deaf mute, an imbecile, and a minor, these classifications also are explicitly stated. [So what can have been omitted in the explicit specification of the pertinent classification, that the framer of the Mishnah passage found it necessary to make use of such amplificatory language as *all*?]

M. If, furthermore, the intent was to include an infant less than a month old, that classification also is explicitly included [below].

N. If, furthermore, the intent was to include an idolator, that classification furthermore is explicitly included as well. [Accordingly, what classification of persons can possibly have been omitted in the framing of the Mishnah passage at hand, that the author found it necessary to add the emphatic inclusionary language to imply that further categories, beyond those made explicit, are in mind?]

Q   In point of fact, [the purpose of adding the emphatic language of inclusion] was to encompass an infant less than a month in age.

P.   [The framer of the passage] taught [that such a category is included by use of the word all] and then he went and stated the matter explicitly [to clearly indicate the inclusion of that category].

II.

A   [When, at M. Men. 9:8, we find the formulation], **All lay hands [on a beast to be slaughtered, that is, including not only the owner of the beast, who set it aside and consecrated it for the present sacrificial purpose, but also some other party]**, whom do we find included [by the inclusionary language, *all* of M. Men. 9:8]?

B.   [It is used to indicate] the inclusion of the heir [of the owner of the beast who consecrated it and subsequently died. The heir of the deceased owner may take his place vis-à-vis his beast, and lay his hands on the beast, and so derive benefit from the sacrifice of that beast, even though he did not originally designate it as holy.]

C.   And that inclusion does not accord with the position of R. Judah [who maintains that, since Scripture specifies at Lev. 1:3 that the person who has designated the beast as a holy sacrifice "shall lay hands on it," excluded are all other parties, who did not designate the beast as holy. Only the owner of the beast may lay hands, and no one else. In so formulating the rule by using the inclusionary language, *all*, the framer of the passage has indicated that he rejects the position of Judah].

D.   [And when, at M. Tem. 1:1, we find the formulation,] **All effect an act of substitution** [so consecrating the beast that is supposed to take the place of the originally consecrated beast, in line with Lev. 27:10, but leaving that originally consecrated beast in the status of consecration nonetheless], what category [of person] do we find included [by the use of such language]?

E   [Once more], the use of such language indicates the inclusion of the heir [of the owner of the beast, who originally consecrated it and died before sacrificing it, just as at B, above].

F.   And that inclusion once more does not accord with the position of R. Judah [for Lev. 27:10 states, "*He* shall not alter it...," thus referring solely to the owner of the beast, and not to an heir or any other third party].

G.   [Now the statements just given accord with] that which has been taught [in a tradition external to the Mishnah but deriving from authorities named in the Mishnah], as follows:

H   An heir lays hands [on a beast originally consecrated by the deceased], an heir effects an act of substitution [in regard to a beast originally consecrated by the deceased].

I.   R. Judah says, "An heir does not lay on hands, an heir does not effect an act of substitution."

J.   What is the scriptural basis for the position of R. Judah?

K.   "His offering..." (Lev. 3:2, 7, 13: "He shall lay his hand upon the head of his offering") – and not the offering that was set aside by his father.

L.   From the rule governing the end of the process of consecrating [the laying on of hands] [R. Judah further] derives the rule governing the beginning of the process of consecrating a beast [e.g., through an act of substitution, which indicates that a given beast is substituted for, therefore shares the status, of another beast that already has been consecrated. In this way the beast put forward as a substitution is itself deemed to be sanctified.] [Accordingly, a single principle governs both stages in the sacrificial process, the designation of the beast as holy and therefore to be sacrificed, e.g., through an act of substitution, and the laying on of hands just prior to the act of sacrificial slaughter itself. Just as the latter action may be performed solely by the owner of the beast, who derives benefit from the act of sacrifice, so the former action likewise is effective only when the owner of the beast carries it out.]

M.   Accordingly, just as, at the end of the process of consecration, the heir does not lay on hands, so at the beginning of the process of consecration, an heir does not carry out an act of substitution.

N.   And as to the position of rabbis [vis-à-vis Judah, who maintain that the heir may do so, how do they read Scripture in such wise as to derive their view?]

O.   [Scripture states,] "And if changing, he shall change" (Lev. 27:10) [thus intensively using the same verb twice, with one usage understood to refer to the owner himself, the other usage to some closely related person].

P.   [The use of the verbal intensive therefore is meant] to include the heir, and, as before, we derive the rule governing the conclusion of the sacrificial process [with the laying on of hands] from the rule governing the commencement of the sacrificial process [the designation of the beast as holy, by its substitution for an already consecrated beast].

Q.   Accordingly, just as, at the beginning of the process of consecration, the heir does carry out an act of substitution, so at the end of the process of consecration, the heir does lay on hands.

R.   Now [given rabbis' reading of the relevant verses], how do these same rabbis deal with Scripture's three references to "*his* offering" [which in Judah's view makes explicit that only the owner of the beast lays hands on his beast, cf. Lev. 3:2, 7, 13]?

S.   They require that specification of Scripture to lay down the rule that [an Israelite] lays hands on his sacrifice, but not on the sacrifice of an idolator, on his sacrifice and not on the sacrifice of his fellow:

T.   on his sacrifice, further, to include all those who own a share in the sacrificial animal, according to each the right to lay hands upon the beast [of which they are partners].

U.   And as to R. Judah? He does not take the view that all those who own a share in the sacrificial animal have a right to lay hands on the beast.

V.   Alternatively, [one may propose that] he does maintain the stated position [concerning the partners in a sacrificial animal].

W.   [But] he derives the rule governing [2B] the idolator['s beast] and that of one's fellow from a single verse of Scripture [among the three verses that make explicit that one lays hands on *his* animal], leaving available for the demonstration of a quite separate proposition two [other] of these same [three] references.

X. [It follows, for Judah's position, that] one of these verses serves to indicate, "*His* offering" and not "the offering of his father," and another of the available verses then serves to include [among those who indeed may lay hands on the sacrificial beast] all shareholders, according to each of them the right to lay hands on the beast held in common partnership.

Y. [Further exploring the thesis of Judah about the scriptural basis for his view, exactly] how does R. Judah interpret the intensive verb used at Lev. 27:10, "And if changing, he shall change?"

Z. He requires that usage to include the participation of the woman [in the process of substitution, so that if a woman makes a statement effecting an act of substitution, that statement is as valid as if a man had made it].

AA. That [view of his reading] is in accord with the following tradition assigned to Tannaitic authority:

BB. Since the entire formulation of the passage concerning an act of substitution speaks of the male, how in the end shall we include the female as well [so that an act of substitution of a woman is regarded as valid]?

CC. Scripture states, "And if changing, he shall change...." [The intensive language serves to include the woman.]

DD. And as to rabbis, [how do they prove the same position]?

EE. It is from the use of the inclusionary words, *and, if,* in the phrase, "And if changing...."

FF. And as to the view of R. Judah [in this same regard]?

GG. The usage, "And if...," in his view is not subject to exegesis at all [and yields no additional information about the rule under discussion. Accordingly, in order to prove that a woman is involved in the process of substitution, as much as a man, Judah must refer solely to the intensive verb construction.]

III.

A. All are obligated [to carry out the religious duty of dwelling in] a tabernacle [on the Festival of Tabernacles].

B. [When the framer of the foregoing statement makes explicit use of the inclusionary language, *all*], what [classification of persons is] encompassed, [that otherwise would have been omitted]?

C. It is to include a minor who does not depend upon his mother [but can take care of himself], in line with the following statement found in the Mishnah [M. Suk. 2:8:] **A child who does not depend upon his mother is liable to [carry out the religious duty of dwelling in a] tabernacle.**

D. All are liable [to carry out the religious duty of taking up] the palm branch [enjoined at Lev. 23:40].

E. [When the framer of the foregoing statement makes explicit use of the inclusionary language, *all*,] what [classification of persons is] included, [that otherwise would have been omitted]?

F. It is to include a minor who knows how to shake [the palm branch, so, with proper intention, making appropriate use of the holy object].

G   That is in line with the following statement found in the Mishnah [M. Suk. 3:15:] **A minor who knows how to shake [the palm branch with proper intention] is liable to [the religious duty of taking up] the palm branch.**

H   All are liable [to carry out the religious duty of affixing] fringes [to the corners of garments].

I   [When the framer of the foregoing statement makes explicit use of the inclusionary language, *all*,] what [classification of persons is] included, [that otherwise would have been omitted]?

J.   It is to include a minor who knows how to cloak himself [in a garment, and so enters the obligation of affixing to said cloak the required fringes, cf. T. Hag. 1:2].

K   For it has been taught [at T. Hag. 1:2]: **A minor who knows how to cloak himself [in a garment] is liable to [affix to that garment the required show] fringes.**

L   All are liable [to carry out the religious duty of wearing] phylacteries.

M   [When the framer of the foregoing statement makes explicit use of the inclusionary language, *all*,] what [classification of persons is] encompassed, [that otherwise would have been omitted]?

N   It is to include a minor who knows how to take care of phylacteries [and therefore may be entrusted with them].

O   For it has been taught [at T. Hag. 1:2]: **As to a minor who knows how to take care of phylacteries, his father purchases phylacteries for him.**

IV.

A   **All are obligated [on the occasion of a pilgrim festival to bring] an appearance-offering [to the Temple and to sacrifice it there in honor of the festival, cf. M. Hag. 1:1].**

B.   [When the framer of the foregoing statement makes explicit use of the inclusionary language, *all*,] what [classification of persons is] included, [that otherwise would have been omitted]?

C.   It is to include a person who is half-slave and half-free. [Such a person is subject to the stated liability of bringing an appearance-offering. But a person who is wholly a slave is exempt from the stated requirement of making the pilgrimage and bringing the offering.]

D.   But in the view of Rabina, who has made the statement that one who is half-slave and half-free [also] is exempt from the obligation of bringing an appearance-offering [in celebration of the pilgrim festival], [in his view] what [classification of persons] is included [by the specification that *all* are subject to the stated obligation]?

E.   It is to include a person who is lame on the first day of the festival but is restored [to full activity] on the second day. [A lame person is exempt from the religious obligation of coming up to Jerusalem on the pilgrim festival, since he obviously cannot make the trip. If, however, as of the second day of the festival, the lame person should be healed, then, according to the formulation of the rule at hand, such a person would become obligated, retrospectively, to bring the required appearance-offering as of the first day.]

F. [The foregoing statement rests on the position that on the successive days of the festival, one has the option of meeting an obligation incurred but not met on the earlier day. Thus if one did not make the required appearance-offering on the first day, he is obligated for it but also may make up for it on the later days of the festival. The obligation for one day pertains to, but then may be made up, on the days following, thus, on day three for day two, on day four for day three, and the like. Accordingly, at E we maintain first, that the person becomes obligated on the second day, and, second, that the obligation then is retroactive to the first. So he can make up what he owes. But the obligation, to begin with, likewise is retroactive. On day two he became obligated for an appearance-offering to cover day one. Accordingly, what we have just proposed] fully accords with the position of him who said that [offerings made on] all [of the days of the festival] serve as a means of carrying out the obligations incurred on each one of them [as just now explained].

G. But in the view of him who says that all of the days of the festival [may serve to make up only for an obligation] incurred on the first day [of the festival alone, so that, first, one does not incur an obligation on a later day of the festival affecting what one owes for an earlier day of the festival, and so that, second, if one is not obligated to bring an appearance-offering on the first day of the festival, he is not obligated to do so on any later day of the festival], what [classification of persons] is included [by use of the inclusionary language, *all*]?

H. It serves to include a person who is blind in one eye. [A person blind in both eyes is exempt from the appearance-offering on the pilgrim festival. One fully sighted, of course, is liable. The intermediate category then is dealt with in the stated formulation.]

I. Now that view would not accord with the following teaching in the authority of sages of the Mishnah, as it has been taught:

J. Yohanan b. Dahabbai says in the name of R. Judah, "One who is blind in one eye is exempt from the religious duty of bringing an appearance-offering, for it is said, 'He will see... he will see...' (Ex. 23:14) [reading the scriptural language not as 'make an appearance,' but, with a shift in the vowels, 'will see,' cf. T. Hag. 1:1].

K. "[The proposed mode of reading the verse at hand yields the following consequence:] Just as one comes to see [the face of the Lord], so he comes to be seen. Just as one sees with two eyes, so one is seen with two eyes" [cf. T. Hag. 1:1F-H]. [The exegesis then excludes a person blind in one eye.]

L. If you prefer, [however, we may revert to the earlier proposal, and] state: Indeed, [the use of the inclusionary language, *all*, is meant] to include a person who is half-slave and half-free.

M. And now as to the question you raised above [D], that that position would not accord with the opinion of Rabina, that indeed poses no problem.

N. [Why not?] The formulation at hand, [which prohibits the half-slave half-free man from bringing the necessary offering] is in line with the original formulation of the Mishnah law [prior to the debate, cited presently, between the Houses of Shammai and

Hillel]. The other formulation [which permits and hence requires the half-slave person, half-free person, in the intermediate status, to bring the appearance-offering] is in line with the posterior formulation of the Mishnah law.

O.   For we have learned [at M. Git. 4:5]:

P.   "He who is half-slave and half-free works for his master one day and for himself one day," the words of the House of Hillel.

Q   Said to them the House of Shammai, "You have taken good care of his master, but of himself you have not taken care.

R.   "To marry a slave girl is not possible, for half of him after all is free [and free persons may marry only other free persons].

S.   "[To marry] a free woman is not possible, for half of him after all is a slave [and slaves may marry only slaves].

T.   "Shall he refrain?

U.   "But was not the world made only for procreation, as it is said, 'He created it not a waste, he formed it to be inhabited' (Isa. 45:18).

V.   "But: For the good order of the world, "they force his master to free him.

W.   "And he [the slave] writes him a bond covering half his value."

X.   And the House of Hillel reverted to teach in accord with the opinion of the House of Shammai. [Accordingly, the law prior to the reversion specified at X treated one who is half-slave and half-free as in a fixed category, and such a one would not bring an appearance-offering, since he was partially a slave. But after the reversion, one who was half-slave and half-free could leave that interstitial category easily and so would not be regarded as essentially a slave. Such a one then would be obligated to bring the appearance-offering, there being no permanent lord over him except for the Lord God.]

V.

A   All are obligated [to the religious duty of hearing] the sounding of the ram's horn [on the New Year] [T. R.H. 4:1].

B.   [When the framer of the passage makes use of the inclusionary language, *all*,] what [classification of persons does he thereby] include?

C   It is to include a minor who has reached the age [at which he is able to benefit from] instruction.

D   For we have learned [in a teaching attributed to the authority of Mishnah sages]: They do not prevent a minor from sounding the ram's horn on the festival day [cf. B. Yoma 72A].

VI.

A   All are subject to the religious obligation of hearing the reading of the Scroll of Esther [T. Meg. 2:7A-B].

B.   All are suitable to read the Scroll of Esther aloud [for the community, thereby fulfilling the religious obligation of all those who are present, M. Meg. 2:4].

C   [When the framer of the passage makes use of the inclusionary language, *all*,] what [classification of persons does he thereby] include [3A]?

D. It is to include women [who may read the Scroll of Esther aloud for the community and thereby carry out the obligation of all present to do so].

E. This view accords with the position of R. Joshua b. Levi. For R. Joshua b. Levi said, "Women are liable [to the religious duty of] the reading of the Scroll of Esther, for they, too, were included in the miracle [of redemption from Israel's enemies, celebrated on Purim, cf. B. Meg. 4A]."

VII.

A. **All are liable to the religious duty of saying Grace in public quorum [if they have eaten together. They thus may not say Grace after meals by themselves, if a quorum of three persons is present. In that circumstance a public recitation, involving a call to Grace, is required, T. Ber. 5:15.]**

B. [When the framer of the rule uses the inclusionary language,] what [classification of persons] does he mean to include?

C. He means to include women and slaves.

D. For it has been taught [in a teaching bearing the authority of Mishnah teachers]: Women say Grace in public as a group [unto] themselves, and slaves do likewise. [Accordingly, both classifications of persons are subject to the liability of saying a public Grace should a quorum of appropriate persons be present].

VIII.

A. All join in the public saying of Grace [responding to the call to say Grace].

B. [When the framer of the ruler uses the cited inclusionary language,] what [classification of persons] does he mean to include?

C. It is to include a minor who has knowledge on his own concerning Him to whom they say a blessing [in the Grace after meals].

D. That is in line with what R. Nahman said, "He who knows to Whom they say a blessing [in the Grace after meals] – they include such a one in the public call to say the Grace after meals."

IX.

A. **All are subject to becoming unclean by reason of the flux [specified at Lev. 15:1ff., M. Zab. 2:1].**

B. [When the framer of the rule uses the cited inclusionary language,] what [classification of persons does he mean to] include?

C. It is to include an infant one day old [who, should he produce a flux, would be deemed subject to flux uncleanness under appropriate circumstances. This form of genital uncleanness is not limited to an adult.]

D. For it has been taught [in a teaching bearing the authority of Mishnah sages]: "[When any] man [produces flux out of his flesh]" (Lev. 15:2).

E. "Now why does the Author of Scripture state, "When any man..." [so indicating an inclusion of some category beyond man]?

F. "It is to include even an infant a day old, who thus is subject to the uncleanness of flux, "the words of R. Judah.

G. R. Ishmael, the son of R. Yohanan b. Beroqah, says, "It is hardly necessary [to interpret Scripture in such wise]. Lo, [Scripture] says,

'And any of them who has an issue, whether it is male or female' (Lev. 15:33).

H   "[The sense is], 'Male,' meaning whoever is male, whether minor or adult. 'Female' [means], whoever is female, whether minor or adult. [Both categories, minor and adult, male and female, fall within the classification of those subject to uncleanness through flux. Scripture is explicit in this matter, without the necessity of interpreting the language important in Judah's view.]

I   "If that is the case, then on what account does [the Author of Scripture] use the language, 'If any man...'? [The Author of] the Torah made use of the language of common speech [and did not mean to provide occasions for exegesis of minor details of formulation]."

X.

A.   All are subject to being made unclean through corpse uncleanness.

B.   [When the framer of the foregoing statement uses the inclusionary word, *all*,] what [classification of persons does he thereby] to include?

C.   It is to include a minor.

D.   [How so?] I might have proposed that [when Scripture states,] "When a man becomes unclean and does not undertake a rite of purification" (Num. 19:20), [the meaning of the Author of Scripture is,] "a man indeed [is subject to the law of corpse uncleanness] but a minor is not [subject to that same law]."

E.   Accordingly [by using the inclusive language, *all are subject*,] [the framer of the passage] informs us [that this is not the case].

F.   [And indeed the same passage continues,] "And upon the persons that were there" (Num. 19:18), [Thus using the language, "persons," which also is inclusive and encompasses a minor, we are able to prove the besought point. Accordingly, we must ask for some other exegetical value to be associated with the language, "When a man...." For we now realize that the minor is included by the language, "persons," and thus we recognize that the further word choice, "man," serves to exclude some classification. So we need to find out – as the passage unfolds – what classification of persons is included by the one, yet excluded by the other, or for what purpose an inclusion and an exclusion are joined. It is to that secondary issue that we now proceed.]

G.   [Accordingly, we ask,] But what [sort of] exclusion [is effected by the language,] "Man" [used at Num. 19:20]?

H.   It serves to exclude a minor from the penalty of extirpation [should he violate the law governing cultic cleanness. Although a minor is expected to observe the laws of flux he would not suffer the penalty specified at Num. 19:20 if he failed to do so, since that verse speaks only of an adult.]

XI.

A.   **All are subject to becoming unclean through the skin ailment [M. Neg. 3:1A].**

B.   [When the author of the foregoing statement uses the inclusionary language, *all*,] what [category of persons does he mean to] include?

C.   [He means] to include a minor.

D. [How so?] I might have entertained the proposition [that the language of Scripture], "A man afflicted by the skin disease" (Lev. 13:44), [means] that a man indeed [is subject to the uncleanness under discussion], but a minor is not [subject to that same form of uncleanness].

E. Accordingly, [by using the language, *all are subject,* the framer of the passage] informed us [that that is not the case].

F. Now may I claim [to the contrary] that that indeed *is* the case, [that Scripture intends to exclude a child from the form of uncleanness at hand]?

G. [No, I may not. For Scripture states,] "As to a person, when there will be on the skin of his flesh..." (Lev. 13:2), [meaning a person], under all circumstances [whether adult or minor].

H. [If that is the case, then] what need do I have for the explicit reference to a man [at Lev. 13:44]?

I. It is to accord with the following teaching in the name of authorities of the Mishnah:

J. "A man [afflicted by] skin disease" (Lev. 13:44).

K. I know only that a man is subject to the stated skin ailment. How do I know [that the same skin ailment affects] a woman?

L. When [the Author of the Torah] states, "*And* the one afflicted by skin disease," lo, [by using the word, *and,* the Author indicates that] subject to the rule are two [classifications of persons, hence both male and female].

M. Why then [does the Author] specify, "...man"?

N. It [is to speak to a matter that comes] later [in the same passage, namely, Lev. 13:45, that the one afflicted by the skin disease tears his clothing and messes up his hair. The point, in particular, is that] a man tears his clothing and messes up his hair, and a woman does not tear her clothing and mess up her hair [should she be afflicted by the skin ailment].

XII.

A. All examine cases of the skin ailment.

B. All are suitable to examine cases of the skin ailment [M. Neg. 3:1B].

C. [When the framer of the foregoing statement used the inclusionary language, *all,*] what [classification of persons did he mean] to include?

D. It was to include [among those suitable to examine cases of the skin ailment even] those who are not expert in such matters and in the [various] classifications among which skin ailments are divided [cf. T. Neg. 1:1C].

E. But has not an authority stated, "[If] one is not expert in them and in the classifications among which skin ailments are divided, he [should], *not* examine [cases of] the skin ailment"?

F. Said Rabina, "[The contradiction between the statements at D and E] does not pose a problem. The former statement refers to someone who understands the matter when it is explained to him, while the latter speaks of one who, even when people explain to him, still will not understand the matter."

XIII.

    A   All are suitable to mix [together the ashes of the red cow when it is burned (Num. 19:1ff.) with the requisite water and so to produce the purification water required for purifying one who has become unclean by reason of corpse uncleanness (M. Par. 5:4)].

    B   [When the framer of the passage at hand uses the inclusionary language, *all,*] what [classification of persons does he mean] to include?

    C   In the view of R. Judah [cited below], it is to include a minor, and in the view of rabbis [of the same passage] it is to include a woman.

    D   For we have learned in the Mishnah [at M. Par. 5:4]:   All [classifications of persons] are suitable to mix [the ashes and the water], except for a deaf mute, an imbecile, and a minor. [The Talmud assumes this statement reflects the view of rabbis.]

    E   R. Judah declares a minor valid, but invalidates a woman and a person who exhibits the sexual characteristics of both sexes.

XIV.

    A   All are valid to sprinkle [purification water on one requiring the rite of purification].

    B   [When the framer of the passage at hand uses the inclusionary language, *all,*] what [classification of persons does he mean] to include?

    C   It is to include an uncircumcised [person], and that accords with the position of R. Eleazar.

    D   For R. Eleazar has stated, "An uncircumcised [person] who sprinkled [purification water] – his act of sprinkling is valid."

XV.

    A   All may carry out a rite of slaughter [of an animal for secular use of the meat. The Mishnah repeats this statement twice, once at M. Hul. 1:1 and a second time at M. Hul. 1:2.]

    B   [When the framer of the passage at hand uses the inclusionary language, *all,*] what [classification of persons does he mean] to include?

    C   The first time [at M. Hul. 1:1], he means to include a Samaritan, the second time [at M. Hul. 1:2], he means to include an apostate Israelite. [Both of these categories are assumed to fulfill the dietary rules and hence may carry them out.]

XVI.

    A   All may impose the requirement of emigrating [from the Exile to] the Land of Israel [M. Ket. 13:11].

    B   [When the framer of that statement uses the inclusionary language, *all,*] what [classification of persons does he mean] to include?

    C   [3B] He means to encompass slaves. [If a person overseas owns a circumcised slave whom he wishes to sell, the slave may impose upon the master the requirement that the sale take place only in the Land of Israel.]

    D   But in the view of him who repeats the tradition at hand in such wise as to make explicit reference to slaves [along with others specified, cf. M. Ket. 13:11 in Albeck, all of whom may impose the requirement of emigrating from the Exile to the Land of Israel], what [classification of persons is to be] included [by the formulation using the inclusionary language, *all*]?

E. It is meant to encompass [a move from] a lovely home [in the Exile] to a mean hovel [in the Land of Israel].

F. [And when the framer of the same passage uses the language,] **But all may not remove [a person from the Land of Israel to the Exile, M. Ket. 13:11],** what [classification of persons does he mean] to include?

G. It is to include a slave who fled from overseas to the Land [of Israel].

H. **All may impose the requirement of going up [to dwell] in Jerusalem [M. Ket. 13:11].**

I. [When the framer of that statement uses the inclusionary language, *all*, he means] to include [one who wishes to move] from a lovely home [in some town in the Land of Israel other than Jerusalem] to a mean hovel [in Jerusalem].

J. [When the framer of the same passage uses the passage,] **But all may not remove [a person from Jerusalem to some other town in the Land of Israel, M. Ket. 13:11],** what [classification of cases does he mean] to include?

K. It would be a case in which one proposed to move from a mean hovel [in Jerusalem] to a lovely home [outside of Jerusalem].

XVII.

A. [The framer now returns to the statement made at III.A.] All are obligated [to dwell during the days of the Festival of Tabernacles] in a tabernacle, [specifically including] priests, Levites, Israelites.

B. [The foregoing statement is] self-evident [and hardly requires specification, for] if these classifications of persons are not subject to the stated obligation, then who [in the world] would be subject to it!

C. [We now proceed to explain why one of the stated categories of person, drawing in its wake the other two, must be explicitly included in the formulation of the rule.] It was necessary to make reference to priests. [Why so?]

D. It is conceivable that I might have reasoned as follows: We know that it is written, "You will dwell in tabernacles" (Lev. 23:42), and [in that connection] a master has explained that dwelling in the tabernacle for seven days is comparable to an ordinary state of habitation, so that, just as under ordinary conditions of habitation, a man lives with his wife, so in the case of the tabernacle, a man should dwell with his wife.

E. [What follows from that fact is simple.] Since priests bear the obligation of carrying on the sacred service [in the Temple], [we might suppose that] they should be exempt from the obligation of dwelling in the tabernacle, [for they cannot do so in the accepted manner, with their wives. Since they must go to the Temple to participate in the rite, they also cannot remain with their wives for the entire period at hand. Accordingly, one might have imagined that priests are exempt from the religious requirement of dwelling in the tabernacle.]

F. [The framer of the passage makes explicit reference to priests] so as to inform us that, while priests are exempt at the time of their service in the Temple from the religious duty of dwelling in the tabernacle, when they are not engaged in the Temple service, they indeed are obligated to do so [since at this time they can fulfill the obligation in the proper manner].

G. This indeed accords with the rule governing those who are engaged in travel.

H. For a master has stated, those who are engaged in travel by day are exempt by day from the religious requirement of dwelling in a tabernacle but obligated by night.

XVIII.

A. [The framer returns to the statement made at III.H.] All are obligated to carry out the religious duty of [affixing to their garments] show fringes: priests, Levites, Israelites.

B. [The foregoing statement is] self-evident [and hardly requires specification, for if these classifications of persons are not obligated, then who in the world would be]?

C. It was necessary to make the specification at hand on account of the priests.

D. [How so?] I might have reasoned as follows: Since it is written, "You will not wear hybrid fabrics [e.g., a garment made from both wool and flax which derive from different categories, vegetable and animal, respectively]....You will make twisted cords [that is, show fringes] for yourself" (Deut. 22:11, 12).

E. [From the juxtaposition of the previous two verses, the framer reasons as follows:] As to one who in no way enjoys remission of the prohibition against wearing hybrid fabrics in his clothing, he is obligated to observe the religious duty of wearing show fringes.

F. Thus, since priests [under cultic circumstances] enjoy remission of the prohibition against wearing hybrid fabrics in their garments [Ex. 39:29 is understood as specifying that the priest wears linen and wool cloth, one might reason that] they ought not to be subject to the religious duty of wearing show fringes [on their garments].

G. Accordingly, [by phrasing the matter to make explicit reference to the priesthood, the author] informs us [that that is not the case].

H. Accordingly, while during the time of their service in the cult, they enjoy a remission [of the stated taboo], at other times they do not.

XIX.

A. All are obligated [to carry out the religious duty of wearing] phylacteries: priests, Levites, and Israelites.

B. [The specification of the three categories is hardly required, for the rule affecting them] is self-evident.

C. [No,] it was necessary to make the explicit specification at hand on account of the priests [in the tripartite formula].

D. [How so?] I might have reasoned as follows: Since it is written, "And you shall bind them for a sign upon your hand, and they shall be for frontlets between your eyes," (Deut. 6:8).

E. [I might conclude that] whoever is subject to the religious duty [of putting a phylactery] upon the hand [arm] also is subject to the religious duty of placing a phylactery upon the] head.

F. So, [it would follow], since priests are not subject to the religious duty of placing the phylactery upon the hand,

G   (for it is written, "[His linen garments] he shall place [directly upon] his flesh," [Lev. 6:3], meaning that nothing should interpose between [the linen garment] and his flesh [thus excluding the possibility of his placing a phylactery upon his arm, for it would interpose between the garment and his flesh],)

H   I might therefore conclude that priests likewise should not be subject to the religious duty of placing a phylactery also upon the head.

I   Accordingly, [by framing the passage as he has, the author] has informed us that that is not the case.

J.   For [the phylactery placed upon one limb] does not form a necessary precondition [for placing the phylactery upon the other limb. The two are separate religious duties, and if one cannot do the one, he remains liable to the other.]

K   This accords with what we have learned in the Mishnah [at M. Men. 3:7]: **The phylactery of the hand [arm] is not indispensable to the one of the head, and the one of the head is not indispensable to the one of the hand.**

L   Now what [really] differentiates the [priest's obligation with respect to the two types of phylacteries]? For concerning [the phylactery] to be placed on the hand it is written, "[His linen garment] he shall place [directly] upon his flesh [implying that a priest may not interpose the phylactery between his arm and his garment]" (Lev. 6:3). Concerning the phylactery of the head, it likewise is written, "And you will place the mitre upon his head" (Ex. 29:6). [Would not the phylactery on the head interpose between the hair of the head and the mitre just as the phylactery on the hand would interpose between the arm and the linen garment? Why then is the priest permitted to wear a phylactery upon his head, while he may not wear one on his arm?]

M   It has been taught: His hair was visible between the plate and the mitre, where he placed his phylactery.

XX.

A   [The framer comments upon the statement made above at V.A.] **All are liable [to carry out the religious duty of hearing] the sound of the ram's horn, [inclusive of] priests, Levites, and Israelites, T. R.H. 4:1.**

B.   [The inclusion of the three castes] is self-evident.

C   [Nonetheless,] it was necessary [to frame matters in such a way] on account of the priests [in particular].

D.   [How so?] I might have imagined the following argument: Since it is written, "You will have a day for sounding [the ram's horn]" (Num. 29:1), one who is subject [to hear] the sounding [of the ram's horn] only one day [in the year] is liable [to carry out the stated religious duty].

E.   But as to the priests, since they are subject [to the religious duty of] hearing the sounding [of the ram's horn] throughout the year, its being written, "And you will sound the trumpets over your burnt-offerings" (Num. 10:10), I might have maintained that they are not liable [to the hearing of the sounding of the ram's horn on the New Year in particular].

F.   But are the two statements parallel [that such reasoning is in order]? For there, "trumpets," while here, "a ram's horn" [is what is specified. Accordingly, the two matters really are not parallel anyhow, and the proposed reason for the formulation at A does not stand.]

G.   [Nonetheless, the inclusion of the priests at A remains] necessary. [How so?] I might have imagined the following argument: Since we have learned [at M. R.H. 3:5]: **The day on which the Jubilee Year begins is equivalent to the New Year's [day in the liturgy as to] the sounding of the ram's horn and also as to the blessings [said in the prayers of both days],** [I might have imagined that] whoever is subject to the religious duties governing the Jubilee Year also is subject to the religious duties governing the New Year, and whoever is not subject to the religious duties governing the Jubilee Year is not subject to the religious duties governing the New Year.

H.   Now, since the priests are not subject to the religious duties governing the Jubilee Year, for we have learned [at M. Ar. 9:8], **"Priests and Levites [but not others] may sell and redeem property at all times [inclusive of the Jubilee Year]," [4A]** I might have maintained that they also should not be held liable for carrying out the religious duties affecting the New Year [inclusive of hearing the sound of the ram's horn].

I.   [The cited formulation, A] serves, therefore, to inform us that even while they are not liable to the religious duty of restoring real estate to the original owners [a duty of the Jubilee Year], they nonetheless are liable to the [other obligation in the Jubilee Year] of remitting debts and releasing slaves.

XXI.

A.   [The framer now takes up the statement above at VI.A.] **All are subject to carry out the religious obligation of hearing the reading of the Scroll of Esther, [inclusive of] priests, Levites, and Israelites [T. Meg. 2:7 A-B].**

B.   [The inclusion of the three castes] is self-evident.

C.   [Nonetheless,] it was necessary [to frame matters in such a way on account of the priests in particular].

D.   [In so stating matters, the framer wishes to indicate] that they must leave off their [sacred] service [at the altar, in order to hear the public reading of the scroll of Esther].

E.   And that view conforms to what Rab Judah said that Samuel said, for Rab Judah said that Samuel said, "Priests in connection with their sacred service [at the altar], Levites in connection with their [singing on] the platform, and Israelites [attending the Temple service as] the delegation [from their particular village, all must] leave off [the performance of their holy] service in order to listen to the public reading of the scroll of Esther.

XXII.

A.   **All are subject to the religious obligation of saying Grace in public quorum if they have eaten together,** [as explained at VII.A], **[inclusive of] priests, Levites, and Israelites [T. Ber. 5:15].**

B.   [The inclusion of the three castes] is self-evident.

C. [Nonetheless,] it was necessary to frame matters in such a way [on account of the priests in particular,] in a case in which the group had eaten Holy Things.

D. [How so?] I might have imagined the following argument: "And they shall eat those [Holy] Things with which atonement has been effected" (Ex. 29:33), has the All-Merciful stated [in Scripture], indicating that [the present act of eating constitutes an act of] atonement.

E. [But in regard to the obligation of saying Grace, the All Merciful said only that "You shall eat and be satisfied and say a blessing" (Deut. 8:10) implying that one only need say Grace when eating in order to satisfy one's hunger and not when eating as an act of atonement. It would seem, therefore, that priests are exempt from Grace when eating for atonement purposes.]

F. [Accordingly, it was necessary] to indicate otherwise [namely that with regard to that which the All Merciful has said, "You shall eat and be satisfied [and say a blessing]," even [priests who are eating for the purposes of atonement] are included.

XXIII.

A. All are liable to join in the public saying of Grace [responding to the call to say Grace, as explained at VII.A, inclusive of] priests, Levites, and Israelites [T. Ber. 5:15].

B. [The inclusion of the three castes] is self-evident.

C. [Nonetheless,] it was necessary [to frame matters in such a way] on account of the case of priests who ate food in the status of priestly rations or Holy Things, while [at the same meal] a nonpriest ate food in secular [not consecrated] status.

D. I might have imagined the following argument: Since, if the nonpriest had wished to eat along with the priest [out of the food that the priest was eating], he could indeed not have done so, the [priest] therefore should not join with him [in responding to the public call to form a quorum to say Grace] since clearly they did not share a meal.

E. [But that argument is invalid, and thus the framer of A] has informed us, [in framing matters as indicated that the priest must join him in saying Grace. This is justified on the basis of the following consideration:] since if it is the case that the nonpriest could not have eaten [the food of] the priest, the priest, nonetheless, may perfectly well eat [the food of] the nonpriest, [the consequence is that all parties join together in the common quorum].

XXIV.

A. All pledge the Valuation [of others] [inclusive of] priests, Levites, and Israelites [M. Ar. 1:1A, C].

B. [The inclusion of the three castes] is self-evident.

C. [Nonetheless,] said Raba, "It was necessary [to frame matters in such a way] on account of the opinion of Ben Bukhri."

D. For we have learned [at M. Sheq. 1:4].

E. Said R. Judah, "Testified Ben Bukhri in Yabneh: 'Any priest who pays the 'sheqel' does not sin.'

F. "Said to him Rabban Yohanan ben Zakkai, 'Not so. But any priest who does not pay the 'sheqel' does sin.

G   "'But the priests expound this scriptural verse for their own benefit: And every meal-offering of the priest shall be wholly burned, it shall not be eaten (Lev. 6:23).

H   "'Since the 'omer', Two Loaves, and Show Bread are ours, how [if we contribute] are they to be eaten?'"

I   [We now spell out the relationship between the opinion of Ben Bukhri, that the priests do not pay the sheqel, and the present matter. Raba resumes discourse,] "Now, in the view of Ben Bukhri, since to begin with [the priests] are not obligated to bring [the sheqel-offering to the Temple], if they actually do bring it, the priests commit a sin. [How so?] They turn out to bring unconsecrated offerings to the Temple courtyard [and that is a sin. One may bring only consecrated offerings, designated for the purpose of the cult, to the Temple courtyard. One can consecrate only something that he is obligated to consecrate in accord with the Temple rules. Ben Bukhri, however, would permit the priest to] bring [the sheqel tax] by handing over ownership to the community at large.]

J.   "Now," [Raba continues,] "I might have supposed that the following argument applies: Since it is written, 'And all your Valuations will be according to the sheqel of the sanctuary' (Lev. 27:25), [it would follow that] whoever is subject to the requirement of bringing the sheqel tax also can pledge the Valuation [of others]. It would then follow that, since the priests are not subject [in Ben Bukrhi's view] to the religious duty of bringing the sheqel tax [in support of the public offerings], they cannot pledge Valuations.

K   "Thus the framer of the cited passage has informed us [that that, in fact, is not the case. Priests may also pledge the Valuation of others.]"

L   [The foregoing explanation of the language used at A is now rejected.] Abbayye said to him, "[The scriptural language,] 'All your Valuations' [cited by Raba at J as part of his proof for the position imputed to Ben Bukhri's principle serves for a quite separate purpose, namely, to indicate that] all the pledges of Valuation that you make should add up to no less than a sela [per Valuation]." [Since a particular verse may bear only one interpretation, the cited verse could not also support the position proposed at J, which, therefore, cannot have been in the mind of the framer of the cited passage, K, when he stated matters as he did.]"

M   "Rather," said Abbayye, "[It still was] necessary [for the framer to make explicit reference to the priesthood at A for another reason]. I might have proposed the following argument:

N   "Since it is written, 'And their redemption money – from a month old you shall redeem them – shall be according to your valuation' (Num. 18:16),

O   "[the use of the word Valuation in the cited verse, which deals with the redemption of the firstborn by ordinary Israelites then would indicate that] whoever is subject to the requirement of redeeming the firstborn can pledge the Valuations [of others]. But since priests are not subject to the law of redemption of the firstborn, they cannot pledge the Valuations [of others]. Accordingly, [by framing matters as he did at A, the author] informed us [that that is not the case]."

P. Said Raba to him, "[If that is the basis for your position], then how do you deal with the following statement made in connection with the ram that is brought as a guilt-offering: 'And he shall bring as his guilt-offering to the Lord a ram without blemish out of the flock, according to your valuation' (Lev. 5:25).

Q "We may then draw the parallel as follows: Whoever can [pledge] Valuations is subject to the law governing the ram brought as a guilt-offering. Then one of concealed sexual traits and one who has the sexual traits of both genders, classifications of persons who are not subject to the law of Valuations at all, also will not be subject to the requirement of bringing the ram brought as a guilt-offering [– a position that is manifestly impossible!]" [Abbayye's proposed interpretation is weak, because the same reasoning would lead to an impossible conclusion, if every time we introduce the word "Valuation," we must exclude those classifications of persons that, for reasons particular to Valuations, are not subject to the possibility of having their Valuation pledge.]

R. "Rather," said Raba – and there are those who maintain that it was stated by R. Ashi, "[The formulation given at A, specifying the obligation of priests] is necessary.

S. [How so?] "I might have imagined the following argument: Since it is written, 'Then he shall be set before the priest' (Lev. 27:8), [I might suppose that only an Israelite would be set before the priest], but not *a priest* before a priest.

T. "Therefore [the framer of the passage] informs us [that that is not the case]."

XXV.

A. **[All] are subject to the pledge of Valuation [by others] [M. 1:1A].**

B. [What classification of persons does the framer of the passage intend] to include [by stressing the word, all]?

C. It is to include a person who is disfigured or afflicted with a skin ailment [= I.C-D].

D. Whence the authority [in Scripture] for that statement?

E. It is in line with that which our rabbis have taught: "According to your valuation" (Lev. 27:8) serves to encompass a generalized statement of Valuation [explained at XXVII, below].

F. Another interpretation of "According to your Valuation": the Valuation of the whole of a person one pays, and he does not pay the Valuation of distinct limbs.

G. Is it possible that I should exclude [from a pledge of Valuation] even some [part of the person's body] on which life depends? [If someone should pledge the Valuation, for example, of the other person's heart, would the foregoing statement excluding limbs from the process of Valuation apply in such a case?]

H Scripture states, "[When a man makes a special vow of] persons [to the Lord at your Valuation]" (Lev. 27:2).

I. [The meaning, then, is that] persons [are subject to the vow of Valuation,] excluding [therefore] a corpse [who would not be subject to such a vow. Hence if a person vows the Valuation of a part of a person on which life depends, the pledge of Valuation is valid and to be paid.]

J. Thus I shall exclude a [pledge of Valuation] of a corpse. But perhaps I should not exclude a dying person [who then may be subject to a vow of Valuation]?

K. Scripture states, "Then he shall be set [before the priest] and the priest shall value him" (Lev. 27:8).

L. Whoever is subject to the condition of being set before the priest also is subject to Valuation, and whoever is not subject to the condition of being set before the priest [such as a dying man, who cannot be moved] also is not subject to Valuation.

M. Another interpretation [of the reference, at Lev. 27:2, to] "persons":

N. I know only that the pledge of Valuation applies to a single individual who pledged the Valuation of a single individual. How do I know that the same obligation applies to a single individual who pledged the Valuation of a hundred persons?

O. Scripture states, "...persons...."

P. Another interpretation [of the reference, at Lev. 27:2, to] "persons":

Q. [4B] I know only that the law applies in the case of a man who pledged the value of either a man or a woman.

R. How do I know that the law applied to a woman who pledged the value of a man, [or to] a woman who pledged the value of a woman?

S. Scripture states, "...persons...."

T. Another interpretation: "...persons..." serves to include one who is disfigured or afflicted with a skin ailment.

U. For it is possible that I might have reasoned as follows: "When a man makes a special vow of persons to the Lord at your valuation" (Lev. 27:2) [means that only] whoever possesses a worth [as above, I.E-F] would be subject to a vow of Valuation. On the other hand, whoever does not possess a worth would not be subject to a vow of Valuation. [Thus excluding the disfigured person or person with skin ailment who could not be sold in the marketplace.]

V. Now when Scripture states, "Persons...," [it serves to include the categories under discussion here].

This dazzling performance, ranging far and wide over the surface of the law, makes a single, superficial point, which is that wherever in the Mishnah we find the inclusionary or augmentative language, "all," there is the occasion to ask what is encompassed within the law at hand that, for some reason or other, we might not have known was covered by said law. There is no argument moving from point to point, no extension or progress in the demonstration of a proposition, but rather, a systematic display of item after item, each free-standing, all of them making the same exegetical point without in any way exploiting it. The difference between the good student and the excellent one finds an apt illustration here: this is the work of a conscientious and industrious compiler. What now follows shows us the difference.

To exemplify the character of discourse that strikes me as not exegetical, but rather abstract, theoretical, and propositional in a sustained way – that is, the discourse I deem essential to the Bavli and indicative of its intellectual might – I present the case that drew my attention to the need to learn more about the kind of writing under discussion here. This is the item that concluded *Sources and Traditions*. The passage directly continues the one just now cited and serves the next clause of the same Mishnah paragraph. The issue comes up somewhat abruptly, in the context of the detailed exposition of the rule at hand. But once the issue is framed, it takes over, and from there to the end, it remains the same. It is to be framed as a debate:

1. A man has not got the right to take the law into his own hands *versus*

2. A man has got the right to take the law into his own hands where there will be an irreparable loss.

At that point, a set of cases will be examined, to uncover what law is implicit in the laws at hand. I should claim that, while the Mishnah commentary is helpful, the sustained debate before us is interesting, and, without what follows, the Bavli would be merely a collection of lessons, rather than a composite of important conclusions, capable of governing in situations to which the laws of the Mishnah would prove monumentally irrelevant.

II.1 A   **And someone else came along and stumbled on it and broke it – [the one who broke it] is exempt:**

B.   *Why should he be exempt? He should have opened his eyes as he walked along!*

C.   *They said in the household of Rab in the name of Rab,* "We deal with a case in which the whole of the public domain was filled with barrels."

D.   Samuel said, "We deal with a case in which the jugs were in a dark place."

E.   R. Yohanan said, "We deal with a case in which the jug was at a corner." [Kirzner: The defendant therefore is not to blame.]

F.   *Said R. Pappa, "A close reading of our Mishnah rule can accord only with the view of Samuel or R. Yohanan. For if it were in accord with the position of Rab, then what difference does it make that exemption is accorded only if the man stumbled over the pitcher? Why not rule in the same way even if he deliberately broke the pitcher?"*

G.   *Said R. Zebid in the name of Raba,* "In point of fact, the same rule really does apply even if the defendant deliberately broke the jug. And the reason that the language, **and stumbled on it,** is used, is that the later clause goes on to say, **And if [the one who broke it] was injured by it, the owner of the barrel is liable [to pay damages for] his injury.** But that would be the case only if he stumbled on it, but not if he deliberately broke the jug. How come? The man has deliberately injured himself. So that is why, to begin with, the word choice was **and stumbled on it.**

II.2   A   Said R. Abba to R. Ashi, "This is what they say in the West in the name of R. Ulla: 'The reason is that people do not ordinarily look out when they walk along the way.'"

II.3   A   *There was a case in Nehardea, and Samuel imposed liability [for the broken utensil]. And, in Pumbedita, Rabbah imposed liability as well.*

       B.   *Now there is no problem in understanding Samuel's ruling, since he acted in accord with his own tradition [if the pitcher was visible, there would be liability]. But shall we then say that Rabbah concurred with Samuel?*

       C.   *Said R. Pappa, "The damage was done at the corner of an oil factory, and, since it is entirely permitted to store barrels there, the defendant should have walked along with his eyes wide open."*

II.4   A   R. Hisda sent word to R. Nahman, "Lo, they have said, 'For kicking with the knee, three selas; for kicking with the foot, five; for a blow with the saddle of an ass, thirteen. *What is the penalty for wounding with the blade of a hoe or the handle of a hoe?*"

       B.   *He sent word, "Hisda! Hisda! Are you really imposing in Babylonia such extrajudicial fines as these [which you have no right to do over there]? Tell me the details of the case as it happened."*

       C.   *He sent word, "There was a well that belonged to two people, who used it on alternate days. One of them then went and drew water on a day that was not assigned to him. The other said, 'This is my day.' The latter ignored him. So the other took the blade of a hoe and struck him with it."*

       D.   *R. Nahman sent word, "Even if he hit him a hundred times with the blade of the hoe [it would not have mattered]. For even in the opinion of one who says, 'Someone may not take the law into his own hands,' where there will be a loss, he has every right to do so."*

       E.   *For it has been stated:*

       F.   *R. Judah said, "A man has not got the right to take the law into his own hands."*

       G.   *R. Nahman said, "A man has got the right to take the law into his own hands where there will be a loss."*

       H.   *Now all parties concur that where there will be a loss, someone may take the law into his own hands. Where there is an argument, it concerns a case in which there will be no loss. R. Judah said, "A man has not got the right to take the law into his own hands." Since there will be no loss, he can go to court. But R. Nahman said, "A man has got the right to take the law into his own hands where there will be a loss." Since he is acting in accord with the law anyhow, why take the trouble to go to court?*

       I.   *Objected R. Kahana [to R. Judah's view],* "Ben Bag Bag says, 'A person should not go and retrieve his own property from the household of someone else, lest he appear to be a thief. But he should be ready in public to break his teeth and you may say to him, "I am seizing what is my own from the thief's possession"' [T. B.Q. 10:38]." [This then would contradict Judah's position.]

       J.   *[Judah] said to him,* [28A] *"True enough, Ben Bag Bag is on your side. But his is a dissenting view, differing from rabbis."*

       K.   *R. Yannai said, "What is the meaning, anyhow, of* **break his teeth?** *It is, in court."*

L.   *If so, the language,* **you may say to him,** *is inappropriate. Rather it should be,* **they [the court] may say to him!** *So too, the language,* **I am seizing what is my own,** *is inappropriate. Rather, it should be,* **he is seizing what is his own!**

M.   *So that's a problem.*

N   *Come and take note:* In the case of an ox that climbed up on another one to kill it, and the owner of the one on the bottom came along and pulled out his ox, so that the one on the top fell and was killed – the owner of the bottom ox is exempt from having to pay compensation. *Does this ruling not pertain to an ox that was an attested danger, in which case there is no loss to be expected?*

O   *No, it speaks of an ox that was deemed innocent, and there is a considerable loss to be expected.*

P.   *If so, then look what's coming:* If he pulled off the ox on top and it died, he is liable to pay compensation. *But if the ox was deemed innocent, why should he have to pay compensation?*

Q   Because he should have pulled his ox out from underneath, and he did not do that. [Kirzner: He had no right to push the ox on top.]

R.   *Come and take note:* He who filled the courtyard of his fellow with jugs of wine and jugs of oil – the owner of the courtyard has every right to break the jugs in order to get out or great the jugs in order to get in.

S   Said R. Nahman bar Isaac, "He breaks the jugs to get out only if a court says he may do so, he may break the jugs to get in only to get whatever documents he needs to prove his case in court."

T.   *Come and take note:* How on the basis of Scripture do we know that in the case of a slave whose ear had been bored [as an indication that he was in perpetual service, to the Jubilee Year], the term of service of which has come to an end [with the Jubilee], the owner of which has been urging him to leave, and, in the process, injured him and done him damage, the owner is exempt from having to pay compensation? Scripture states, "You shall not take satisfaction for him who is...come again..." (Num. 35:12), meaning, for one who is determined to come again [as a slave, continuing his service], you will not take a ransom.

U.   *Here with what sort of a case do we deal? It is a slave who was a thief* [Kirzner: so the owner is protecting himself from a genuine loss].

V.   *Well, up to now he hasn't stolen anything, but now he's expected to go and steal?*

W.   *Yes, that's quite plausible, since up to now he was afraid of his master, but now that he is about to go free, he isn't afraid of his master anymore.*

X.   R. Nahman bar Isaac said, "At issue is a slave to whom his master gave a Canaanite serving girl as a wife. *Up to this time it was a legitimate relationship, but once he is freed, it is not legitimate*" [Kirzner: so the master may use force to eject him].

Y.   *Come and take note:* **He who leaves a jug in the public domain, and someone else came along and stumbled on it and broke it – [the one who broke it] is exempt.** *So the operative consideration is that he stumbled on it. Lo, if he had deliberately broken it, he would have been liable.* [This is contrary to Nahman's view.]

Z.   *Said R. Zebid in the name of Raba, "In point of fact, the same rule really does apply even if the defendant deliberately broke the jug. And the reason that the language,* **and stumbled on it,** *is used, is that the latter clause goes on to say,* **And if [the one who broke it] was injured by it, the owner of the barrel is liable [to pay damages for] his injury.** *But that would be the case only if he stumbled on it, but not if he deliberately broke the jug. How come? The man has deliberately injured himself. So that is why, to begin with, the word choice was* **and stumbled on it.**

AA.   *Come and take note:* "Then you shall cut off her hand" (Deut. 25:12) – that refers to a monetary fine equivalent in value to the hand. *Does this not speak of a case in which* the woman has no other way of saving her husband but doing what she did [proving one may not take the law into one's own hands]?

BB.   No, it involves a case in which she can save her husband in some other way.

CC.   Well, if she cannot save her husband in some other way, would she be free of all liability? *Then why go on to say,* "And puts forth her hand" (Deut. 25:11) – excluding an officer of the court [from liability for humiliation that he may cause when acting in behalf of the court]? *Rather, why not recast matters by dealing with the case at hand, thus:* Under what circumstances? When she can save her husband by some other means. But if she cannot save him by some other means, then she is exempt.

DD.   *This is the sense of the passage:* Under what circumstances? When she can save her husband by some other means. But if she cannot save him by some other means, then her hand serves as the agency of the court and she is indeed exempt.

EE.   *Come and take note:* **He who had a public way passing through his field, and who took it away and gave [the public another path] along the side, what he has given he has given. But what is his does not pass to him [M. B.B. 6:7A-D].** *Now if you maintain that someone may take the law into his own hands, then let the man just take a whip and sit there [and keep people out of his property]!*

FF.   Said R. Zebid in the name of Raba, "It is a precautionary decree, lest he assign to the public a crooked path."

GG.   R. Mesharshayya said, "It is a case in which he gives them a crooked path."

HH.   R. Ashi said, "Any path that is over off to the side is classified as a crooked path to begin with, since what is nearer for one party will be farther for another."

II.   *If that's so, then why specify,* **But what is his does not pass to him?** *Why can't he just say to the public, "Take what is yours and give me what is mine?"*

JJ.   *That is because of what R. Judah said, for* said R. Judah, "A path that the public has taken over is not to be disrupted."

KK.   *Come and take note:* A householder who designated *peah* at one corner of the field, and the poor come along and take the *peah* from another side of the field – both this and that are classified as *peah. Now if you maintain that a person may take the law into his own hands,*

why should it be the fact that both this and that are so classified? *Just
let the man take a whip and sit there [and keep people out of his property]!*

LL.   *Said Raba, "What is the meaning of the phrase,* both this and that are so
classified? *It is for the purpose of exempting the designated produce from
the requirement of separating tithes. For so it has been taught on Tannaite
authority:* He who declares his vineyard to be ownerless and then
gets up early in the morning and harvests the grapes is liable to
leave for the poor the grapes that fall to the ground, the puny
bunches, the forgotten ones, and the corner of the field, but is
exempt from having to designate tithes."

No one can imagine that the framer of this passage took as his task
the explanation of the details of the Mishnah paragraph to which the
composite is appended. The rather ambitious, free-standing composition
is inserted only because the framer has drawn upon our Mishnah's rule
as part of his repertoire of cases and evidence. It could have appeared
more or less anywhere without any alteration of its character, since what
we have is a propositional essay on a problem of broad intelligibility and
more than narrowly episodic interest. It is at 4.D that the real point of
debate takes over. We see that the issue is tangential to the exegetical
problem, but critical in its own terms. It is further noteworthy that the
issue is specified in a free-standing debate, set forth at 4.E-G. The
sequence of cases moves toward the illustration of arguments one might
propose, but, the Bavli being what it is, we shall work through cases that
illustrate arguments, precedents that constitute facts to be addressed and
held together in equilibrium, not arguments framed in a philosophical
manner. Our cases emerge at 4.I, N, R, T, Y, AA, EE, KK. The Mishnah
paragraph before us is cited in the context of the debate, at Z. It is not
distinguished in this context, and the formation of the whole goes
forward entirely within the terms of the broadest nature; we never lose
sight of what is at issue. Our eight cases, spread across the face of the
laws of the Mishnah, are shown to address a single problem, and any
eight other cases, far beyond the details of the Mishnah's law, can have
served with equal effect.

The case before us has been chosen because of its simplicity and
accessibility; no special, technical knowledge is required to grasp the
issue of whether or not one may take the law into his own hands.
Furthermore, while the eight cases remain deeply embedded in the
Mishnah's specificities, the relevance of each is clearly articulated. In the
nineteen tractates we shall examine are yet others. So the basic inquiry is
well justified: we most certainly do have in the Bavli a type of writing
that is critical to the purpose of the document, unlike the materials
classified in *Sources and Traditions,* but that is also irrelevant to the
exegetical program of the document, exactly like those same materials.

Let me now lay out the results of a survey of nineteen tractates, answering questions of generalization and conclusion. These are three, and they are systematically addressed to each tractate that has given us pertinent material:

1. Rhetoric: Do we identify recurrent patterns of word choice, syntax, or other indicative traits of form?
2. Logic: How cogent are the composites? Is a single issue paramount, or do we find a tendency to weigh a discussion down with footnotes, excurses, and irrelevant filler, such as not uncommonly characterizes the Bavli's larger and more paramount composites?
3. Proportion: What really concerns me is how considerable a part of a given chapter is made up of the composites I call essential. By proportion I do not mean volume, for example, Does our discursive composite cover a large part of a given chapter or tractate? but rather, importance: Can we say that the composite has asked a question of formidable consequence in its tractate? In the broader context of the Bavli's re-presentation of the law?

These seem to me to indicate objective points of differentiation between and among the items that have struck me as pertinent. If we find recurrent patterns of word choice, then we may posit that a literary convention has guided framers of thought of an abstract order to set forth their ideas in a distinctive way. If not, then what we have classified as "essential discourse" forms a mode of thought not assigned a distinctive manner of formulation and expression. If the composites are cogent, with a clear beginning and end, then we may say that a purposive mind has set forth a problem and worked it out. If not, then what we have is simply a collection of relevant cases, not a well-composed argument. Finally, if the kinds of discourse we have now reviewed form important parts in their respective chapters, then we may conclude that a sustained effort – if not (as we realize) a ubiquitous one – formed for the Bavli a layer of abstract thought and inquiry above and beyond the concrete and exegetical one.

What is at stake in the answers? The results of the present exercise of synthesis will lead us to the answers to two basic questions:

1. Are the essays on problems of abstraction and general intelligibility part of a sustained and systematic exercise? Do we deal with a "layer" or a distinguishable component of the document as a whole?
2. Do the essays of discursive character appear to form part of the main work of the Bavli – systematic amplification of selected tractates of the Mishnah – or do they form a distinct stage in the unfolding of the document, and, if they do, can we estimate whether this type of writing comes before or after the work of Mishnah commentary?

What is at stake is clear in the exposition of these final questions. Is the kind of discourse I have called "essential" in fact adventitious or part of a clearly attested program in the formation of the Bavli? The description of the Bavli as writing, hence also an account of the formation of the materials that have found their way into the Bavli, in part depends upon the results of this experiment.

In my survey, the passages that have struck me as different from the standard exegesis and extension of the Mishnah paragraphs – generalizing, abstract, addressed to issues of general intelligibility – prove random and episodic. There is no evidence that a coherent literary program has guided writers of passages of the present classification, and all the evidence points in the opposite direction. Just as no uniform rhetoric governs, so there is no pronounced tendency either to amplify, gloss, and footnote, or not to do so. Some of the entries fall into the class of sustained compositions, others of mere composites of similar materials, not subjected to sustained analysis, from which no conclusions are drawn. Some of the entries define the broader configuration of which they form a part; some do not. Most interesting, some prove sustained and systematic and free-standing; others address issues of Mishnah exegesis, following along the theoretical lines contained within the pertinent Mishnah paragraph itself. The contrast, for instance, between the entry for tractate Niddah and Keritot and the discussion of intentionality in Zebahim, on the one side, and that taking the law into one's own hands in Baba Qamma or the study of comparability and exegesis in Zebahim, shows what is at issue. On the one side the Mishnah sets the issue through a case, and the Bavli's composites then give us more cases to the issue. On the other, the issue is original to the composition in which it appears; it is not demanded for the purposes of Mishnah exegesis; it is also not imposed upon the labor of Mishnah exegesis. From an intellectual viewpoint it is simply a fresh initiative, taken entirely within its own framework and precipitated by deep thought on issues that the Mishnah's rule in context has not framed.

Only a few of the items I have been able to find provide anything other than another kind of Mishnah commentary. The few free-standing composites and compositions suggest only that, within the circles of authors who prepared materials that found their way into the Mishnah were speculative minds, capable of sustained and systematic thinking about principles exemplified by cases but not, in the end, initially framed as cases: philosophers capable of thinking philosophically, not merely lawyers of some perception and depth, capable only of identifying the premises of cases and through them comparing case to case. There were, indeed, a few such pieces of writing, but not very many, and what strikes me as an essential mode of discourse, this inquiry into the law behind the laws, more often than not proves, if not mechanical, then also not very radical. But the few instances of truly independent inquiry, inquiry beginning with not cases and examples but a profound problem, itself then choosing cases and examples for analysis, not demonstration and proof, would give to the Bavli as a whole that promise of something more that, through ages to come, would be kept by philosophical minds of equal wit. These first-rate minds would find each other out, in each succeeding age.

Now to state the upshot of this approach to the description of the writing of the Bavli. The Bavli is not a layered document, in which one kind of thinking (about the Mishnah) is succeeded by another, literally distinct and intellectually distinctive mode of thinking, generated by that earlier layer or responding to it. There is no distinct "layer" of writing of the kind we have analyzed; all objective evidence points in fact to the opposite conclusion. What we have is simply a different kind of thinking, set forth within the conventional and routine structures of the Bavli in its reading of the Mishnah. Important later on, impressive in its own context, the essential discourse defined a dimension of the existing writing, not a way toward a distinctive kind of writing altogether. The search for the law behind the laws begins, in point of fact, not so much or mainly with the Bavli as with the Mishnah; and, in this context, I may say very simply that that search more nearly characterizes the framers of the Mishnah than the authors of compositions, compilers of composites, and authorship of the tractates of the Bavli overall.

The very simple fact that the inquiry into the law behind the law commonly continues with the Mishnah's own statements shows us that what we have is nothing more (but nothing less) than evidence of one kind of intellect, among the many that made up the continuous authorship responsible for the canon of the Mishnah, Tosefta, Yerushalmi, and Bavli: a mode of thought, not a medium of literary expression. Were our task an intellectual history, detached from problems of literary evidence and its traits, that result would yield consequence. But ours is a labor of the description of the traits of an enormous and complex piece of writing, and for that purpose, formal, literary traits are the necessary, if not the sufficient, indicators. This writing does not reveal those indicative traits alone, but them and their opposites; hence, as I said, the experiment has yielded a negative result. It remains, then, to correlate these results with the ones found in the complementary studies.

The upshot is simple. The Bavli is not much more than a Mishnah commentary. Where the type of thinking and writing of an other than exegetical character, such as we have examined, yielded compositions and composites now in the Bavli, it was not seldom in response to problems set forth in the Mishnah itself; and it was ordinarily in the context and in the rhetoric of an established exegetical exercise devoted to the Mishnah. So, in a large part of our very small set of cases, the paramount purpose of Mishnah exegesis was realized in these inquiries into the law behind the laws. What is other than Mishnah exegesis, rhetorically and topically, forms only a portion of the whole. What is other than Mishnah exegesis, if not topically (for that is, by definition, excluded from this type of writing, which is not topical at all) is balanced, even in analytical proposition, by what merely carries forward an inquiry begun in the Mishnah itself. So no, the evidence treated here tells us, once again, that the Bavli is not much more than a Mishnah commentary, even though, in my view, that additional component will prove remarkably interesting in due course.

The Bavli is a systematic writing, occasionally using composites drawn together by principles of agglutination that do not in general govern in the Bavli, but then ordering these agglutinative composites entirely in accord with the Bavli's own program of Mishnah commentary. Even the apparently miscellaneous composites, which seem to grow not purposefully but only haphazardly and episodically, in fact cohere to a few simple rules of formation. These miscellanies are made up of compositions joined together around a common topic, and the common topic is made relevant to the context, in the Bavli, in which such miscellanies make their appearance, by the simple fact that, in the main, the Mishnah has touched upon that same topic. So I found that – from the perspective of the formation of the Bavli – there is nothing miscellaneous in these large and rather random appearing composites. The one way in which they differ from the materials that predominate in the Bavli is that ordinarily a composite undertakes either an exegetical or an analytical task, and only rarely provides a mere repertoire of thematically tangential entries. That result is sustained here. The entries we have examined without exception prove purposive and internally coherent, all of them displaying that sustained analytical and systematic, argumentative purpose that characterizes the Bavli overall. The quest for the law behind the laws yields writings that in every detail underline the systematic character of the writing of the Bavli.

The Bavli utilizes available sources, but among them was not a set of inquiries, worked out on their own terms and within their own framework, into the law behind the law. There is no question that, here and there, work on that interesting question was undertaken; but this was mainly, though not exclusively, in the framework of Mishnah commentary, and nearly always expressed within the rhetorical framework established by a prior program of Mishnah commentary. If the Bavli does draw upon available sources, composed independently of the composition of the Bavli as a whole and then utilized by the framers of the Bavli, a set of sources that, because of their independence of the Bavli's main kind of writing, can have antedated that writing, then it is important to identify other sources, besides those discussed in my address to the distinction between sources and traditions. Indeed, my initial expectation was that, through routine procedures of literary analysis, I could show that there was a "layer" of the Bavli, however thin, made up of a distinctive and essential discourse of an other than exegetical kind: writing that served an entirely distinct purpose from that that defined the structure and system of the Bavli overall. But the opposite result is now before us. The essential discourse comprising an inquiry into the law behind the laws is not a distinct source, whether early, whether late, upon which the framers of the Bavli drew; it is a discourse that is essential in a different, unanticipated sense altogether. It is essential to the exegetical purpose of the framers of the Bavli, in some few contexts, to move quite beyond their exegetical frame of reference. But when they chose to do so, they in no way differentiated in the signs of rhetoric (let alone logic in the odd sense used in this chapter and elsewhere in this book) that writing from any other. All proves uniform; all is set forth as essential in its context. A mere handful of our entries stands on its own, and, if these represent not components of the Bavli's own tradition but sources upon which the Bavli has drawn, then those other, perhaps prior, sources made so slight a contribution to the Bavli as to represent nothing of consequence or influence within the Bavli. So when we describe the Bavli, we have to begin with the simple statement: the Talmud of Babylonia is a commentary on the Mishnah.

If I may now state very simply what I find remarkable about the Bavli: it is the power of original minds to say what this wished in so unexceptional a way as to appear merely as extension and refinement of someone else's writing. As we have seen, even when authors of compositions or authorships of composites are working entirely on their own, asking questions not required for the exegesis of the Mishnah, they remain well within the exegetical parameters of the Mishnah. And yet – and yet these exegetes at every point turned out to have made a statement of their own, on a program of their own devising, in a framework of their own definition. How people can have succeeded, as these writers did, in insinuating their own enormous conceptions into the framework of a received and revered document, so that what they set forth laid a compelling claim upon the status of "tradition," remains to be discovered. But it is the simple fact that the Bavli's authorship did make a statement of its own, proportioned in accord with its own sense of what is fitting, addressing in the language of their choice the issues they found urgent, and all of this they did in such a way as to make what was theirs appear simply to extend and to clarify the formation of someone else. The secret of the Judaism that would unfold from, and within the disciplines of, the Bavli is captured, in literary form, in that fact. The Bavli forms considerably more than a reprise and a paraphrase of the Mishnah, but its authors would have us believe their work is a mere commentary, a clarification and refinement of this and that.

Part Three
THE LESSONS OF THE BAVLI:
MESSAGE AND MEANING

6

The Bavli's One Statement

Now that we know that the Bavli speaks for some one group of authors (an "authorship") is a document of remarkable integrity, repeatedly insisting upon the harmony of the parts within a whole and unitary structure of belief and behavior, we want to know what the authorship of the Bavli repeatedly says. So the question is, within the restricted rhetorical vocabulary of the document, can we identify the one thing that is repeated – always in some one simple rhetorical pattern – in regard to many things? If the limits of my language are the limits of my world, may I also say that the limits of my rhetoric restrict the thoughts that I may think about that world? Dismantling ("deconstructing") its components and identifying them, perhaps even describing the kinds of compilations that the authors of those components can have had in mind in writing their compositions – these activities of literary criticism yield no insight into the religious system that guided the document's framers. It is time to reconstruct, to see things whole, having carefully examined the parts.

I have now demonstrated that the Talmud of Babylonia in formal terms adheres to a few entirely visible rhetorical patterns, which time and again, without limitation by reason of subject matter, made possible a limited inquiry into some few problems and propositions. In adhering to a restricted repertoire of rhetoric, the writing speaks for an authorship, serving as a formally coherent statement, not merely a collection of received opinions. The framers of the document not only chose and reframed what they inherited but placed the stamp of their own rhetorical and logical program upon the writing they produced. Since that is now the fact, moving on from issues of rhetoric and logic, I have to ask about its implications upon the topical and propositional program of the document. When a document says the same thing about many things, it presents not only propositions but a metaproposition, a substrate that frames the teleology of its recurrent propositions. Since I now have proved that the Talmud of Babylonia, a.k.a. the Bavli, says a great many things in only a single manner, everywhere appealing to a severely restricted rhetorical repertoire that serves throughout, I ask the question, How are we to know whether, in saying in one way a great many things, the document's authors propose also to say one thing about a great many things? At stake in the answer to that methodological question is the identification of the metapropositional statement implicit in an exceptionally diverse and intellectually prolix piece of writing. I wish now to show how to identify the metapropositional program to which propositional inquiries repeatedly point and even suggested one of the main points of that program.

To explain what I now seek – how the authors say a single thing about many things – I have to spell out what I mean here by a metapropositional statement or program. Only then will I offer a single example of such a metapropositional statement, with the promise that, when the necessary *Vorstudien* are complete, a much richer account of the matter will become possible. A proposition presents the result of an analysis of a given problem. When analyses of a variety of problems yield diverse propositions that as a matter of fact turn out to say the same one thing about many diverse things, that one thing said in many ways about many things forms not a proposition but a metaproposition. It is a proposition that derives from all subsets of propositions and states in an abstract and general way – whether explicitly or merely by indirection – the one proposition contained within many demonstrations of propositions. We know that we have identified the metapropositional program of a writing when we can say what we think is at stake, in the most general terms, in a variety of specific syllogisms and turn out to be saying the same thing again and again. We may test our hypothetical metaproposition by asking whether, in those many things, we may identify any other proposition to define the stakes of a demonstration; or whether some other encompassing proposition may serve as well as the one we propose over as broad a range of data as we examine. Where may we expect to find not only propositions but a statement that coheres throughout: a statement in behalf of all propositions? A coherent legal system, for one example, not only sets forth rules for diverse circumstances but, through the rules, also may lay out a philosophy of the social order, an account of what is always fair and just; then all of the cases, each with its generalization, turn out to repeat in different ways a single encompassing statement.

So, too, while the author of a document makes statements about a great many subjects, a well-crafted document by a strong-minded writer will find the author saying much the same thing about all things. Then the key to good writing will be the power to make the same point again and again without boring the reader or belaboring the obvious. Indeed, an important and truly well-conceived piece of writing addressed to a long future will precipitate productive debates about not only details but what that some one thing said in many ways is meant to propose. Great writing leaves space for readers. That is the mark of a strong argument, a well-crafted formulation of a considered viewpoint, the expression of a deeply reflected upon attitude, or, in intellectual matters, a rigorously presented proposition. To find out what we might imagine some one thing a writer may say about many things, we ask simply, "What is at stake if this point is validated?" or simply, "If so, so what?" If time and again we find that treatment of a given subject yields as its final and most general and abstract point a proposition that turns out also to emerge from an unrelated treatment of some other subject, altogether, then we have what I call a metaproposition, meaning, a proposition that transcends a variety of propositions and that occurs in all of them.

Obviously, defining the metapropositional statement that an author repeatedly sets forth involves an element of eisegesis – and even subjectivity. That is invariably a starting point. On the one side, others may see some other metaproposition that circulates throughout a piece of writing, different from one that I might proposed. On the other, still others may perceive no metaproposition at all. How to test a thesis on the metaproposition of a diverse piece of writing? One irrefutable demonstration is that a single rhetoric prevails, for that legitimates asking whether saying everything in some one way, writers also say one thing about many things. To define that some one thing, and to find out whether or not a proposed metaproposition in fact circulates throughout such a writing, first of all, a massive survey must show where, how, and why one proposes that one and same proposition that – according to a proposed metaproposition – an author persists in setting forth in the context of a great many diverse discussions. If it can be shown that most, or even all, of a large and various corpus of writing turns out to be saying that one thing through its treatment of a great many things, then one is justified in claiming to have set forth that proposition beyond the propositions that animates a document. It is the one that the authors have composed the document to set forth and in a vast number of ways to demonstrate. But let me forthwith turn to the two problems just now noted. What about the possibility that another metaproposition may be shown to inhere, different from the one that as a matter of hypothesis is set forth at the outset? Or what if a proposed metaproposition is not found to be present at all? Then the experiment has failed. And how are we going to test the validity of two or more proposed metapropositions, and so to know whether or not the metaproposition that is suggested is the right one? The answer lies in a detailed demonstration that the proposed metaproposition is the best one possible, in the context of a variety of possibilities, to encompass the data at hand. And God lives in the details.

Have we an example of a metapropositional statement set forth in a single, public, anonymous, and authoritative writing, and can we define the contents of one such statement? Indeed we do and we can. I already have shown the remarkably cogent and simple metaproposition, the recurrent statement that defines what is at stake in detailed syllogistic argument, which inheres in the Mishnah and proves paramount throughout. The pervasive telos of thought in the Mishnah is such that many things are made to say one thing, which concerns the nature of being. Specifically, the Mishnah's authority repeatedly demonstrates that all things are not only orderly, but are ordered in such wise that many things fall into one classification. So one thing may hold together many things of diverse classifications. These two matched and complementary propositions – [1] many things are one, [2] one thing encompasses many – complement each other. In forming matched opposites, the two provide a single, complete and final judgment of the whole of being, social, natural, supernatural alike. Nearly the whole of the document's tractates in one way or another repeat that simple point. The metaproposition is never expressed but it is everywhere demonstrated by showing, in whatever subject is treated, the possibility always of effecting the hierarchical classification of all things: each thing in its taxon, all taxa in correct sequence, from least to greatest.

What about the Bavli? Can I point to a sustained passage that talks about a variety of things, but deals with only one thing? One principal concern in the Bavli is the metaproposition that encompasses the numerous specific propositions: How do we make connections between rules and their point of origin? Every time we ask, "What is the source [in Scripture] for this statement?" we find an answer that is left to stand. So one fundamental and ubiquitous metaproposition of the Bavli may be set forth in this language:

1. It is important to link laws that occur in one source to those that occur in another.
2. Among the compilations [components of "the one whole Torah of Moses, our rabbi," in later mythic language] that enjoy canonical status [in our language], the premier is Scripture.
3. So whenever we find a statement of a rule in the Mishnah and ask for its source, the implicit criterion of success will be, "the rule is founded on language of Scripture, properly construed."

4. So, consequently, the proposition implicit in numerous propositions, common to them all and holding them all together, is this: all rules cohere, and the point of origin of nearly all of them is the written part of the Torah revealed by God to Moses at Sinai.

But I think that the rather formal issues outlined here form only the surface. To grasp the metapropositional program that, in my view, defines the stakes of discourse, let me specify what I conceive to be the counterpart program, pertaining to not connecting rules to Scripture, but rather, connecting principle to (consequent) principle: how thought really takes place, which is, not in a stationary pool but in a moving stream. To state the result up front: the Mishnah portrays all things at rest, a beautifully composed set in stasis, a stage on which nothing happens. The Bavli portrays all things in motion, a world of action, in which one thing leads to some other, and nothing stands still. All of this is accomplished in a shift in the received mode of thought, and the shift is set forth in the metaproposition, fully exposed, in the reading of two paragraphs of the Mishnah. We now consider what I conceive to be the counterpart program to the one that, in my view, the Bavli's sages inherited from the Mishnah and spelled out in tedious and unending particulars. To understand what is fresh and important in the Bavli's metapropositional program concerning the nature of thought, we have to call to mind what they inherited, for what they did was to impose the stamp of their own intellect upon the intellectual heritage that the Mishnah had provided for them.

To set forth the basic theory of the framers of the Mishnah on how thought takes place, which is to say, how we may understand things and know them, we must recall a simple fact. The Mishnah teaches the age-old method of scientific thought through comparison and contrast. Like things follow like rules, unlike things, the opposite rules, and the task of thought is to show what is like something else and therefore follows the rule that governs that something else; or what is unlike something else and therefore follows the opposite of the rule that governs that something else. So the Mishnah's mode of thought establishes connections between and among things and does so, as is clear, through the method of taxonomy, comparison and contrast, list making of like things, yielding the rule that governs all items on the list.

List making places on display the data of the like and the unlike and implicitly (ordinarily, not explicitly) then conveys the rule. The Mishnah is then a book of lists, with the implicit order, the nomothetic traits of a monothetic order, dictating the ordinarily unstated general and encompassing rule. And all this why? It is in order to make a single statement, endless times over, and to repeat in a mass of tangled detail precisely the same fundamental judgment. The framers of the Mishnah appeal solely to the traits of things. List making then defines a way of proving propositions through classification, so establishing a set of shared traits that form a rule which compels us to reach a given conclusion. Probative facts derive from the classification of data, all of which point in one direction and not in another. A catalogue of facts, for example, may be so composed that, through the regularities and indicative traits of the entries, the catalogue yields a proposition. A list of parallel items all together point to a simple conclusion; the conclusion may or may not be given at the end of the catalogue, but the catalogue – by definition – is pointed. All of the catalogued facts are taken to bear self-evident connections to one another, established by those pertinent shared traits implicit in the composition of the list, therefore also bearing meaning and pointing through the weight of evidence to an inescapable conclusion. The discrete facts then join together because of some trait common to them all. This is a mode of classification of facts to lead to an identification of what the facts have in common and, it goes without saying, an explanation of their meaning. What is at stake in the making of lists, that is, the formation of classes of things, is the comparison and contrast of one class of things with some other, yielding at the end the account of the hierarchization of all classes of things in correct sequence and grade. The following abstract shows us through the making of connections and the drawing of conclusions the propositional and essentially philosophical mind that animates the Mishnah and makes explicit what that authorship always wants to know: the relationships, in hierarchical order, between classes of things.

If I had to specify a single mode of thought that established connections between one fact and another, it is in the search for points in common and therefore also points of contrast. We seek connection between fact and fact, sentence and sentence in the subtle and balanced rhetoric of the Mishnah, by comparing and contrasting two things that are like and not alike. At the logical level, too, the Mishnah falls into the category of familiar philosophical thought. Once we seek regularities, we propose rules. What is like another thing falls under its rule, and what is not like the other falls under the opposite rule. Accordingly, as to the species of the genus, so far as they are alike, they share the same rule. So far as they are not alike, each follows a rule contrary to that governing the other. So the work of analysis is what produces connection, and therefore the drawing of conclusions derives from comparison and contrast: the *and*, the *equal*. The proposition then that forms the conclusion concerns the essential likeness of the two offices, except where they are different, but the subterranean premise is that we can explain both likeness and difference by appeal to a principle of fundamental order and unity. To make these observations concrete, we turn to the case at hand. The important contrast comes at the outset. The high priest and king fall into a single genus, but speciation, based on traits particular to the king, then distinguishes the one from the other. Now if I had to specify the deepest conviction at the most profound layers of thought, it is that things set in relationship always stand in that same relationship. The work of making connections and drawing conclusions produces results that are fixed and final. If we establish a connection between one set of things and another, that connection forms the end of matters – that, and not a series, by which the connection between A and B serves as a guide to a movement from C to A via B, that is, as we shall now see, the formation of not a connection but a series of things that are connected only to one another, but not to other components of the same series – which is to say, a series. To put matters very simply, If A is like B, and B is like C, then is C like A? And if we entertain the possibility of a series, then, *what are the rules of connection that form the links of the results of comparison and contrast?* In other words, in the aftermath of classification comes not hierarchization but movement, this thing in relationship to that, that in relationship to the other, all things in movement, nothing at rest. So, if a series is possible, then how is a series composed? That is the question answered by the Bavli, the question no one in the Mishnah asked, because the Mishnah's framers contemplated a world at rest, and the Bavli's, a world in motion.

In so stating, I have leapt over each of the necessary stages of my exposition, so let us begin from the beginning. Now that the Mishnah's position is in hand, we revert to my claim that the Bavli's own statement in the chapter under discussion concerns the nature of thought. Let us first of all review the points that are made, and the sequence in which they are set forth. We begin with the point of intersection:

1. It is important to know how to connect rules to Scripture.
2. The principles that govern the making of connections to Scripture are those that govern making connections not between words and words ("the hermeneutical principles") but rather between one thing and something else, that is, defining a genus and its species; so when we know how to compare and contrast, find what is like something else and what is different from something else, we know how to conduct the passage from rules to Scripture.
3. Exegetical rules tell us how to form classes of things in relationship to Scripture.
4. Dialectical rules tell us how to move from one class of things to another class of things.

No. 2 then marks the point of departure, and Nos. 3 and 4, the remarkable shift in the passage. We go not only from rule to generalization, or from case to principle. That, to be sure, takes place and forms an everywhere present metaproposition. But that is banal, in light of other results already set forth, and the passages run on in a tedious way. Rather, we go from thinking about things and their connections (comparison and contrast) to thinking about thought itself. So what I have represented as the rules of dialectical thinking – not merely argument! – turn out to tell us how thought happens; the Bavli's reading of Mishnah-tractate Zebahim 5:1-2 forms a fundamental exercise of thought about thinking (Bavli Zebahim 47B-52A). For, when we review the principal steps in the sustained and unfolding inquiry, we realize that, in particulars and in detail, the framers of the passage have set forth a profound essay on thought. In the terms just now given, if A=B, and B=C, then does C=A? Is a series possible? Are there limits to the extension of a series? And on what basis do we construct a series? Do the media of linkage between A and B, that is, A=B, have to be the same as those that link B to C, for C to stand in the series that A has begun? These abstract questions have to become concrete before the sense of matters will emerge. So let us now review the sequence of points that represent the inquiry into the making of connections, which is to say, the Bavli's metapropositional statement on the character of a series. For it is the series, first this, then that, finally the third thing, and the rules that govern the movement from this, to that, to the third thing, that defines what is the center of deep thought in the Bavli's reading of the specified Mishnah paragraphs.

Let me now present the text under discussion, then explain how I think we must interpret it so as to identify its metapropositional program. The Babylonian Talmud's exposition of Mishnah-tractate Zebahim 5:1-2 in a systematic and amazingly orderly way sets forth principles of comparison and contrast within the discipline of dialectical thinking. As we follow the discussion, we shall see beneath the surface – but not very far – the issue of the dialectics of analogical contrastive thought. That is, the question facing us is the logic of a series. Then I shall spell out in detail the context in which the metapropositional statement before us is made and show what is remarkable and fresh in the thought of the Bavli's framers. As we shall see, they are trying to show the logic, and limits, of a series, or, as I shall explain, if A=B and B=C, then does C=A, and, if so, why? To state matters in words rather than symbols, if we say something equals something else, what more are we saying, that is, what is the implication of the claim of equivalency? Let us first consider the documentary evidence in my form-analytical translation, then turn to investigate the metapropositional inquiry that I claim is before us. I indent material that occupies a subordinate position in the exposition at hand; in a contemporary re-presentation, what is indented would be a footnote or an appendix; such secondary and supplementary material forms only a tiny proportion of the whole.[1] Italics in the translation signify the presence of Aramaic, plain type, Hebrew; boldface type, the citation of a sentence of the Mishnah or the Tosefta.

5:1

A. What is the place [in which the act of sacrifice] of animal-offerings [takes place]?

B. **Most Holy Things [the whole-offering, sin-offering, and guilt-offering] – the act of slaughtering them is carried out at the north [side of the altar].**

C. **The bullock and the he-goat of the Day of Atonement – the act slaughtering them is at the north.**

D. **And the receiving of their blood is carried out in a utensil of service, at the north [side of the altar].**

E. **And their blood requires sprinkling over the space between the bars [of the ark], and on the veil, and on the golden altar.**

F. **One act of placing of their [blood] [if improperly done] impairs [atonement].**

G. **And the remnants of the blood did one pour out at the western base of the outer altar.**

H. **[But] if he did not place [the remnants of their blood at the stated location], he did not impair [atonement].**

5:2

A. **Bullocks which are to be burned and he-goats which are to be burned –**

B. **the act of slaughtering them is at the north [side of the altar].**

C. **And the receiving of their blood is in a utensil of service at the north.**

D. **And their blood requires sprinkling on the veil and on the golden altar.**

E. **[47B] [The improper sprinkling of] one act of placing of their [blood] impairs [atonement].**

F. **The remnants of their blood did one pour out on the western base of the outer altar.**

G. **If he did not place [the remnants of the blood at the stated location], he did not impair [atonement].**

H. **These and those are burned in the ash pit.**

---

[1] I explain this matter at some length in my *The Rules of Composition of the Talmud of Babylonia. The Cogency of the Bavli's Composite* (Atlanta, 1991: Scholars Press for South Florida Studies in the History of Judaism).

I.1   A   *But why should the Tannaite author of the passage not state in the opening clause [A-B] as he does later on [Cff.]:* **And the receiving of their blood is carried out in a utensil of service, at the north [side of the altar]***!*

B   *Since there is the matter of the guilt-offering presented by the person healed of the skin ailment [which is classified also as Most Holy Things], the blood of which is received in the hand [not in a utensil of service], he leaves out that item.*

C   *But is the blood not received in a utensil of service? And lo, it is taught later on,* **The peace-offerings of the congregation and the guilt-offerings – What are the guilt-offerings? (1) The guilt-offering for false dealing, and (2) the guilt-offering for acts of sacrilege, and (3) the guilt-offering [because of intercourse with] a betrothed bondwoman, and (4) the guilt-offering of a Nazir, and the (5) guilt-offering of the person healed of the skin ailment, and (6) the suspensive guilt-offering – the act of slaughtering them is at the north [side of the altar]. And the receiving of their blood is with a utensil of service at the north [M. 5:5]***!*

D   *To begin with he took the position that the receiving of the blood was to be done by hand. So he omitted reference to the item here [just as has been explained]. But when he realized that the collection of the blood cannot be done unless a utensil is used, he included it later on. For it has been taught on Tannaite authority:*

E   "And the priest shall take of the blood of the guilt-offering" – might one think that this is done with a utensil?

F   Scripture states, "and the priest shall put it" (Lev. 14:14) – just as the putting on of the blood is to be done by the priest's hand itself, so the taking of the blood also should be done by the priest's hand itself.

G   Might one suppose that that is the same for the altar [so that blood to be sprinkled on the altar is received not in a utensil but in the hand]?

H   Scripture states, "For as the sin-offering so is the guilt-offering" (Lev. 14:13) – just as the sin-offering requires a utensil for receiving the blood, so the guilt-offering requires a utensil for receiving the blood.

I   You must then draw the conclusion that two priests received the blood of the guilt-offering of the one healed of the skin ailment, one in his hand, the other in a utensil. The one who received the blood in a utensil went to the altar and put the blood there, and the one who received it in his hand went to the person who had been healed of the skin ailment and put it on the specified parts of his body.

II.1   A   [48A] **Bullocks which are to be burned and he-goats which are to be burned – the act of slaughtering them is carried out at the north side of the altar. And the receiving of their blood is in a utensil of service at the north. And their blood requires sprinkling on the veil and on the golden altar:**

B   *Now take note that the requirement that the rite be carried out at the north side of the altar is written in regard to the burnt-offering, so let the framer* of the passage formulate the rule by making reference first of all to the burnt-offering.

C. [The reason that he treats the sin-offering first is that] since the rule covering the sin-offering derives from exegesis of Scripture [rather than being stated explicitly therein], it is regarded by him as of greater value.

D. But then let him present the rules governing the sin-offerings that are offered on the outer altar!

E. Since the blood of those listed first is taken into the inner sanctum, it is regarded by him as of greater value.

We open with two entirely conventional questions, namely, analysis of the formulation of the Mishnah's rule, within the premise that the wording in all of its patterns yields meaning. The solution of the initial problem, in appeal to a verse of Scripture, provides only a routine demonstration of the metaproposition that Scripture forms the court of final appeal. The second entry follows suit. Now begins the chapter's great, sustained project.

I.2   A.   Where in Scripture is reference made to the rule governing the burnt-offering?

B.   "And he shall kill it on the side of the altar at the north" (Lev. 1:11).

C.   So we have found the explicit rule that treats a beast deriving from the flock. How do we know that the same rule governs what comes of the herd?

D.   Scripture states, "And if his offering be of the flock," and the word "and" continues the preceding statement, with the result that the subject that is prior may be deduced from the one given following. [Freedman: When a passage commences with "and" the conjunction links it with the previous portion, and a law stated in one applies to the other too. Here the subject above is the burnt-offering of the herd and the subject below is the flock.]

E.   That answer is satisfactory for him who takes the view that one may indeed derive a rule governing a prior subject from one that is given later on, but from the perspective of him who denies that fact, what is to be said?

The question before us is startling. In the materials just now examined, no one has told us that there are rules of exegesis, which provide signposts on the road from Scripture to the Mishnah, or from Scripture to the law. Now we encounter the first of the chapter's sustained and systematic discussions of rules of reading Scripture.

F.   For it has been taught on Tannaite authority:

G.   "'And if any one [commits a breach of faith and sins unwittingly in any of the holy things of the Lord]' (Lev. 5:15) – this ['and if'] serves to impose liability for a suspensive guilt-offering in the case of an act of sacrilege that is subject to doubt," the words of R. Aqiba.

H.   And sages declare him exempt.

I.   May not one say that this is what is subject to dispute: R. Aqiba takes the view that we derive the rule for a prior matter from one that is mentioned later on, and rabbis maintain that we do not derive the rule governing a

prior matter from a matter that is mentioned later on. [The prior matter
is the one regarding sacrilege, the one that follows deals with the
suspensive guilt-offering, so Lev. 5:17: "If anyone sins, doing any of
the things that the Lord has commanded not to be done, though he
does not know it, yet he is guilty and shall bear his iniquity." Aqiba
then derives the rule governing the case of an act of sacrilege that is
subject to doubt from the rule governing unwitting sins that are
subject to doubt, and consequently requires a suspensive guilt-
offering, and that explains his position: **R. Aqiba declares [a
person] liable to a suspensive guilt-offering in the case of a
matter of doubt regarding acts of sacrilege.** Sages do not read the
rule of the latter passage into the definition of the former.]

J.   Said R. Pappa, *"All parties concur that we derive the rule for a prior
topic from one that comes later on,* [B. Ker. 22B adds:] *for otherwise we
should have no basis for the law that the bullock has to be slaughtered on
the north side of the altar* [for that rule derives from the fact that while
the rule on the bullock-offerings, Lev. 1:3-4, comes prior to the rule
on offering small cattle, Lev. 1:10f., and only the latter requires the
slaughter to take place on the north side of the altar, we do indeed
slaughter the bullock-offerings on the north side of the altar as
well]. *But this is the reason for the position of rabbis, who declare one
exempt [from having to present a suspensive guilt-offering in the case of a
matter of doubt regarding acts of sacrilege]: they derive an verbal analogy
to a sin-offering based on the appearance of the word 'commandments'
with reference to both matters.* There [at Lev. 4:27, with reference to a
sin-offering] there is an offense for which one is liable to extirpation
in the case of a deliberate violation of the law, and to a sin-offering
in the case of an inadvertent violation of the law, and to a
suspensive guilt-offering in the case of doubt. So in every case, for
which one is liable to extirpation in the case of a deliberate violation
of the law, and to a sin-offering in the case of an inadvertent
violation of the law, and to a suspensive guilt-offering in the case of
doubt, the same rule applies; *but this excludes sacrilege, for in that
case,* a deliberate violation of the law does not bring on the penalty
of extirpation." [B. Ker. 22B adds: *For it has been taught on Tannaite
authority,* He who deliberately committed an act of sacrilege – Rabbi
says, "He is subject to the death penalty." And sages say, "He is
subject to an admonition."]

K.   And how about the position of R. Aqiba?

L.   *He maintains that when we draw a verbal analogy between the reference
here to "commandments" and the reference to "commandments" with
regard to the sin-offering [thus yielding the position outlined at E], it
serves for the eating of prohibited fat, and accomplishes the following
purpose:* just as in that matter, reference is made to a sacrifice of
fixed value, so all of the sacrifices must be of fixed value, *thus
excluding sacrifices of variable value [such as those listed at Lev. 5:1-13],
e.g., a sin-offering brought on account of imparting uncleanness to the
sanctuary and its Holy Things, which is expiated by an offering of variable
value.*

M.   *And rabbis?*

N   They take the view that one may not derive from an argument by
analogy established through the use of a word in common only a
limited repertoire of conclusions [but once the analogy is drawn,
then all of the traits of one case apply to the other].

Now we find something that captures our attention, which is
evidence of a sustained and systematic inquiry. First we have
introduced our guideline on moving from Scripture to law. Then,
second and by consequence, we have introduced a refinement on the
guideline. At stake is the limits of analogy: Is something like something
else in one way analogous in all other ways, so that every rule pertaining
to the one thing applies also to the other? Or is an analogy limited,
determinate only for itself? That seems to me a question of sufficient
abstraction to impress the thinkers before us, since it has to do with, not
the rules of argument or guidelines in an exegetical venture, but the rules
of thought and guidelines on right reason. Once people think in a deep
system of analogy and contrast, the issue before us becomes urgent and
unavoidable.

O   *Then does it follow that* R. Aqiba holds that one may derive from an
argument by analogy established through the use of a word in
common only a limited repertoire of conclusions? [Not at all.] *All
parties concur that* one may not derive from an argument by analogy
established through the use of a word in common only a limited
repertoire of conclusions [but once the analogy is drawn, then all of
the traits of one case apply to the other].

P.   *And this is the operative consideration for the position of R. Aqiba:*
Scripture has said, "And if anyone," with the result that the use of
the "if" serves to complement the matter that is treated first and to
impose upon that matter a rule that is presented only later on.
[Thus: "'And if anyone [commits a breach of faith and sins
unwittingly in any of the Holy Things of the Lord]' (Lev. 5:15) – this
'and if' serves to impose liability for a suspensive guilt-offering in
the case of an act of sacrilege that is subject to doubt," the words of
R. Aqiba.]

Q   *Now surely rabbis have to take account of the fact that* Scripture has
said, "And if anyone," [with the result that the use of the "if" serves
to complement the matter that is treated first and to impose upon
that matter a rule that is presented only later on].

R.   *May one propose that it is in the following point that they differ:*

S.   *One authority maintains that proof supplied by analogy [here: the analogy
sustained by the use of "and" to join the two subjects] takes priority, and
the other party maintains that the proof supplied by the demonstration of a
totality of congruence among salient traits takes precedence. Rabbis prefer
the latter, Aqiba the former position.*

T.   *Not at all! All parties concur that proof supplied by analogy [here: the
analogy sustained by the use of "and" to join the two subjects] takes
priority. But rabbis in this context will say to you that the rule governing
the subject treated below derives from the rule governing the subject*

> *treated above, so that the guilt-offering must be worth at least two silver sheqels. This is established so that you should not argue that the doubt cannot be more stringent than the matter of certainty, and just as where there is certainty of having committed a sin, one has to present a sin-offering that may be worth even so little as a sixth of a zuz in value, so if there is a matter of doubt, the guilt-offering worth only a sixth of a zuz would suffice.*

What I said a moment ago pertains here as well. The same issue is now restated and refined. Do we have to show that things that are alike are alike in all respects, or is it sufficient to show likeness in only salient, therefore indicative and determinative, ones?

U.   *And how does R. Aqiba derive that same theory?*

V.   *He derives it from the verse,* "And this is the Torah of the guilt-offering" (Lev. 7:1), meaning, there is a single Torah that covers all guilt-offerings.

W.   *You may then leave off considering the issue from the view of him who maintains that "Torah" is to be interpreted in that way, but on the view of him who maintains that "Torah" is not to be interpreted in that way, what is to be said?*

X.   *Such a one derives the matter from the use of* "according to your valuation" at Lev. 5:15 and Lev. 5:18 [and that yields a verbal analogy based on congruence of shared traits].

Y.   *That poses no problems in the context in which* "according to your valuation" *occurs, but what about the guilt-offering that is presented in the case of the violation of a maidservant who has been promised in marriage (Lev. 19:20-22), in which no reference is made to* "according to your valuation"?

Z.   *There we find the repetition of* "with the lamb" (Lev. 5:16, 19:22) [which yields the same rule on the minimum value of the beast offered for this purpose].

It suffices at this point to observe that this rather long and complex inquiry is cogent, and the cogency is both on the surface and underneath. The sustained sequence of moving questions and answers ("dialectic"), with a question's answer raising its own question, carries the surface discourse from point to point, beginning to end. But at the deep structure is also a program of inquiry, exemplified at the surface, and the inquiry concerns principles of the reading of Scripture, which can obviously serve for the reading of any other writing to which the standing and stylistic power of Scripture are imputed, within a logic of comparison and contrast. What we want to know in the subtext (if that is the right term for the here articulated program exemplified by the text) is that logic: If we find similarity, what conclusions do we draw from that similarity?

III.1   A   [Supply: Most Holy Things (...sin-offering...) – the act of slaughtering them is carried out at the north side of the altar:]

B.   *How on the basis of Scripture do we know that the sin-offering has to be prepared at the north side of the altar?*

C.   *As it is written,* "And he shall kill the sin-offering in the place of the burnt-offering" (Lev. 4:24).

D.   *So we have found that the act of slaughter must take place in the designated place, but how on the basis of Scripture do we know that the same rule applies to the act of receiving the blood?*

E.   *As it is written,* "And the priest shall take of the blood of the sin-offering" (Lev. 4:25). ["...Take" means to receive the blood, and the "and" joins this to the immediately preceding verse (Freedman).]

F.   *What about the rule governing the location of the priest himself who receives the blood? How on the basis of Scripture do we know that rule?*

G.   *Said Scripture,* "And he shall take to himself" [in the place where the blood is received, that is, at the north of the altar].

H.   *So we have found the manner in which the religious duty is optimally carried out. But how do we know that these rules are absolutely indispensable to the rite [so that if they are not observed, the offering is ruined]?*

I.   *A further verse of Scripture states,* "And he shall kill it for a sin-offering in the place where they kill the burnt-offering" (Lev. 4:33), *and it has been taught on Tannaite authority:*

J.   Where is the burnt-offering slaughtered? It is in the north. This, too [the sin-offering], also is slaughtered in the north.

K.   [48B] Now is it from this verse that the rule is to be derived? Is it not in point of fact stated, "In the place where the burnt-offering is killed shall the sin-offering be killed" (Lev. 6:18) [referring to all sin-offerings]? So why is this [sin-offering presented by a ruler] singled out? It is to establish the place in which it is to be killed, so to prove that if one did not slaughter it in the north, it is invalid [and that repetition teaches the rule just now stated, yielding the fact that the keeping these rules is indispensable to the valid performance of the rite].

L.   You maintain that that is the reason that the matter has been singled out. But perhaps it is not the case, but rather to indicate that this offering alone [the ruler's sin-offering] is the only one that requires the north, but no other sin-offering has to be killed at the north side of the altar? Therefore Scripture states, "And he shall kill the sin-offering in the place of the burnt-offering," so stating an encompassing rule in regard to all sin-offerings: all have to be slaughtered in the north.

M.   *So we have found the rule governing the sin-offering presented by the ruler: it is both described as properly carried out in this way and also prescribed as indispensably carried out in this way. And we also know that other sin-offerings are properly carried out in this way. But how do we know that it is necessary to carry out other sin-offerings in this way [so that if they are not slaughtered at the north, they are invalid]?*

N.   Because the same requirement is specified in Scripture in regard to both the lamb (Lev. 4:33) and the she-goat (Lev. 4:29).

Here is a model of the familiar inquiry into the linkage between Scripture and the law presented in the Mishnah. What we now are beginning to perceive is that our entire chapter is doing this to tell us the answer to the one question: What is the scriptural basis for the rule before us? Why the subject matter of this chapter of the Mishnah persuades the framers of the Talmud to the chapter of the Mishnah that the issue of scriptural sources of the law in the Mishnah is a compelling and dominant theme is clear: the question can be asked, because, on this subject, Scripture is prolix and abundant, rich in rules, prolix in their formulation. Consequently, where the question can be asked, it is asked; our authors would have had a very difficult time pursuing the same question in connection with, e.g., writs of divorce, where a couple of verses of Scripture pertain, all the more so the many Mishnah tractates to which no verses of Scripture allude at all. It is because the subject matter of the Mishnah chapter coincides with numerous and well-articulated verses of Scripture that we are able to address what I claim to be the deeper issues throughout: not only exegesis or rules of exegesis, but rather, analogical contrastive thinking and the rules of the logic of comparison and contrast. It is the point at which these deeper issues of thought are articulated that the Talmud moves away from the obvious program of linking law to Scripture; and that same point, moreover, concerns not rules of exegesis at all, but rules of right thinking.

III.2   A   [As to the verse, "And he shall kill *it* for a sin-offering in the place where they kill the burnt-offering" (Lev. 4:33),] what is the purpose of the word "it"?

        B.   *It is required in line with that which has been taught on Tannaite authority:*

        C   "...It..." is slaughtered at the north side of the altar, but the goat presented by Nahshon is not slaughtered at the north side of the altar [that is, the goats brought as a sin-offering at the consecration of the altar. These are not really sin-offerings at all.]

        D.   *And it has been taught on Tannaite authority:*

        E.   "'And he shall lay his hand upon the head of the goat' (Lev. 4:24) [the goat brought by the ruler] – this encompasses the goat brought by Nahshon under the rule of the laying on of hands," the words of R. Judah.

        F.   R. Simeon says, "It serves to encompass under the rule of laying on of hands the goats brought on account of inadvertent idolatry."

        G   [Reverting to the question of A,] *You might have supposed that since they are encompassed under the rule of laying on of hands, they also are encompassed under the rule of being slaughtered in the north. So we are informed to the contrary.*

        H   *To this proposition Rabina objected, "That conclusion serves full well for R. Judah, but from R. Simeon's perspective, what is there to be said?"* [Freedman: He does not include it in respect of laying hands, so a text is not required to show that the north does not apply to it.]

What follows is of special interest, because it articulates another (rather obvious) rule of analogical thinking, which is, rules can be derived not only by appeal to Scripture but also by reference to analogy not made explicit by the verbal formulations of Scripture. The main point here is that, once an analogy serves, it serves everywhere an analogy can be drawn; there is no a priori that limits the power of an analogy to govern all like cases.

I. *Said Mar Zutra b. R. Mari to Rabina, "And does that conclusion serve so well for R. Judah anyhow? Where it is included under the law, it is included under the law, where not, not [so no verse of Scripture is required]. And should you say that if Scripture had not included the matter, we should have reached the same conclusion by argument for analogy, then if that is the case, we can infer by analogy also the rule on laying on of hands. So you must answer that a temporary sacrifice [done once, as with Nahshon's] cannot derive its law by inference from a permanent one, and so here too, a sacrifice brought only on a special occasion cannot find its rule by analogy to the rule governing a sacrifice that is permanent. [There is no reason to suppose that the sin-offering of Nahshon, which was for an occasion, had to be done at the north, and therefore why is a text needed to exclude it? So we do not know the answer to our question, As to the verse, "And he shall kill it for a sin-offering in the place where they kill the burnt-offering" (Lev. 4:33), what is the purpose of the word "it"?]*

J. "*Rather:* 'It' is slaughtered in the north, but the one who does the slaughtering does not have to stand in the north."

K. *But the law on the slaughterer derives from what R. Ahia said. For it has been taught on Tannaite authority:*

L. R. Ahia says, "'And he shall kill it on the side of the altar at the north'': Why is this stated? It is because we find that the priest who receives the blood must stand in the north and also must receive the blood in the north. If he stood in the south and received the blood in the north, the offering is invalid. So you might have thought that the same rule governs slaughtering the animal. Scripture says, 'And he shall kill it,' meaning, 'it' must be in the north, while the one who does the act of slaughter need not be in the north."

M. [Reverting again to the question of A,] "It" must be killed in the north, but a bird does not have to be killed in the north [when the neck of the bird is wrung to kill it as a sacrifice]. *For it has been taught on Tannaite authority:*

N. Might one suppose that killing a bird-offering must be done in the north?

O. That conclusion, after all, stands to reason, for if killing a lamb, which does not have to be done by a priest, must be done in the north, killing a bird, which does have to be done by a priest, surely should be done in the north!

P. Accordingly, it is necessary to specify "it," to bear the meaning, "it" must be killed in the north, but a bird does not have to be killed in the north.

Q   No, what is particular to the lamb is that Scripture has required the use of a utensil in killing it [while no knife is required for a bird]!

R.   Rather, [reverting again to the question of A,] "it" must be killed in the north, but a Passover-offering does not have to be slaughtered in the north. *For it has been taught on Tannaite authority:*

S.   R. Eliezer b. Jacob says, "Might one suppose that slaughtering the Passover-offering must take place in the north? For it stands to reason. If Scripture required that the burnt-offering be slaughtered at the north, though it did not specify a fixed time for slaughtering the burnt-offering, surely the Passover-offering, for which Scripture did prescribe a fixed time for slaughter, should have to be slaughtered in the north.

T.   "Accordingly, it is necessary to specify 'it,' to bear the meaning, 'it' must be killed in the north, but a Passover-offering does not have to be killed in the north."

U.   Not at all. The distinctive trait of the burnt-offering is that it is wholly burned up.

V.   Then derive the matter from the sin-offering [which is not wholly burnt up but yields meat to the priest].

W.   What is distinctive about the sin-offering is that it achieves atonement for those who are liable to the penalty of extirpation.

X.   Then derive the matter from the guilt-offering.

Y.   What is distinctive about the guilt-offering is that it falls into the classification of Most Holy Things, and, as a matter of fact, you cannot derive the rule from the cases of the burnt-offering, guilt-offering or sin-offerings, for all of them are in the classification of Most Holy Things.

Z.   *So, in the end, it must be as we originally said:*

AA.   "It" is slaughtered in the north, but the one who does the slaughtering does not have to stand in the north."

BB.   *And as to the question that you raised based on what R. Ahia said* [R. Ahia says, "'And he shall kill it on the side of the altar at the north': why is this stated? It is because we find that the priest who receives the blood must stand in the north and also must receive the blood in the north. If he stood in the south and received the blood in the north, the offering is invalid. So you might have thought that the same rule governs slaughtering the animal. Scripture says, 'And he shall kill it,' meaning, 'it' must be in the north, while the one who does the act of slaughter need not be in the north."] – *the answer is, the sense is not to exclude the slaughterer from the requirement that the rite be done in the north, but rather,* "While the one who does the slaughtering need not be in the north, the one who receives the blood must be in the north."

CC.   *The receiver? But surely that is deduced from the language,* "and he shall take," meaning, "let him take himself to the north"!

DD.   The authority at hand does not accept the sense, "and he shall take," meaning, "let him take himself to the north."

It is hardly necessary to remind ourselves that we are dealing with a sustained and continuous exposition, one that holds together from start to finish: the same question, addressed in sequence to successive statements of the same base text (the Mishnah's paragraph), and answered in a consistent way throughout.

III.3   A   *So we have found that, so far as fulfilling the religious duty, the act of slaughtering of the burnt-offering must be done in the north, and the act of receiving, so far as fulfilling the religious duty, must be done in the north. How do we know that it is indispensable that the act of slaughtering and receiving the blood be done in the north [and if not, the offering is invalid]?*

     B   Said R. Adda b. Ahbah – others say, Rabbah b. Shila, "It is an argument a fortiori: If slaughtering and receiving the blood at the north form an indispensable part of the rite of offering the sin-offering, the rule of which in any event is derived from the rule governing the burnt-offering, then surely it is reasonable to suppose that these same procedures' being done in the north are indispensable in the case of the burnt-offering, from which the rules governing the sin-offering derive!"

     C   But the distinctive trait of the sin-offering is that it effects atonement for those who are liable to extirpation.

     D   *Said Rabina, "[The reason that nonetheless Adda utilizes the argument a fortiori is as follow:] This is what R. Adda bar Ahbah found troubling: Do we ever find the rule governing a derivative matter more stringent than the rule governing the primary matter?"* [The sin-offering here is secondary to the burnt-offering, since the requirement of offering the sacrifice at the northern side of the altar occurs primarily in connection with the burnt-offering (Freedman).]

     E   Said Mar Zutra b. R. Mari to Rabina, "Do we not find such a case? [49A] Lo, there is the matter of second tithe, which itself can be redeemed, while what is purchased with money exchanged for produce in the status of second tithe cannot be redeemed. *For we have learned in the Mishnah:* [Produce] purchased with coins [in the status] of second tithe, which becomes unclean [and therefore may not be eaten as second tithe] – let it be redeemed. R. Judah says, "Let it be buried." They said to R. Judah, "If it is the case that when produce which is designated as second tithe itself becomes unclean, lo, it must be redeemed, is it not logical that produce purchased with coins in the status of second tithe which becomes unclean also should be redeemed?" He said to them, "No! If you say this in regard to [produce designated as] second tithe itself, which, if in a state of cleanness, may be redeemed when it is outside Jerusalem, can you say so as regards produce purchased with coins [in the status of second tithe which, when it is [in a state of] cleanness, may not be redeemed when outside Jerusalem?" [M. M.S. 3:10].

     F   *In that case the power of the sanctification is insufficient to govern its redemption.* [Freedman: An object must possess a certain degree of sanctity before the sanctity can be transferred to something else, while the sanctity of this is too light to permit such a transfer. Hence Judah's ruling arises out of the lesser, not the greater, sanctity of what has been purchased.]

G   *And lo, there is the case of a beast declared as a substitute for a consecrated beast, for while an act of consecration does not affect a beast that is permanently blemished, an act of substitution does affect a beast that is permanently blemished!*

H   *The consecration of the beast declared as a substitute derives from the consecration of the consecrated beast itself, while the sanctification of a consecrated animal for its part derives from its originally unconsecrated status. [Another animal already has been sanctified.]*

I   *And lo, there is the case of the Passover, which itself does not require the laying on of hands, drink-offerings, and the waving of the breast and shoulder, while a beast purchased with the remainder of funds set aside for the purchase of a Passover-offering, when it is offered up on that occasion, does require the laying on of hands, drink-offerings, and the waving of the breast and shoulder.*

J   *But the animal purchased with the remainder of funds set aside for the purchase of a Passover-offering during the rest of the year is classified simply as a peace-offering [and it is not a Passover-offering at all; it is a different sacrifice, subject to its own rules (Freedman)].*

K   *If you prefer, I shall say,* Scripture has said, "the burnt-offerings," meaning, "it must be in its appointed place." [That means doing so in the northern area is essential to the rite, not merely recommended.]

IV.1 A   [Supply: **Most Holy Things (…guilt-offering) – the act of slaughtering them is carried out at the north side of the altar**].

Here we go again: How on the basis of Scripture do we know the law that the Mishnah has stated without a prooftext?

B   *How on the basis of Scripture do we know that the guilt-offering has to be prepared at the north side of the altar?*

C   *As it is written,* "In the place in which they kill the burnt-offering shall they kill the guilt-offering" (Lev. 7:1).

D   *So we have found that the act of slaughter of the guilt-offering must take place at the northern side of the altar. How on the basis of Scripture do we know that the collecting of the blood also must take place there?*

E   "And the blood thereof shall be dashed" (Lev. 7:2).

F   *So the receiving of the blood must also be in the north. How about the location of the one who receives the blood?*

G   *That is indicated by the use of* <u>*the accusative particle et*</u> *[which extends the law to the one who receives the blood] in the verse,* "And the blood thereof shall be dashed" (Lev. 7:2).

H   *So we have found that that is the recommended manner of carrying out the rite. But how do we know that it is indispensable to the proper performance of the rite that matters be done in this way?*

I   *There is another verse that is written in this same connection:* "And he shall kill the he lamb in the place where they kill the sin-offering and the burnt-offering" (Lev. 14:13) [repeating the rule in regard to another guilt-offering shows that it is indispensable to the proper carrying out of the rite].

IV.2   A.   *But does the cited verse really serve the stated purpose in particular? Surely it serves another purpose altogether, as has been taught on Tannaite authority:*

       B.   If a matter was covered by an encompassing rule but then was singled out for some innovative purpose, you have not got the right to restore the matter to the rubric of the encompassing rule unless Scripture itself explicitly does so.

       C.   How so?

       D.   "And he shall kill the lamb in the place where they kill the sin-offering and the burnt-offering, in the holy place; for the guilt-offering, like the sin-offering, belongs to the priest; it is most holy" (Lev. 14:13) –

       E.   Now what need does Scripture have to state, "for the guilt-offering, like the sin-offering"? [Freedman: For if it is to teach that it is slaughtered in the north, that follows from the first half of the verse; if it teaches that sprinkling of the blood and eating the meat follow the rules of the sin-offering, that is superfluous, since it is covered by the general regulations on guilt-offerings given at Lev. 7:1-10.] And why does Scripture state, "for the guilt-offering, like the sin-offering"?

       F.   The reason is that the guilt-offering presented by the person healed of the skin ailment was singled out for the innovative purpose of indicating the following:

       G.   In regard to the thumb of the hand, big toe of the foot, and right ear, you might have thought that the rite does not require the presentation of the blood of the offering and the parts to be burned up on the altar. Scripture therefore states, "for the guilt-offering, like the sin-offering," to show that just as the sin-offering's blood and sacrificial parts have to be presented on the altar, so the blood and sacrificial parts of the guilt-offering presented by the person healed of the skin ailment have to be presented on the altar.

       H.   *If [you claim that the purpose of the verse is as stated and not to teach that doing the rite at the north is indispensable, as originally proposed,] then Scripture should have stated only the rule governing the rite for the one healed from the skin ailment but not the earlier version of the rule.*

       I.   *Quite so – if we take the view that when something becomes the subject of a new law, it cannot then be covered by an encompassing rule that otherwise would apply,* [49B] *while the encompassing rule still can be derived from that special case. But if we take the view that when something becomes the subject of a new law, then it cannot be covered by an encompassing rule that otherwise would apply, and the encompassing rule also cannot be derived from that special place, then the law [Lev. 7:1-10, indicating that the guilt-offering must be killed in the north] is needed for its own purpose!*

       J.   *Since Scripture has restored the matter to the rubric of the encompassing rule explicitly, that restoration has taken place.*

       K.   *Said Mar Zutra b. R. Mari to Rabina, "But why not say, when Scripture restored the matter to the rubric of the encompassing rule, that was solely in regard to having to present the blood and the sacrificial parts on the altar, since the priest is necessary to perform that rite. But as to*

>   *slaughtering the animal, which does not have to be done by a priest, that*
>   *does not have to be done at the northern side of the altar?"*
>
> L.   *[He said to him,] "If so, Scripture should say simply, 'for it is like the*
>   *sin-offering.' Why say, 'or the guilt-offering, like the sin-offering'?*
>   *It is to teach, let it be like other guilt-offerings [that must be slaughtered at*
>   *the northern side of the altar]."*
>
> IV.3 A. *Why must a verbal analogy [for the burnt-offering] be drawn to both a sin-*
>   *offering and also a guilt-offering?*
>
> B.   *Said Rabina, "Both are necessary. If a verbal analogy had been drawn to a*
>   *sin-offering but not to a burnt-offering, I should have reached this*
>   *conclusion: from what source did we derive the rule that a sin-offering is*
>   *slaughtered at the north side of the altar? It is on the basis of the analogy*
>   *to the burnt-offering. The consequence is that a rule that has been derived*
>   *by analogy in turn generates another rule through analogy [so to avoid*
>   *such a circularity, Scripture adds the matter of the burnt-offering, to prove*
>   *that that is not the case]."*
>
> C.   *Said Mar Zutra b. R. Mari to Rabina, "Then draw the analogy to the*
>   *burnt-offering and omit reference to a verbal analogy to the sin-offering*
>   *altogether!"*

Now we come to one of the great moments of our chapter: the truly dialectical question, that is generated by the dialectical mode of thought. What we want to know, stated narrowly, is the limits of verbal analogy. To explain what is at issue, we have to proceed in a moving argument, hence, the issue is the dialectics of analogy. Specifically: I have two items, A and B. I claim that B is like A, therefore the rule governing A applies also to B. Now I turn forward, to C. C is not analogous to A; there are no points of congruence or (in the exegetical formulation that our authors use) verbal intersection. But C is like B because there is an analogy by reason of verbal intersection (the same word being used in reference to C and B). The question is, may I apply to C, by reason of the verbal intersection between C and B, the lesson that I have learned in regard to B only by reason of B's similarity by reason of congruence, not verbal intersection, to A? This is formulated (as best as I can translate the Hebrew/Aramaic) as, "Can a conclusion that is derived on the basis of a verbal analogy go and impart a lesson by reason of analogy to a third item?" This issue is going to occupy us for quite some time.

> D.   *[He said to him,] "Then I might reach the conclusion that [elsewhere] what*
>   *is derived on the basis of a verbal analogy turns around and imparts a*
>   *lesson by means of a verbal analogy [and there would be nothing in the*
>   *text to show the contrary (Freedman)]. And if you should say, then draw*
>   *the analogy to a sin-offering, I would reply: Scripture prefers to draw the*
>   *analogy to what is primary rather than to what is secondary [and the sin-*
>   *offering is the primary source of the law, since that is where the*
>   *requirement that the rite take place at the north is specified, and the sin-*
>   *offering is derivative of he burnt-offering]. That is why the analogy is*
>   *drawn to the sin-offering and also to the burnt-offering, bearing the sense*

that that which is derived on the basis of a verbal analogy does not in turn go and impart a lesson by means of a verbal analogy."

IV.4   A   *Raba said, "[The proposition that that which is derived on the basis of a verbal analogy does not in turn go and impart a lesson by means of a verbal analogy] derives from the following proof:*

    B   "It is written, 'As is taken off from the ox of the sacrifice of peace-offerings' (Lev. 4:10) [namely, the sacrificial parts of the anointed priest's bullock brought for a sin-offering] – *now for what purpose is this detail given? That the lobe of the liver and the two kidneys are to be burned on the altar [as is the case with those of the sin-offering], that fact is specified in the body of the verse itself. But the purpose is to intimate that the burning of the lobe of the liver and the two kidneys of the he-goats brought as sin-offerings for idolatry are to be derived by analogy from the bullock of the community brought on account of an inadvertent sin. That law is not explicitly stated in the passage on the bullock that is brought for an inadvertent sin, but is derived from the rule governing the bullock of the anointed priest. 'As is taken off' is required so that it might be treated as something written in that very passage [on the bullock of inadvertence, being superfluous in its own context], not as something derived on the basis of a verbal analogy does not in turn go and impart a lesson by means of a verbal analogy."*

    C   *Said R. Pappa to Raba, "Then let Scripture inscribe the rule in that very passage, and not trouble to draw a verbal analogy to the bullock of the anointed priest at all."*

    D   *"If the rule had been inscribed in its own context and not been presented by means of a verbal analogy to the bullock of the anointed priest, I might have said that that which is derived on the basis of a verbal analogy does in turn go and impart a lesson by means of a verbal analogy. And if you should object, 'Then let Scripture present the rule by analogy without making it explicit,' I could answer that Scripture prefers to make an explicit statement in the proper context rather than to present a law through a verbal analogy. Scripture therefore inscribed the matter in the passage dealing with the anointed priest and established the analogy so as to demonstrate that that which is derived on the basis of a verbal analogy does not in turn go and impart a lesson by means of a verbal analogy."*

My claim that this chapter is systematic and orderly, composed with a broader program in mind and not narrowly limited to the exegesis of phrases of the Mishnah read in sequence, is now demonstrated by what is to follow. We have proven one point. It bears a consequence. We go on to the consequence. The mode of thought is dialectical not only in form, but also in substance: if A, then B. If B, then what about C? But we see that matters are not only continued, but also refined. It is one thing to have shown that if B is like A, and C, unlike A, is rendered comparable to B by a verbal analogy, then may I take the next step and draw into the framework of B and C, joined by verbal analogy and assigned a common rule by B's congruent analogy to A, also D, E, F, and G, that is, other classes of things joined to C by verbal analogy – but not necessarily the same verbal analogy that has joined C to B? That indeed is the obvious next step to be taken, and it is now taken.

IV.5 A Now it is a fact that that which is derived on the basis of a verbal analogy does in turn go and impart a lesson by means of a verbal analogy, *demonstrated whether in the manner of Raba or in the manner of Rabina.*

B Is it the rule, however, that *that which is derived on the basis of a verbal analogy may in turn go and impart a lesson by means of an argument on the basis of congruence?* [Freedman: Thus the law stated in A is applied to B by analogy. Can that law then be applied to C because of congruence between B and C?]

C [Indeed it can.] *Come and take note:* R. Nathan b. Abetolomos says, "How on the basis of Scripture do we know that when there is a spreading of disease signs [cf. Lev. 13-14] in clothing, [if it covers the entire garment], it is ruled to be clean? The words 'baldness on the back of the head' and 'baldness on the front of the head' are stated in respect to man, and 'baldness on the back' and 'baldness on the front' are mentioned in connection with clothing. Just as is in the former case, if the baldness spread throughout the whole, the man is clean, so here too, if the baldness spread throughout the whole, the garment is clean."

D And in that context how do we know the rule [that that which spreads and covers the whole head is clean, since Lev. 13:12-13 refers to what is on the skin, not the head? And furthermore, the symptoms differ (Freedman)]? Because it is written, "And if the skin ailment...cover all the skin...from his head even to his feet" (Lev. 13:12) – so the head is treated as analogous to the feet. Just as if the feet have all turned white, the ailment have spread over the whole of the body, the man is clean, so here, too, when it spreads over the whole of the head and beard, he is clean. [Thus we derive the rule by a verbal analogy that the specified marks covering the whole head are clean, and then the same rule is applied to the garments by the argument resting on congruence, as stated at C (Freedman).]

E [To the contrary,] said R. Yohanan, "Throughout the Torah we infer one rule from another that has itself been derived by inference, except for the matter of consecration, in which we do not derive a rule from another that has itself been inferred."

F. *Now if it were the fact that we did so, then let the reference to "north" not be stated in the context of the guilt-offering at all, and it could be inferred from the rule governing sin-offerings, by means of the argument based on the congruence of the language, "It is most Holy" [which is stated in the setting of the sin-offering at Lev. 7:18 and the guilt-offering at Lev. 7:1]! Does that not bear the implication that that which is derived on the basis of a verbal analogy may not in turn go and impart a lesson by means of an argument on the basis of congruence?*

G *But perhaps the reason that we do not learn the lesson at that passage is that there is an ample refutation: the reason that the sin-offering has to be offered in the north is that it achieves atonement for those who are liable to the penalty of extirpation?*

H   *Still, in context, there is nonetheless a superfluous reference to "most Holy"* [at Num. 18:9]. [Freedman: Since this is superfluous, an argument from congruence is plausible, even though the guilt-offering is dissimilar to the sin-offering; that we do not do so proves that in the case of sacrifices that which is derived on the basis of a verbal analogy may not in turn go and impart a lesson by means of an argument on the basis of congruence.]

What follows simply proceeds to the logically next question: we have now linked B to C via a verbal analogy. C stands in relationship to other classes of things, but not for the same reason that it stands in relationship to B, that is, through other than verbal analogical relationships. It forms a relationship a fortiori, for instance, with D, E, and F. If something applies to C, the lesser, it surely should apply to D, the greater. So now we want to know the permissible grounds for drawing relationships – comparisons and contrasts – of classes of things. The deeper issue of comparative contrasting thinking is now right on the surface: What constitutes the proper basis for establishing the plausibility of comparison and contrast anyhow? We obviously do not want to compare things that do not bear comparison because they are not species of the same genus, but distinct genera. But then on what basis do we move from species to species and uncover the genera of which they form a part (if they do form a part)? Is it only verbal correspondence or intersection, as has been implicit to this point? Or are there more abstract bases for the same work of genus construction (in our language: category formation and re-formation)? This simple issue is going to keep us busy from here to nearly the end of the chapter, because there is a rich repertoire of principles that establish of discrete data classes of data and that then link one class to another. The first was, we recall, deriving a rule by analogy and then moving on to transmit the rule to classes linked by not analogy but rather verbal intersection. We proceed to the next problem, which is, whether or not a rule shown to apply to two or more classes of things linked by verbal analogy may then be applied to further classes of things that relate to the foregoing by not verbal analogy but a relationship a fortiori.

IV.6   A   That which is learned by a verbal analogy may in turn go and impart a rule by an argument a fortiori .
       B.   [50A] That is in line with that which the Tannaite authority of the household of R. Ishmael set forth.
IV.7   A   Can that which is learned by verbal analogy in turn go and impart a rule by an analogy based on the congruence of other shared traits [but not verbal ones in context]? [This mode of argument depends not on verbal analogy supplied by Scripture but an analogy drawn from similarity of the traits of two subjects.]

B.   *Said R. Jeremiah, "Let Scripture omit reference to slaughtering the guilt-offering at the north of the altar, and that rule can have been inferred by appeal to an analogy based on the congruence of other shared traits [but not verbal ones in context] from the rule governing a sin-offering. [Both offerings expiate sin. So the rule governing the one will pertain to the other.]*

C.   "So why has Scripture stated that law? Is it not to indicate that that which is learned by verbal analogy established may not in turn go and impart a rule by an analogy based on the congruence of other shared traits [but not verbal ones in context]??"

D.   *But in accord with your reasoning, let the rule be inferred by an analogy based on the congruence of other shared traits [but not verbal ones in context] from the one governing a burnt-offering! [The rule is explicitly stated in that context, and the intermediate analogy based on verbal similarities is not required at all (Freedman).]*

E.   *So why is it not inferred in that way?*

F.   *It is because one may present the following challenge: the distinguishing trait of the burnt-offering is indeed that it is turned to ashes on the altar! [That is not the case of the guilt-offering.]*

G.   *In reference to the sin-offering, one may also present a challenge, namely: the distinguishing trait of the sin-offering is that it expiates sins that bear the sanction of extirpation.*

H.   *While, therefore, admittedly one cannot learn the rule on a one to one basis, why not derive the rule by imputing to the third classification the law governing two other classifications of sacrifice [so that Scripture can have intimated that slaughter at the north is required for two of the three classifications, and by an argument based on the congruent of other shared traits, we should derive the rule governing the third of the three]?*

I.   *From which two of the three can the rule have been derived for the third? If Scripture had not written the rule in connection with the burnt-offering, you might have derived the rule for that classification from the one covering the sin-offering and the guilt-offering.*

J.   *Not at all, for the distinguishing trait of these is that they effect atonement [which is not accomplished by the burnt-offering].*

K.   *Then let Scripture not state the rule in connection with the sin-offering, and derive it from the other two.*

L.   *Not at all, for the distinguishing trait of these is that they require male animals [which is not the case of the sin-offering, which is a female].*

M.   *Then let Scripture not state the rule in connection with the guilt-offering, and derive it from the other two.*

N.   *Not at all, for the distinguishing trait of these is that they may be brought as much in behalf of the community as in behalf of an individual. [A guilt-offering is presented only by an individual.]*

Not surprisingly, we now move forward once more – but by taking a step backward. We have shown that we may move from a class of things joined to another through analogy based on congruence, that is, from A to B, onward to other classes of things joined to the foregoing by verbal analogy or intersection, that is, from B to C and beyond. But can we then move from C, linked to B via verbal analogy, to D, linked to C, but not to

A or B, by congruence, for example, comparable and shared traits of a salient order? The issue then is, May we move forward to further classes of things by moving "backward," to a principle of linkage of classes that has served to bring us to this point, in other words, reversing the course of principles of linkage? What our framers then want to know is a very logical question: Are there fixed rules that govern the order or sequence by which we move from one class of things to another, so that, if we propose to link classes of things, we can move only from A to B by one principle (comparison and contrast of salient traits), and from B to C by a necessarily consequent and always second principle (verbal intersection)? Then may we move (by this theory) from C to D only by verbal intersection but not by appeal to congruence? Why not? Because, after all, if C is linked to B only by verbal intersection but not by congruence, bearing no relationship to A at all, then how claim that D stands in a series begun at A, if it has neither verbal connection, nor, as a matter of fact, congruence to link it to anything in the series? Is then a series substantive, in that we ask that there be some "natural logic" holding the parts together, a "natural logic" that derives from the sequence of operative principles of comparison and contrast? Or is a series merely formal, in that if we can link D to C in one way but D to A in no ways, D still has been shown, in the course of argument but not by the reason or internal logic of the argument, to relate to A not at all? This enormously engaging question dictates everything that is coming, and I do not have to repeat the point, since there is no grasping a line from here to nearly the end of the chapter if we do not understand that what our sages are trying to find out is whether a series is a series because of its external form alone or because of its internal, inherent traits as well. If I were a mathematician, I could appeal to the issue of whether the symbolic representation of, for example, spatial relations is limited by tests out there, as Euclid supposed, so that we move from data to symbol, or may there be a symbolic representation of "things" for which there is not "out there" there, as non-Euclidean geometries claim. But I am not a mathematician.

IV.8 A.   Can a rule that is derived by analogy based on the congruence of other shared traits [but not verbal ones in context] turn around and teach a lesson through an analogy based on verbal analogy?

      B.   *Said R. Pappa, "'This is the law of the sacrifice of peace-offerings...if he offers it for a thanksgiving-offering' (Lev. 7:11ff.): in this verse we learn the rule that funds for the purchase of an animal offered for a thanksgiving-offering may derive from money exchanged for produce in the status of second tithe, since we find, in point of fact, that peace-offerings themselves [into the class of which the cited verse assimilates thanksgiving-offerings] may be purchased from money exchanged for produce in the status of second tithe."*

C. *And how do we know, as a matter of fact, that peace-offerings themselves [into the class of which the cited verse assimilates thanksgiving-offerings] may be purchased from money exchanged for produce in the status of second tithe?*

D. *The reason is that the word "there" is written in the context of both a beast purchased for use as a peace-offering and also second tithe, [at Deut. 27:7 and Deut. 14:23, respectively].* [It follows that the rule governing the peace-offering derives from an argument based on an analogy established through verbal congruence, and that rule is then applied to a thanksgiving-offering by an analogy based on other than verbal congruence.]

E. *Said Mar Zutra b. R. Mari to Rabina, "But tithe of grain is in the status of unconsecrated food in general [but the issue at hand addresses tithe of the corral, which is in the status of Holy Things]!"*

F. *He said to him, "Who has claimed that* that to which a rule is transferred [by means of the exegetical principle at hand] must be in the class of Holy Things and that that from which a rule is transferred likewise must be in the class of Holy Things?"

IV.9 A Can a rule that is derived by an analogy based on the congruence of other shared traits [but not verbal ones in context] turn around and teach a lesson through an analogy based on the congruence of [other] shared traits?

B. *Said Rami bar Hama, "It has been taught on Tannaite authority:*

C. *""Of fine flour soaked"* (Lev. 7:12) – this teaches that the soaked cake [one that is made of boiled flour] must be made of fine flour.

D. *"'How do we know the rule that applies to the ordinary unleavened cakes [hallot]?*

E. *"'Scripture in both contexts [speaking of the cakes that are soaked as well as the unleavened ones] speaks of hallot.*

F. *"'How do we know that the same rule applies to thin wafers?*

G. *"'Because Scripture in both contexts speaks of unleavened bread.'"* [Freedman: Thus we first learn by an analogy based on shared traits that the ordinary unleavened cakes must be made of fine flour, and then by a further such argument we learn from the ordinary unleavened cakes that the thin wafers likewise must be of fine flour.]

H. *Said to him Rabina, "How do you know that he derives the rule governing unleavened cakes from the one governing ordinary unleavened cakes? Perhaps he derives the rule from the law governing oven baked cakes (Lev. 2:4) [without appeal to the analogy that has been drawn here]?"*

I. Rather, said Raba, "It has been taught on Tannaite authority:

J. *"""And its innards and its dung, even the whole bullock shall he carry forth outside of the camp"* (Lev. 4:11) – this teaches that they carry it out whole.

K. *"'Might one suppose that they burn it whole?*

L. *"'Here we find a reference to "its head and its legs," and elsewhere* (Lev. 1:8-9, 12-13) we find reference also to "its head and its legs." Just as in that other case, this is done only after cutting up the beast, so here, too, it means only after cutting up the beast.

M   "'If so, then just as there this is after flaying the hide, so here, too, is it to be after flaying the hide? Scripture states, "and its innards and its dung."'"

N.   *What conclusion is supposed to be drawn here?*

Q   Said R. Pappa, "Just as its dung is kept within the innards, so the meat must be held within the hide."

P.   *And so, too, it has been taught on Tannaite authority:*

Q   Rabbi says, "Here [with reference to the bullock and he-goat of the Day of Atonement] we find a reference to 'hide and meat and dung,' [50B] and elsewhere, we find a reference to hide and meat and dung [in connection with the bullock of the anointed priest]. Just as there, the beast was burned only after being cut up, but without flaying the hide, so here, too, the beast was burned only after being cut up, but without flaying the hide." [Thus the result of one such argument is transferred to another case by another such argument (Freedman)].

IV.10 A.   Can a rule that is derived by an analogy based on the congruence of other shared traits [but not verbal ones in context] go and teach a lesson through an argument a fortiori?

B.   Indeed so, by reason of an argument a fortiori:

C.   If an argument deriving from an analogy based on verbal congruence, which cannot go and, by an argument based on verbal congruence, impart its rule to some other class – *as has been shown by either Raba's or Rabina's demonstration* – nonetheless can go and by an argument a fortiori impart its rule to some other class – *as has been shown by the Tannaite authority of the household of R. Ishmael* – then a rule that is derived by an argument based on analogy based on other than verbal congruence, which can for its part go and impart its lesson by an argument based on an analogy resting on verbal congruity – *as has been shown by R. Pappa* – surely can in turn teach its lesson by an argument a fortiori to yet another case!

D.   *That position poses no problems to one who takes the view that R. Pappa's case has been made. But for one who takes the view that R. Pappa's case has not been made, what is to be said?*

E.   *Rather, this is an argument a fortiori in favor of the same point:*

F.   If an argument deriving from an analogy based on verbal congruence, which cannot go and, by an argument based on verbal congruence, impart its rule to some other class – *as has been shown by either Raba's or Rabina's demonstration* – nonetheless can go and by an argument a fortiori impart its rule to some other class – *as has been shown by the Tannaite authority of the household of R. Ishmael* – then a rule that is derived by an argument based on analogy based on other than verbal congruence, which can for its part go and impart its lesson by an argument based on an analogy resting on verbal congruity which is like itself – *as has been shown by Rami bar Hama* – surely can in turn teach its lesson by an argument a fortiori to yet another case!

IV.11 A.   Can a rule that is derived by an analogy based on the congruence of other shared traits [but not verbal ones in context] go and teach a lesson through an argument constructed by analogy based on the

	congruence of other shared traits among two or more classifications of things?
B.	*That question must stand.*
IV.12 A	Can a rule derived by an argument a fortiori go and teach a rule established through analogy of verbal usage?
B.	The affirmative derives from an argument a fortiori:
C.	If an argument deriving from an analogy based on points of other than verbal congruence, which cannot go and, by an argument based on verbal congruence, impart its rule to some other class – *as has been shown by either R. Pappa's demonstration* – then a rule that is derived by an argument a fortiori, which can be derived by an argument based on the shared verbal traits of two things – *as has been shown by the Tannaite authority of the house of R. Ishmael* – surely should be able to impart its rule to another classification of things by reason of an argument based on a verbal analogy!
D.	*That position poses no problems to one who takes the view that R. Pappa's case has been made. But for one who takes the view that R. Pappa's case has not been made, what is to be said?*
E.	*The question then must stand.*
IV.13 A	Can a rule that is derived by an argument a fortiori go and teach a lesson through an argument based on the congruence of other shared traits [but not verbal ones in context]?
B.	The affirmative derives from an argument a fortiori:
C.	If an argument deriving from an analogy based on points of other than verbal congruence, which cannot be derived from an argument based on verbal congruence, impart its rule to some other class – *as has been shown by R. Yohanan's demonstration* – can go and teach a lesson by an argument based on an analogy established through other than verbal traits, *as has been shown by Rami bar Hama* – a rule based on an argument a fortiori, which can be derived by an argument based on an analogy resting on verbal coincidence, surely should be able to impart its rule to another classification of things by reason of an argument based on an other than verbal analogy!
IV.14 A	Can a rule based on an argument a fortiori turn around and teach a lesson through an argument based on an argument a fortiori?
B.	Indeed so, and the affirmative derives from an argument a fortiori:
C.	If an argument deriving from an analogy based on points of other than verbal congruence, which cannot be derived from an argument based on verbal congruence, impart its rule to some other class – *as has been shown by R. Yohanan's demonstration* – can go and teach a lesson by an argument a fortiori, as we have just pointed out, then an argument that can be derived from an analogy based on verbal congruence – *as has been shown by the Tannaite authority of the household of R. Ishmael* – surely should be able to impart its rule by an argument a fortiori!
D.	But would this then would represent what we are talking about, namely, a rule deriving from an argument a fortiori that has been applied to another case by means of an argument a fortiori? Surely this is nothing more than a secondary derivation produced by an argument a fortiori!
E.	Rather, argue in the following way:

F.   Indeed so, and the affirmative derives from an argument a fortiori:

G.   if an argument based on an analogy of a verbal character cannot be derived from another such argument based on an analogy between two classes of things that rests upon a verbal congruence – *in accordance with the proofs of either Raba or Rabina* – nonetheless can then go and impart its lesson by an argument a fortiori – *in accordance with the proof of the Tannaite authority of the household of R. Ishmael* – then an argument a fortiori, which can serve to transfer a lesson originally learned through an argument based upon verbal congruence, *in accordance with the proof of the Tannaite authority of the household of R. Ishmael* – surely should be able to impart its lesson to yet another classification of things through an argument a fortiori.

H   And this does represent what we are talking about, namely, a rule deriving from an argument a fortiori that has been applied to another case by means of an argument a fortiori.

IV.15 A.   Can a rule based on an argument a fortiori turn around and teach a rule through an argument constructed on the basis of shared traits of an other than verbal character among two classifications of things?

B.   *Said R. Jeremiah, "Come and take note:* [If] one pinched off the neck and [the bird] turned out to be terefah – R. Meir says, 'It does not impart uncleanness of the gullet [since slaughtering a beast is wholly equivalent to pinching the neck of a bird].' R. Judah says, 'It does impart uncleanness of the gullet.' [Birds and beasts in no way are comparable; neither slaughtering an unconsecrated clean bird nor pinching the neck of a consecrated one will exempt from uncleanness a bird which turns out to be terefah.] Said R. Meir, 'It is an argument a fortiori: now if in the case of the carrion of a beast, which imparts uncleanness through contact and through carrying, proper slaughter renders clean from its uncleanness that which was terefah, [in the case of] the carrion of fowl, which to begin with does not impart uncleanness through contact and through carrying, it should logically follow that its proper slaughter should render clean from its uncleanness that which was terefah. Just as we find that its proper slaughter [in the case of a bird or beast] renders it valid for eating [51A] and renders it clean from its uncleanness in the case of terefah, so proper pinching of the neck, which renders it valid for eating, should render it clean from its uncleanness in the case of terefah.' R. Yosé says, 'It is sufficient that it [the slaughtering of the bird] be equivalent to the carrion of a beast: its [a beast's or a bird's] slaughtering renders clean [what is terefah], but the pinching of the neck [of a bird does] not [render clean what is terefah]' [M. Zeb. 7:6]. [The language 'just as we find then represents an argument based on shared traits of two distinct classifications of things, and so we see that a rule derived by an argument a fortiori then through such an argument based on shared traits is transferred to another class of things altogether.]"*

C.   *But that is not so. For even if we concede that that is the case there, then still the rule derives from the act of slaughter of unconsecrated beasts* [Freedman].

IV.16 A   Can a rule derived by an argument based on shared traits of an other than verbal character shared among two classes of things then turn around and teach a lesson by an argument based on an analogy of a verbal character, an analogy not of a verbal character, an argument a fortiori, or an argument based on shared traits?

B.   *Solve at least one of those problems by appeal to the following:*

C.   On what account have they said that if blood of an offering is left overnight on the altar, it is fit? Because if the sacrificial parts are kept overnight on the altar, they are fit. And why if the sacrificial parts are kept overnight on the altar are they fit? Because if the meat of the offering is kept overnight on the altar it is fit. [Freedman: Thus the rule governing the sacrificial parts is derived by an appeal to an argument based on shared traits of an other than verbal character shared among two classes of things, and that rule in turn is applied to the case of the blood by another such argument based on shared traits of an other than verbal character shared among two classes of things].

D.   What about the rule governing meat that is taken outside of the Temple court? [If such meat is put up on the altar, it is not removed therefrom. Why so?]

E.   Because meat that has been taken out of the holy place is suitable for a high place.

F.   What about the rule governing unclean meat? [If such meat is put up on the altar, it is not removed therefrom. Why so?]

G.   Since meat that is unclean is subject to a remission of the prohibition affecting it in the case of an offering made in behalf of the entire community.

H.   What about the rule governing the sacrificial parts of a burnt-offering that the officiating priest subjected to the intention of being burned after the proper time? [If such meat is put up on the altar, it is not removed therefrom. Why so?]

I.   Since the sprinkling of the blood is effective and propitiates in making such meat refuse by reason of the improper intentionality [we leave the sacrificial portions on the altar once they have been put there].

J.   What about the rule governing the sacrificial parts of a burnt-offering that the officiating priest subjected to the intention of being eaten outside of the proper place? [If such meat is put up on the altar, it is not removed therefrom. Why so?]

K.   Since sacrificial meat in that class is treated as analogous to sacrificial meat that has been subjected to an improper intentionality in respect to eating the meat outside of the proper time.

L.   What about the rule governing the sacrificial parts of a burnt-offering the blood of which unfit priests have received and tossed, when such unfit persons are eligible for an act of service in behalf of the community...? [This question is not answered.]

M.   [Reverting to C-E:] Now can an analogy be drawn concerning something that has been disposed of in the proper manner for something that has not been disposed of in the proper manner? [If the sacrificial parts are kept overnight, they are not taken off the

> altar, and therefore the meat kept overnight is fit; but the meat may be kept overnight, while the sacrificial parts may not. So, too, when the Temple stood, the flesh might not be taken outside, but where there was no Temple and only high places, the case is scarcely analogous!]

N   *The Tannaite authority for this rule derives it from the augmentative sense, extending the rule, deriving from the formulation, "This is the Torah of the burnt-offering"* (Lev. 6:2). [Freedman: The verse teaches that all burnt-offerings, even with the defects catalogued here, are subject to the same rule and do not get removed from the altar once they have been put there; the arguments given cannot be sustained but still support that proposition.]

The simple order of the whole allows the answer to one question to precipitate the consequent and necessary next question. I need hardly review what our authors have made so clear through their own exposition. I cannot imagine anybody's not seeing that a sustained methodological inquiry is taking place at the very surface of discourse on the bloody rite of the Temple!

V.1   A.   **The remnants of their blood did one pour out on the western base of the outer altar. If he did not place [the remnants of the blood at the stated location], he did not impair [atonement]:**

B.   *What is the Scripture basis for this rule?*

C.   Scripture has said, "And all the remaining blood of the bullock shall he pour out at the base of the altar of the burnt-offering which is at the door of the tent of meeting" (Lev. 4:7).

D.   *That speaks of the first altar that one meets [as you enter from the door, and that is the western base].*

What needs to be said once does not have to be repeated: the work of the framers of the Talmud is sometimes thought about thinking, but always inquiry into the relations between Scripture and law (in the Mishnah, as elsewhere). The former must be done once, it serves then throughout; but the latter has to be repeated many times. It would therefore vastly misrepresent the Talmud were I to present only Parts I-IV or to claim that the deep structure of discourse of Parts I-IV is present throughout; that is contrary to fact. The reason is that the Talmud's authorship remains bound within the limits of the medium it has chosen for the expression of its ideas, which is the form of a commentary to the Mishnah. And that means, the Mishnah will be commented upon! Now that commentary proves quite cogent, pursuing a few and limited questions over and over again. And one of these is, we recall very well, the scriptural basis for the Mishnah's law. That question overrides any intent to expound the principles of comparison and contrast among genera, the linkage between genus and genus, let alone to set forth the deep structure of abstract thought on the nature of the series, that is, on the movement of an argument from point to point. All of that wonderful thought, shown in Part IV, now subsides, as we revert to our work. Once we have finished one job, we now undertake the same job, in the setting of another statement of the Mishnah. The competition between the wonders of sheer thought, at which our sages excel, and exegesis always is won by exegesis. These geniuses of ours were very modest men.

V.2 A. *Our rabbis have taught on Tannaite authority* [Freedman: There are five passages that deal with the sin-offering, Lev. 4: the sin-offering of the anointed priest, Lev. 4:1-12, the sin-offering of the entire congregation, Lev. 4:13-22, the sin-offering of a rule, Lev. 4:22-26, the female goat of an ordinary person, Lev. 4:27-32, and the lamb of an ordinary person, Lev. 4:32-35. The first two were offered on the inner altar, the other three on the outer. In regard to the first three Scripture states that the residue of the blood is to be poured out "...at the base of the altar of the burnt-offering..." (Lev. 4:7, 18, 25), and in connection with the other two there is an allusion to the base of the altar without reference to "of the sin-offering." Here rabbis explain why Scripture specifies the altar of the burnt-offering in the first three cases. The first teaches that the residue is poured out at the base of the outer altar, the altar of the burnt-offering, but not at the base of the inner altar, even though the blood was sprinkled on the horns of the inner altar. The second is superfluous, and it teaches that only the outer altar had such a base, not the inner altar. The third reference intimates that the residue of the blood of all sacrifices whose blood is sprinkled on the altar of burnt-offering must be poured out at its base. Thus:]

      B. "...At the base of the altar of the burnt-offering..." (Lev. 4:7) – and not at the base of the inner altar.

      C. "...At the base of the altar of the burnt-offering..." (Lev. 4:18) – the inner altar has no base anyhow.

      D. "...At the base of the altar of the burnt-offering..." (Lev. 4:25) – apply the laws governing the base to the altar of the burnt-offering.

      E. But perhaps that is not the sense, but rather, let there be a base around the altar of the burnt-offering? [Freedman: Perhaps the verse says nothing about the residue of the blood but indicates that the two sprinklings of the blood of the burnt-offering must be made at that part of the altar that had a special base, excluding the southeastern horn, which did not have a special base.]

      F. Said R. Ishmael, "The proposition can be shown to derive from an argument a fortiori: if the residue of the blood of the sin-offering, which does not make atonement, has to be poured out at the base, then the sprinkling of the blood of the burnt-offering itself, which does make atonement, surely would require the base [meaning, it must be a corner of the altar at which the horn has been provided with a base]." [Then a verse is not required to make that point, if the teaching is as proposed. Hence the proposed proof is null.]

      G. Said R. Aqiba, "[Along the same lines,] the proposition can be shown to derive from an argument a fortiori: If the residue of the blood of the sin-offering, which does not make atonement and which is not presented for the purposes of atonement in any way, has to be poured out at the base, then the sprinkling of the blood of the burnt-offering itself, which does make atonement, and which is presented for the purposes of atonement, surely would require the base [meaning, it must be a corner of the altar at which the horn has been provided with a base]. So why does Scripture state, 'at the base of the altar of burnt-offering'? It is to indicate that the laws of the base should pertain to the altar of the burnt-offering."

V.3   A.   A master has said, "'...at the base of the altar of the burnt-offering...' (Lev. 4:7) – and not at the base of the inner altar':

      B.   *Surely that clause is required to make its own point [and not to prove the derivative, "and not...," point]!*

      C.   That point itself derives from the language, "which is at the door of the tent of meeting" [indicating that the outer altar is what is required, so the specification "of the burnt-offering" is superfluous and serves the specified purpose].

V.4   A.   [Supply: A master has said,] "'...at the base of the altar of the burnt-offering...' (Lev. 4:25) – [51B] apply the laws governing the base to the altar of the burnt-offering":

      B.   *For if it should enter your mind that the passage is to be read literally as written, then what need do I have for a verse of Scripture dealing with the residue, since pouring out the residue was an act done in the outer courtyard and not in the inner sanctum?*

      C.   *And if you should say that without that verse, I might have concluded that it is indeed to be reversed, [52A] with the residue of the inner-offering to be poured at the outer altar and the residue of the outer altar to be performed at the inner altar, in point of fact, the inner altar had no base [so the interpretation is possible only as given].*

V.5   A.   **[Supply: A master has said,] "But perhaps that is not the sense, but** rather, let there be a base around the altar of the burnt-offering": [Freedman: Perhaps the verse says nothing about the residue of the blood but indicates that the two sprinklings of the blood of the burnt-offering must be made at that part of the altar that had a special base, excluding the southeastern horn, which did not have a special base.]

      B.   But is it not written, "At the base of the altar of burnt-offering"? [Freedman: If the verse intimated that the sprinkling itself must be performed on that part of the altar that has a base, it could not refer to sin-offerings, the blood of which was sprinkled on all the horns of the altar, including the southeast. Hence it would have to refer to the burnt-offering alone. But in that case, Scripture should write, "at the base of the burnt-offering," which would intimate that the blood of the burnt-offering must be sprinkled over against the base. The word "altar" then becomes redundant.]

      C.   *If the verse stated, "At the base of the burnt-offering," I might have supposed that the sense was, on the top of the base [right up by the altar itself]. But since it is written, "at the base of the altar of burnt-offering," the meaning is, "at the top of the base."*

D.   Said R. Ishmael, "What need do I have for a verse to tell me that it is to be spilled out at the top of the base? It would follow through an argument a fortiori: if the residue of the blood of the sin-offering, which does not make atonement, has to be poured out at the top of the base, then the sprinkling of the blood of the burnt-offering itself, which does make atonement, surely would require the top of the base."

E.   Said R. Aqiba, "[Along the same lines,] the proposition can be shown to derive from an argument a fortiori: if the residue of the blood of the sin-offering, which does not make atonement and which is not presented for the purposes of atonement in any way, has to be poured out at the top of the base, then the sprinkling of the blood of the burnt-offering itself, which does make atonement, and which is presented for the purposes of atonement, surely would require the top of the base. So why does Scripture state, 'at the base of the altar of burnt-offering'? It is to indicate that the laws of the base should pertain to the altar of the burnt-offering."

V.6   A.   *In what regard do the two authorities differ?*

        B.   *Said R. Adda b. Ahbah, "At issue between them is whether or not the pouring out of the residue of the blood is indispensable to the rite. One authority maintains that pouring out of the residue of the blood is indispensable to the rite. The author takes the view that pouring out of the residue of the blood is not indispensable to the rite."*

        C.   *R. Pappa said, "All parties maintain that pouring out of the residue of the blood is not indispensable to the rite. But here what is at issue is whether or not the draining out of the blood of a bird that has been presented as a sin-offering is indispensable to the rite. One authority takes the view that it is, the other, that it is not, indispensable to the rite."*

        D.   *There is a Tannaite formulation in accord with the theory of R. Pappa:*

        E.   "'And all the remaining blood of the bullock [of the offering of the anointed priest] shall he pour out at the base of the altar': (Lev. 4:7) – Why does Scripture make reference to 'the bullock' [since the context makes clear that that is what is at issue]? It teaches concerning the bullock that is offered on the Day of Atonement that the blood has to be poured out at the base of the altar," the words of R. [Aqiba].

        F.   Said R. Ishmael, "It is an argument a fortiori [that that is the case, and a prooftext is not required]. If the blood of an offering that is not obligatory [the bullock presented by a sin-offering by the anointed priest, which is not an obligatory-offering in that the man does not have to have said], presented on the inner altar, has to be poured out at the base, the blood of an offering that is obligatory, [the bullock presented on the Day of Atonement, which is required, whether or not the high priest has sinned], presented on the inner altar, surely should have to be poured out at the base!"

        G.   Said R. Aqiba, "If an offering that is neither obligatory nor even a matter of a mere religious duty, the blood of which is not brought into the inner sanctum [the Holy of Holies], has to be poured out onto the base of the altar, an offering that is a statutory obligation, the blood of which is taken into the inner sanctum, surely should require a base!"

H   "Now you might have supposed that the pouring out of the residue is indispensable for the rite [of the bullock on the Day of Atonement], and therefore Scripture states, 'And he shall make an end of atoning' (Lev. 16:20), meaning, all of the rites of atonement are now complete," the words of R. Ishmael.

I   [Reverting to the claim of D:] Now it is an argument a fortiori in regard to the bullock of the anointed priest, namely, if the blood of an offering that is neither obligatory nor even a matter of religious duty which is not taken to the inner altar but still has to be poured out at the base of the altar, surely the blood of an offering whether obligatory or a matter of religious duty surely should have to be poured out at the base of the altar!

J.   Might one suppose that it is indispensable to the rite?

K.   Scripture states, "And all the remaining blood of the bullock he shall pour out," and in this way Scripture turns the matter the residual aspect of a religious duty, indicating that pouring out the residue is not indispensable to the correct carrying out of the rite.

V.7 A   *But does R. Ishmael really take the position [as Pappa has claimed] that* draining out of the blood of a bird that has been presented as a sin-offering is indispensable to the rite? And has it not been set forth as a Tannaite rule by the Tannaite authority of the household of R. Ishmael, "'And the rest of the blood shall be drained out': – what is left is to be drained out, [52B] but what is not left is not drained out"? [Freedman: All the blood may be used in sprinkling, so that nothing is left for draining, hence draining cannot be indispensable.]

B   *There is a conflict among Tannaite versions of the opinions of R. Ishmael.*

V.8 A   *Said Rami bar Hama, "The following Tannaite authority takes the view that pouring out the residue of the blood is indispensable. For it has been taught on Tannaite authority"*:

B   "This is the law of the sin-offering...the priest who offers it for sin [having correctly carried out the rite in every detail] shall eat it" (Lev. 6:18-19) – "it" meaning, the one, the blood of which has been tossed above the red line around the altar, and not the one the blood of which was tossed below the red line around the altar.

C   Now explain [why might you have supposed that even though the blood was not properly sprinkled, the meat nonetheless still may be eaten, absent a prooftext to the contrary]!

D   It is a conclusion that can have been implied by the following verse, "and the blood of your sacrifices shall be poured out...and you shall eat the meat" (Deut. 12:27) – thereby we have learned concerning a case in which it is required to toss the blood four times, that if one has tossed the blood in a single action, he has achieved atonement.

E.   Might one therefore suppose that if the blood that was supposed to be sprinkled above the red line was sprinkled below, the offering might also have achieved atonement for the donor?

F.   For it is a matter of logic: there is blood that is to be tossed above the red line [a sin-offering made of a beast], and there is blood that is to be tossed below the red line [a sin-offering of a bird], so, just as the blood that is supposed to be tossed below the red line does not atone if it is tossed above, so blood that is supposed to be tossed above the red line will not atone if it is sprinkled below it.

G.   Not at all. If you invoke that rule in the case of blood that is supposed to be sprinkled below the red line, it is because in the end it will not be above at all, but will you say the same of blood that is to be sprinkled above the red line, which ultimately will be located down below [in the form of the residue]. [Freedman: Hence when he sprinkles the blood below the line, he is putting it where it will eventually be located and so effects atonement.]

H.   Let blood that is to be tossed on the inner altar prove the case, for it is going in the end to be brought outside [where the residue is poured out around the base of the outer altar], and yet if the blood that is to be tossed on the inner altar to begin with is tossed on the outer altar, the priest has not effected atonement.

I.   Not at all, for if you raise the issue of blood to be tossed on the inner altar, that is because the rite performed on the inner altar does not complete the ritual attached to the entire liturgy [since after the blood is sprinkled on the inner altar, the residue has to be poured out at the base of the outer altar]. But can you say the same of the tossing of the blood on the upper part of the altar, in which case putting the blood on the horns complete the rite [and no further action is indispensable once the blood has been sprinkled on the horns of the altar]. Since sprinkling the blood on the horns of the altar completes the rite, if the priest sprinkled below the red line, the rite also is fit.

J.   [Because of the possibility of composing such an argument,] Scripture states, "This is the law of the sin-offering...the priest who offers it for sin [having correctly carried out the rite in every detail] shall eat it" (Lev. 6:18-19) – "it" meaning, the one, the blood of which has been tossed above the red line around the altar, and not the one the blood of which was tossed below the red line around the altar.

K.   *What is the meaning of the phrase,* the rite performed on the inner altar does not complete the ritual attached to the entire liturgy? *Surely this refers to the residue of the blood [and that proves that pouring out the residue of the blood is an indispensable part of the rite].*

L.   *Said Raba to him, "If so, then you may prove the point through an argument a fortiori:* If to begin with blood of an offering performed on the inner altar which is poured out on the outer altar does not make atonement, even though in the end it will be obligatory to pour out that blood on the outer altar, then as to blood that is to be sprinkled above the red line, which in the end is not subject to the obligation of being poured out below the line for the sacrifice to achieve its goal of atonement, if to begin with one sprinkled such blood below the red line, the offering should not secure atonement. [Freedman: The sacrifice is invalid, and the meat may not be eaten. So why is a verse of Scripture required to prove the point? Hence the premise of this argument, that pouring out of the residue is essential, must be false.]

M Rather, this is the sense: It is not tossing the blood on the altar alone that completes the rite, but tossing the blood on the veil as well.

V.9 A. *Our rabbis have taught on Tannaite authority:*

B. "'And he shall make an end of atoning for the holy place and the tent of meeting and the altar' (Lev. 16:20) – if he atoned [by carrying out the rites required for atonement in other matters, e.g., the four sprinklings on the altar, the seven before the veil (Freedman)], he has completed the rite, but if he has not atoned, he has not completed the rite," the words of R. Aqiba.

C. Said to him R. Judah, "Why should we not say, 'if he made an end to the rite, he has atoned, and if not, he did not atone'? [So the rites, including the four applications, are necessary, and it is on that basis that that fact is to be demonstrated]."

D. *What is at issue between them?*

E. R. Yohanan and R. Joshua b. Levi:

F. *One said, "At issue is the correct interpretation of Scripture."* [Freedman: But not in law. Both hold that all four applications of blood are indispensable, and that pouring out the residue is not. Aqiba holds that the conclusion, atoning, illumines the beginning, make an end, so completion depends on atonement, on the four applications. Judah maintains that "atoning" might merely refer to a single application of blood, and therefore the interpretation must be revised, and the beginning of the verse illuminates the end; only when he completely finishes the rite, having done the four applications, is atonement done.]

G. *The other said, "At issue is whether or not pouring out the residue of the blood at the base is indispensable to the rite."*

H. *Now you may draw the conclusion that it is R. Joshua b. Levi who took the position that at issue is whether or not pouring out the residue of the blood at the base is indispensable to the rite.* For said R. Joshua b. Levi, "In the opinion of the one who said that the pouring out the residue of the blood is an indispensable part of the rite, one must bring another bullock and begin the rite on the inner altar." [Freedman: If the residue of the blood was spilled after the four applications, another bullock must be slaughtered and its blood first sprinkled at the inner altar, and then the residue poured out at the base of the outer altar. But the priest cannot simply pour out all the blood at the base, for then it is not a residue, and it is indispensable that a

residue be poured out. Thus Joshua b. Levi holds that there is a
view that pouring out of the residue is indispensable.]

I.   *But does R. Yohanan not maintain this same theory of matters? And has
not R. Yohanan said,* "R. Nehemiah taught as a Tannaite authority in
accord with the opinion of one who maintains that the pouring out
of the residue of the blood is indispensable to the rite"?

J.   *Rather, you have to say, "In accord with the words of him who says...,"
but not, "in accord with those of these Tannaite authorities in particular
[Aqiba and Judah], and so, too, here [in the matter of Joshua b. Levi], "In
accord with the words of him who says...," but not, "in accord with those
of these Tannaite authorities in particular."*

To see the composite whole: Part IV is the important component of
this astonishingly coherent piece of writing. Nos. 5-16 build on No. 4,
systematically and patiently working through the entire repertoire of
possibilities on the exegetical rules for deriving lessons from Scripture.
The range of exegetical principles – argument a fortiori, argument based
on analogy established through shared verbal choices, argument based
on analogy established through other than shared verbal choices,
analogy based on the congruence of other shared traits [but not verbal
ones in context] – is entirely systematic, with each exegetical technique
compared to all of the others. The unified and accumulative effect of the
whole is demonstrated by No. 10, which appeals to foregoing materials
to make its point. Obviously this beautifully articulated composition –
not a mere composite – has been worked out prior to insertion here; but
the relevance to our chapter's rules and interests is obvious, and we have
been prepared to anticipate just such a theoretical exercise. But the
chapter as a whole turns out to provide a laboratory case on that matter.

I cite the pertinent language, reviewing what has already been given,
and then provide my comments that specify what I conceive to be the
metapropositional issues under discussion. The stages in the argument
of the Talmud are marked by boldface capital letters.

A.   II.2   E.   That answer is satisfactory for him who takes the view that one
may indeed derive a rule governing a prior subject from one
that is given later on, but from the perspective of him who
denies that fact, what is to be said?

The opening question contains the entirety of what is to follow: the
conviction that anterior to conclusions and debates on fixed propositions
is a premise, and the premise concerns not issues but thought itself. For
what is before us is not a hermeneutical principle that guides the
exegesis of Scripture, the movement from a rule back to a scriptural
formulation deemed to pertain. It is a rule of how to think. And the
issue is explicit: Does thought flow, or does it stand still? Does it flow
backward from conclusion to a conclusion already reached? In the

context of the document at hand, the issue is one of arrangements of words, that is, a literary and therefore an exegetical question. That is, then, the proposition. But the metaproposition is otherwise, though that is not yet explicit.

B.   II.2.   J.   But this is the reason for the position of rabbis, who declare one exempt [from having to present a suspensive guilt-offering in the case of a matter of doubt regarding acts of sacrilege]: they derive an verbal analogy to a sin-offering based on the appearance of the word 'commandments' with reference to both matters.

         N.   They take the view that one may not derive from an argument by analogy established through the use of a word in common only a limited repertoire of conclusions [but once the analogy is drawn, then all of the traits of one case apply to the other].

Here is an issue not of exegesis, therefore of hermeneutics, but of the rules of right thinking: thinking about thought. And what is concerns, as I have suggested in context, is how we establish not classes of things but linkage between and among classes of things.   Let me state the centerpiece in simple words but with heavy emphasis: *since I make connections through analogy and contrast, may I proceed to make connections beyond the limits of the original connection?   And the answer is, I must proceed, because thought does not come to rest.   Comparison and contrast yield connections, which then govern.*

In the language before us, once I draw an analogy, do all traits of the two classes of things that have been linked through analogy – of necessity only partial, since were the analogy entire, both classes would constitute a single class! – pertain to each class?   In the present context, what we establish is the anonymous, therefore the governing, rule.   The norm is that once we draw an analogy, the connection established by the (mere) analogy takes over, so that we treat as analogous traits not covered by the analogy at all.   The analogy establishes the connection; but then the movement of thought is such that the connection is deemed to have established a new class of things, all of them subject to one rule. The movement – the dialectic – therefore is not a mere trait of argument, "If you say this, I say that," but a trait of thought: If this is the result of step A, then step B is to be taken – out from, without regard to, the limitations of step A. Thought then is continuous, always in motion, and that metaproposition states in the most abstract terms possible the prior and generative metaproposition that, when we compare classes of things, the comparison initiates a process that transcends the limits of comparison. That is to say, again with emphasis, *we can effect a series.*

C.   II.2   S.   *One authority maintains that proof supplied by analogy [here: the analogy sustained by the use of "and" to join the two subjects] takes priority, and the other party maintains that the proof supplied by the demonstration of a totality of congruence among salient traits takes precedence. Rabbis prefer the latter, Aqiba the former position].*

                T.   *Not at all! All parties concur that proof supplied by analogy [here: the analogy sustained by the use of "and" to join the two subjects] takes priority. But rabbis in this context will say to you that the rule governing the subject treated below derives from the rule governing the subject treated above, so that the guilt-offering must be worth a least two silver sheqels. This is established so that you should not argue that the doubt cannot be more stringent than the matter of certainty, and just as where there is certainty of having committed a sin, one has to present a sin-offering that may be worth even so little as a sixth of a zuz in value, so if there is a matter of doubt, the guilt-offering worth only a sixth of a zuz would suffice.*

Once the connection is made, linking an earlier rule (in Scripture's orderly exposition) to a later one, then the connection is such that movement is not only forward but backward. We have established not a connection between one thing and something else, but a series that can encompass a third thing and a fourth thing, onward – but with, or without, formal limit? This principle of right thinking that the hypothesis of the series requires is revealed by Scripture, as is made explicit once more in the following:

D.   III.1   I.   *...And should you say that if Scripture had not included the matter, we should have reached the same conclusion by argument for analogy, then if that is the case, we can infer by analogy also the rule on laying on of hands....*The main point here is that, once an analogy serves, it serves everywhere an analogy can be drawn; there is no a priori that limits the power of an analogy to govern all like cases.

A series is possible once the work of thought moves beyond contrast and analogy. And it is the rule of right thought that, once we have established a comparison and a contrast, that fact validates drawing conclusions on other aspects of the classes of things that have been connected through the comparison and contrast – analogical contrastive thinking is then not static but in motion. Is the motion perpetual? Not at all, for Scripture, for its part, has the power to place limits on a series.

E.   IV.2   B.   If a matter was covered by an encompassing rule but then was singled out for some innovative purpose, you have not got the right to restore the matter to the rubric of the encompassing rule unless Scripture itself explicitly does so. [That means that the encompassing rule does not apply to an item that Scripture, for its own purposes, has singled out. The upshot is that the identified item is now exceptional in some aspect, so it is no longer subject to a common rule governing all other items in context; then the limits of analogy are set by Scripture's treatment of the items of a series. It is worth while reviewing the pertinent example:]

The series is subjected to limits, if an item in the sequence of connections that forms the series proves exceptional: this is connected to that, that to the other thing, but the other thing is other in some other way, so there the series ends.

F. IV.4 A. *Raba said, "[The proposition that that which is derived on the basis of a verbal analogy does not in turn go and impart a lesson by means of a verbal analogy] derives from the following proof:*

We go over familiar ground. Raba takes the view that a series is simply not possible. Others allege that if we connect one class of things to some other by means, for example, of a verbal analogy, then making that same connection once again, where another verbal analogy connects the second class of things to yet a third, is not correct. Scripture shows that verbal analogies do not validate the making of series.

B. "It is written, 'As is taken off from the ox of the sacrifice of peace-offerings' (Lev. 4:10) [namely, the sacrificial parts of the anointed priest's bullock brought for a sin-offering] – *now for what purpose is this detail given? That the lobe of the liver and the two kidneys are to be burned on the altar [as is the case with those of the sin-offering], that fact is specified in the body of the verse itself. But the purpose is to intimate that the burning of the lobe of the liver and the two kidneys of the he-goats brought as sin-offerings for idolatry are to be derived by analogy from the bullock of the community brought on account of an inadvertent sin. That law is not explicitly stated in the passage on the bullock that is brought for an inadvertent sin, but is derived from the rule governing the bullock of the anointed priest. 'As is taken off' is required so that it might be treated as something written in that very passage [on the bullock of inadvertence, being superfluous in its own context], not as something derived on the basis of a verbal analogy does not in turn go and impart a lesson by means of a verbal analogy."*

To repeat my exposition of this matter: I have two items, A and B. I claim that B is like A, therefore the rule governing A applies also to B. Now I turn forward, to C. C is not analogous to A; there are no points of congruence or (in the exegetical formulation that our authors use) verbal intersection. But C is like B because there is an analogy by reason of verbal intersection (the same word being used in reference to C and B). The question is, may I apply to C, by reason of the verbal intersection between C and B, the lesson that I have learned in regard to B only by reason of B's similarity by reason of congruence, not verbal intersection, to A? Can a conclusion that is derived on the basis of a verbal analogy go and impart a lesson by reason of analogy to a third item? Raba now maintains that that is not the case. But the matter has gone in the other direction: a series is possible. But if a series is possible, then what limits are to be placed on the media by which a series is effected?

G   IV.5   A.   Now it is a fact that that which is derived on the basis of a verbal analogy does in turn go and impart a lesson by means of a verbal analogy, *demonstrated whether in the manner of Raba or in the manner of Rabina.*

Now we revert to our basic issue: the validity of a series. Here we move into as yet unexplored ground, which is the basis for my claim that the order of problems is dictated by an interest in a systematic presentation of the rules of right thinking. We have been exposed to the case in favor of a series: once the analogy makes the connection, then all traits of the things connected are brought into relationship with all other such traits. Scripture then provides one limit to the length of a series: a series cannot be infinite. But there is another limit proposed, and it is not scriptural but substantive, in the nature of things, a trait of thought itself. Here is the point at which I find this sustained exposition of thinking about thought simply remarkable.

B.   Is it the rule, however, that *that which is derived on the basis of a verbal analogy may in turn go and impart a lesson by means of an argument on the basis of congruence?* [Freedman: Thus the law stated in A is applied to B by analogy. Can that law then be applied to C because of congruence between B and C?]

We have proven one point. It bears a consequence. We go on to the consequence. The mode of thought is dialectical not only in form, but also in substance: if A, then B. If B, then what about C? It is one thing to have shown that if B is like A, and C, unlike A, is rendered comparable to B by a verbal analogy. But then may I take the next step and draw into the framework of B and C, joined by verbal analogy and assigned a common rule by B's congruent analogy to A, also D, E, F, and G, that is, other classes of things joined to C by verbal analogy – but not necessarily the same verbal analogy that has joined C to B? That indeed is the obvious next step to be taken, and it is now taken. It is taken in the simple words just now given, and the same point is now going to be made, in a systematic way, for each medium by which classes of things are formed and then connected to one another. Analogical-contrastive thinking therefore is not static but always in motion, since, once a connection is made, other connections made follow. If we make a connection between A and B on the basis of one set of shared traits, we may proceed to make a connection between C and A, via B, on the basis of traits shared by B and C but not by A and C. Not only so, but the same mode of thought extends to the media of connection. If I connect A to B by verbal analogy, I may connect B to other classes of things, for example, C, D, E, by other media of connection, for example, verbal analogy connects A to B, and an argument based on congruence connects B to C, and backward to A; and an argument a fortiori may connect C to D, and backward to A and B – series without end, or series that end only in the dictates of revelation, the ultimate arbiter of the classification and hierarchy of all things. What is truly impressive in what follows is the rigorous order by which each possibility is raised in its turn, the connections fore and aft, such that the framer of the whole not only makes his point in words, but also illustrates it in his own representation of matters: a series is not only possible, it is also compelling. So we see as we move forward, now with no need for further exposition, from H to M.

H	IV.6	A	That which is learned by a verbal analogy may in turn go and impart a rule by an argument a fortiori.
I.	IV.7	A	Can that which is learned by verbal analogy in turn go and impart a rule by an analogy based on the congruence of other shared traits [but not verbal ones in context]? Once more to review: we have now linked B to C via a verbal analogy. C stands in relationship to other classes of things, but not for the same reason that it stands in relationship to B, that is, through other than verbal analogical relationships. It forms a relationship a fortiori, for instance, with D, E, and F. If something applies to C, the lesser, it surely should apply to D, the greater. So now we want to know the permissible grounds for drawing relationships – comparisons and contrasts – of classes of things. So on what basis do we move from species to species and uncover the genera of which they form a part (if they do form a part)? Is it only verbal correspondence or intersection, as has been implicit to this point? Or are there more abstract bases for the same work of genus construction (in our language: category formation and re-formation)?
J.	IV.8	A	Can a rule that is derived by analogy based on the congruence of other shared traits [but not verbal ones in context] turn around and teach a lesson through an analogy based on verbal analogy?
K	IV.9	A	Can a rule that is derived by an analogy based on the congruence of other shared traits [but not verbal ones in context] turn around and teach a lesson through an must be held within the hide."
L	IV.10	A	Can a rule that is derived by an analogy based on the congruence of other shared traits [but not verbal ones in context] go and teach a lesson through an argument a fortiori?

M   IV.10 F.   If an argument deriving from an analogy based on verbal
congruence, which cannot go and, by an argument based on
verbal congruence, impart its rule to some other class – *as has
been shown by either Raba's or Rabina's demonstration* –
nonetheless can go and by an argument a fortiori impart its
rule to some other class – *as has been shown by the Tannaite
authority of the household of R. Ishmael* – then a rule that is
derived by an argument based on analogy based on other than
verbal congruence, which can for its part go and impart its
lesson by an argument based on an analogy resting on verbal
congruity which is like itself – *as has been shown by Rami bar
Hama* – surely can in turn teach its lesson by an argument a
fortiori to yet another case!

So at stake throughout is the question of how a series is composed: the
media for the making of connections between one thing and something
else (that is, one class of things and some other class of things, in such
wise that the rules governing the one are shown by the analogy to
govern the other as well). We want to know not only that a connection is
made, but how it is made. And some maintain that if the connection is
made between one thing and something else by means, for example, of a
verbal analogy dictated by Scripture's wording, then a connection
between that something else and a third thing must also be made in a
manner consistent with the initial medium of connection, verbal analogy.
It cannot be made by means of some other medium of connection. But
the paramount position is otherwise: dialectics affect not only argument
but thought itself, because connections are made through all media by
which connections are made. We now reach the end of the matter, in a
set of ultimately theoretical issues:

N   IV.11 A.   Can a rule that is derived by an analogy based on the
congruence of other shared traits [but not verbal ones in
context] go and teach a lesson through an argument
constructed by analogy based on the congruence of other
shared traits among two or more classifications of things?
B.   *That question must stand.*
Q   IV.12 A.   Can a rule derived by an argument a fortiori go and teach a
rule established through analogy of verbal usage?
B.   The affirmative derives from an argument a fortiori:
C.   If an argument deriving from an analogy based on points of
other than verbal congruence, which cannot go and, by an
argument based on verbal congruence, impart its rule to some
other class – *as has been shown by either R. Pappa's demonstration*
– then a rule that is derived by an argument a fortiori, which
can be derived by an argument based on the shared verbal
traits of two things – *as has been shown by the Tannaite authority
of the house of R. Ishmael* – surely should be able to impart its
rule to another classification of things by reason of an
argument based on a verbal analogy!

D. *That position poses no problems to one who takes the view that R. Pappa's case has been made. But for one who takes the view that R. Pappa's case has not been made, what is to be said?*

E. *The question then must stand.*

P. IV.13 A. Can a rule that is derived by an argument a fortiori go and teach a lesson through an argument based on the congruence of other shared traits [but not verbal ones in context]?

B. The affirmative derives from an argument a fortiori:

C. If an argument deriving from an analogy based on points of other than verbal congruence, which cannot be derived from an argument based on verbal congruence, impart its rule to some other class – *as has been shown by R. Yohanan's demonstration* – can go and teach a lesson by an argument based on an analogy established through other than verbal traits, *as has been shown by Rami bar Hama* – a rule based on an argument a fortiori, which can be derived by an argument based on an analogy resting on verbal coincidence, surely should be able to impart its rule to another classification of things by reason of an argument based on an other than verbal analogy!

Q IV.14 A. Can a rule based on an argument a fortiori turn around and teach a lesson through an argument based on an argument a fortiori?

B. Indeed so, and the affirmative derives from an argument a fortiori:

C. If an argument deriving from an analogy based on points of other than verbal congruence, which cannot be derived from an argument based on verbal congruence, impart its rule to some other class – *as has been shown by R. Yohanan's demonstration* – can go and teach a lesson by an argument a fortiori, as we have just pointed out, then an argument that can be derived from an analogy based on verbal congruence – *as has been shown by the Tannaite authority of the household of R. Ishmael* – surely should be able to impart its rule by an argument a fortiori!

D. But would this then would represent what we are talking about, namely, a rule deriving from an argument a fortiori that has been applied to another case by means of an argument a fortiori? Surely this is nothing more than a secondary derivation produced by an argument a fortiori!

E. Rather, argue in the following way:

F. Indeed so, and the affirmative derives from an argument a fortiori:

G. if an argument based on an analogy of a verbal character cannot be derived from another such argument based on an analogy between two classes of things that rests upon a verbal congruence – *in accordance with the proofs of either Raba or Rabina* – nonetheless can then go and impart its lesson by an argument a fortiori – *in accordance with the proof of the Tannaite authority of the household of R. Ishmael* – then an argument a fortiori, which can serve to transfer a lesson originally learned through an argument based upon verbal congruence, *in accordance with the proof of the Tannaite authority of the household of R. Ishmael* – surely should be able to impart its lesson to yet another classification of things through an argument a fortiori.

H   And this does represent what we are talking about, namely, a rule deriving from an argument a fortiori that has been applied to another case by means of an argument a fortiori.

R.   IV.15   A   Can a rule based on an argument a fortiori turn around and teach a rule through an argument constructed on the basis of shared traits of an other-than-verbal character among two classifications of things?

C   *But that is not so. For even if we concede that that is the case there, then still the rule derives from the act of slaughter of unconsecrated beasts [Freedman].*

S.   IV.16   A   Can a rule derived by an argument based on shared traits of an other than verbal character shared among two classes of things then turn around and teach a lesson by an argument based on an analogy of a verbal character, an analogy not of a verbal character, an argument a fortiori, or an argument based on shared traits?

B   *Solve at least one of those problems by appeal to the following:*

C   On what account have they said that if blood of an offering is left overnight on the altar, it is fit? Because if the sacrificial parts are kept overnight on the altar, they are fit. And why if the sacrificial parts are kept overnight on the altar are they fit? Because if the meat of the offering is kept overnight on the altar it is fit. [Freedman: Thus the rule governing the sacrificial parts is derived by an appeal to an argument based on shared traits of an other than verbal character shared among two classes of things, and that rule in turn is applied to the case of the blood by another such argument based on shared traits of an other than verbal character shared among two classes of things].

D   What about the rule governing meat that is taken outside of the Temple court? [If such meat is put up on the altar, it is not removed therefrom. Why so?]

E   Because meat that has been taken out of the holy place is suitable for a high place.

M   [Reverting to C-E:] Now can an analogy be drawn concerning something that has been disposed of in the proper manner for something that has not been disposed of in the proper manner? [If the sacrificial parts are kept overnight, they are not taken off the altar, and therefore the meat kept overnight is fit; but the meat may be kept overnight, while the sacrificial parts may not. So, too, when the Temple stood, the flesh might not be taken outside, but where there was no Temple and only high places, the case is scarcely analogous!]

N   *The Tannaite authority for this rule derives it from the augmentative sense, extending the rule, deriving from the formulation, "This is the Torah of the burnt-offering"* (Lev. 6:2). [Freedman: The verse teaches that all burnt-offerings, even with the defects catalogued here, are subject to the same rule and do not get removed from the altar once they have been put there; the arguments given cannot be sustained but still support that proposition.]

The movement from point to point, first things first, second things in sequence, is so stunning in the precise logic of the order of issues – we must know A before we can contemplate asking about B – that only a brief review is called for. We have shown that we may move from a class of things joined to another through analogy based on congruence, that is, from A to B, onward to other classes of things joined to the foregoing by verbal analogy or intersection, that is, from B to C and beyond. But can we then move from C, linked to B via verbal analogy, to D, linked to C, but not to A or B, by congruence, for example, comparable and shared traits of a salient order? The issue then, is may we move forward to further classes of things by moving "backward," to a principle of linkage of classes that has served to bring us to this point, in other words, reversing the course of principles of linkage? What our framers then want to know is a very logical question: Are there fixed rules that govern the order or sequence by which we move from one class of things to another, so that, if we propose to link classes of things, we can move only from A to B by one principle (comparison and contrast of salient traits), and from B to C by a necessarily consequent and always second principle (verbal intersection); then we may move (by this theory) from C to D only by verbal intersection but not by appeal to congruence. Why not? Because, after all, if C is linked to B only by verbal intersection but not by congruence, bearing no relationship to A at all, then how claim that D stands in a series begun at A, if it has neither verbal connection, nor, as a matter of fact, congruence to link it to anything in the series. What is clear in this reprise is that the issue is drawn systematically, beginning to end. By simply seeing the sequence of questions, we grasp the whole: the program, the method, the order, all dictated by the inner requirements of sustained inquiry into the logic of comparison and contrast, read as a dialectical problem.

The metapropositional program contributed by the Bavli's framers concerns how series are made, which is to say, whether connections yield static or dynamic results, which is to say, at the deepest layers of intellect, how thought happens. Now, at the end, we ask the framers of the Mishnah to address the question before us. And in answer, they give us silence. So we know that here we hear what is distinctive to, and the remarkable discovery of, the authorship of the Bavli. Since, it is clear, that discovery has taken place within the words of the Written Torah, and, since their deepest metaproposition maintained that the words of the Written Torah are the words of God to Moses, our rabbi, at Sinai –

the words, not just the gist – we have to conclude with what I conceive to be the bedrock of the metapropositional program before us: the Torah teaches us not only what God said, but how God thinks. When we understand the Torah rightly, we engage in thinking about thought. And that is how we know God: through thought. So Spinoza was not so heretical after all.

7

The Bavli and Judaism

The Bavli shaped the mind of Judaism. All authoritative Judaic intellects mastered the Bavli, and their minds were shaped in, and by, that document. By "intellect" or "mind" I mean in particular two traits among many that may characterize how people think. The first is how they connect one thing to something else, one fact to another, or, in literary terms, one sentence to another. When people find self-evident the relationship between one thing and another, we want to know why: the self-evidence of the obvious. Second come the ways in which they form the connections that they make into large-scale conclusions, encompassing statements, even entire systems of thought on the social order. Drawing conclusions from connections, people propose explanations for why things are one way, rather than some other. These two then go together to form a principal component of mind or intellect. For when we know how people are thinking, from the knowledge of the process of thought we also can describe propositions they are likely to reach. That is to say, how does the result of connection generate large-scale composition of ideas? These two stages – the perception of connection, the discernment of (to the engaged, the self-evidently valid) conclusions based on the connection – characterize mind or intellect, for they dictate how people think: in one way, rather than in some other. They further allow us to explore the potentialities and also the limitations of intellect, that people are likely to see one thing or to miss some other. But processes of thought lead us to the boundaries between mind and the systems that link mind to social reality. When processes of the organization of data and the interpretation of the result come to fruition, they yield a large-scale system, a view of the world, an account of how people are to conduct life, and a theory of the social entity that embodies that worldview and way of life.

If we want to understand how the intellectuals of a social entity make sense of things, we examine the language they use in order to speak sensibly. That language presents the evidence on how people both reach and convey conclusions of consequence. When we can understand how people discern relationship between one fact, that is, one sentence, and another fact or sentence and further set forth conclusions to be drawn from the relationship or connection, we know not only what they think, but, from the character of the connection, how they think. So when we want to know "the mind of Judaism," we start our inquiry with the logic of the language of the most important statement of Judaism, which is the Talmud of Babylonia.

And why not? For the sages of the Talmud believed that the Torah represents not only God's word, but also – and especially – God's wording, that is, the exact language that God used to set forth God's will. God in the Torah speaks intelligibly; so we can grasp the principles of intelligible discourse that God sets forth, by example, in the Torah. Our minds correspond to God's mind, and the points of correspondence are limned in language, specifically, in the rules of making connections between one thing and some other, and drawing conclusions from those connections that transcend the things that are connected: syllogistic thinking. In the Torah's language of proposition, syllogism, and proof, therefore, we enter into the mind of God, and the task of theology in Judaism is to make our thinking conform to God's thinking, so that our actions may conform to God's will. Then through the intellectual media that govern the formation of attitude and conscience, we use our minds to discover what it means to be "in our image, after our likeness." The stakes therefore are considerable.

For God lives in the syntax of cogent thought and intelligible statement of thought, and Judaism – the Torah – is the statement of the process, yielding, of course, the proposition as well. The propositions may vary from document to document (though of course cogent all together), but the intellectual process uniformly imposes its connections and ubiquitously generates its conclusions. Accordingly, by definition the logic of intelligible discourse, the premise of self-evident comprehension, above all, the intangible sensibility that makes connections between one thing and something else and yields conclusions transcending them both – these form matters of acute theological concern, because they not only hold together many minds in one community of shared and mutually intelligible speech, but they join the mind of creation to the mind of the Creator; when we speak of being "in our image and after our likeness," our sages hear the message: in intellect. The evidence for that shared intellect, that mind in common, therefore comes to us in how God speaks to humanity in the Torah, and also, how people speak to one another, in the connections each makes between two or more sentences and in the connections all make with one another. The formation of a shared intellect, the making of a mind in common among humanity and between God and humanity – these derive from process and connection.

The mind of Judaism therefore comprises those processes of thought that tell people why one thing is self-evidently connected with some other and that furthermore instruct them how to draw conclusions from the connection. The modes of thought paramount in the canonical writings of the Judaism of the Dual Torah in its formative age are what I now propose to describe, analyze, and interpret. The reason I think I can do so is that we have in those canonical writings of Judaism, from the first through the seventh century, ample evidence of the results of how people have thought deeply and abstractly, the concrete evidences, in language, of the conduct of thought. From the language people used to say what they were thinking, I propose to move backward to the processes of thought encapsulated in that language. If people state a proposition, I want to know the argumentation in behalf of that proposition, the kind of evidence and the manner of marshalling that evidence. Still more to the point, if people see a connection, I want to ask what makes the connection self-evident to them, so that one thing fits with some other, and another thing does not. For the mind of Judaism is not abstract, and the Judaism that that mind defines does not deal solely in abstractions. The authors of the canonical writings of the Judaism of the formative age mastered the requirements of applied reason and practical logic. But that means they also were masters of intellect and logical acumen. Consequently, we have in hand ample evidence, in concrete terms, of both the decisions people reached and the ways in which they framed their propositions. That is why I claim the mind of Judaism finds ample documentation in the writings of Judaism. And – so I maintain – we may reconstruct how people think from what they say. And because, for long centuries, all Judaists read the same books and communicated within the patterns of thought inculcated by those books, we may speak not only of the mind of Judaism but also the textual community that embodied and realized that mind.

The bridge from proposition, that is, *what* people think, to process, *how* they think, therefore is built of modes of discourse preserved and transmitted in writing: mutually intelligible exchanges of ideas, in fully articulated language made up of words and sentences that follow a public syntax. Discourse thus refers to the way in which people make their statements so that the connections within their thought are intelligible and cogent to others (and that by definition, hence the stress on the public). To describe the modes of discourse which attest to modes of thought at the deep structure of mind, we ask how people place on display not only the conclusions they have reached but also the manner in which they wish to announce and argue in favor of those conclusions – all together, the way in which they make their statement of their position. Accordingly, it is in cogent argument concerning proposition that mind becomes incarnate, and the incarnate mind in the Torah is God's.

To make matters more concrete, let me say what I mean by making connections and drawing conclusions. The simple sequence of intellect that moves us from two unrelated facts to two connected facts and thence to a proposition or the drawing of a conclusions, is so:

1. I threw a rock at a dog. It rained.
2. I threw a rock at a dog, then it rained.
3. If I throw a rock at a dog, it will rain.

Some facts are inert, others bear consequence. Facts that fail to intersect with others in general gain slight notice; those that form structures and convey sense gain systematic consequence and ultimately form an encompassing account of how things are and should be, why we do things one way and not another: an ethos, an ethics, an account of a "we," altogether, a system. Mind moreover explains to people about the consequences of the connections that they are taught to perceive, yielding conclusions of one sort, rather than another, based on one mode of drawing conclusions from the connections that are made, rather than some other. Accordingly, while the social entity undergoes change, processes endure to preserve the rules of deliberation that dictate the range of permissible deed. The realm of choice honors limits set by sense deemed common. What follows explains the urgency of the inquiry before us. *How* people think dictates the frontiers of possibility. The mind of Judaism, that is to say, *process*, is what defined, and will define, Judaism.

For the working or structure of "intellect" or "mind" I use as a synonym a simple word, logic, but that is not in a technical sense. I mean the word "logic" to stand for the determinative principle of intelligibility of discourse and cogency of thought represented by stage [2] above. Logic is what tells people that one thing connects or intersects with another, while something else does not, hence, making connections; and logic further tells them what follows from the connections that they make, generating, as at stage [3] above, the conclusions that they are to draw. Accordingly, the first thing we want to know about any intellect, that is, in this context any piece of writing, is its logic of cogent discourse. Logic is what joins one sentence to the next and forms the whole into paragraphs of meaning, intelligible propositions, each with its place and sense in a still larger, accessible system. And logic as a matter of fact makes possible the sharing of propositions of general intelligibility and therefore forms the cement of a social system. For, because of logic, one mind connects to another, so that, in writing or in orally formulated and orally transmitted teaching, public discourse becomes possible. Because of logic debate on issues of general interest takes place. Still more to the point, because of logic a mere anthology of statements about a single subject becomes a composition of theorems about that subject, so that facts serve to demonstrate and convey propositions. Through logic the parts, bits and pieces of information, add up to a sum greater than themselves, generate information or insight beyond what they contain. What people think – exegesis of discrete facts in accord with a fixed hermeneutic of the intellect – knows no limit. How they think makes all the difference. In order to spell out the logic or principle of cogent discourse I therefore choose to focus upon the simple matter of making connections and drawing conclusions from those connections.

The way in which people add up two and two to make four always requires the appeal to the *and,* and that is what endures, that *and* of the two and two equal four, and, too, the *equal,* which is to say, the conclusion yielded by the *and.* The logic lasts: the *and* of making connections, the *equal* of reaching conclusions. This endures: the certainty that X + Y are connected and generate conclusion Z, but (for purposes of discussion here) the symbol # and the number 4 are not connected and therefore, set side by side, produce a mere nonsense statement. The intellect of any Judaism flourishes in processes of thought and comes to expression in the premises of self-evidence, more lastingly and more certainly than in the propositions of conviction and confession. Whatever people propose to state should resort to a highly limited range of putting two *and* two together to *equal* four. In due course I shall survey some of the possibilities of answers to the question: How do two and two validate that *and* that stands between them, and why do two and two *equal* four: connection, conclusion?

In the canonical literature of Judaism, I identify three paramount different "logics" (used in the somewhat loose sense defined just now) by which two sentences are deemed to cohere and to constitute a statement of consequence and intelligibility. One mode of making connections and drawing conclusions from those connections is familiar to us as philosophical logic, the second is equally familiar as the logic of cogent discourse attained through narrative. In both cases the connection between one sentence or fact and another derives from the inherent sense of what is set forth, the one for syllogistic discourse, the other for narrative. The linkages are different, but the connections fall into the same classification. These two, self-evidently, are logics of a propositional order. The third logic yielded by the sample document before us is not propositional, and, as a matter of fact, it also is not ordinarily familiar to us at all. It is a mode of joining two or more statements – sentences not inherently or intrinsically by appeal to sense, that is, on the foundation of meaning or sense or proposition, such as the first two logics utilize. Rather, the joining of facts or sentences rests on foundations of a different order altogether.

Philosophical discourse is built out of propositions and arguments from facts and reason. The cogency of discourse – the *and* that joints two sentences together into a cogent statement – derives from the argument we wish to make, the fact we wish to establish, the proposition we wish to prove. The tension in this mode of thought arises from the trait of mind that derives from two facts a third, one that transcends the givens. The resolution, then, comes from the satisfying demonstration, out of what we know, of something we did not know but wish to find out, or of something we think we know and wish to prove. The syllogistic character of philosophical discourse is familiar to us all. That is why commonplaces such as "[1] All Greeks are liars, [2] Demosthenes is a Greek, [3] (therefore) Demosthenes is a liar," need not detain us. In that sequence, fact [1] and fact [2] come together to prove a fact that is not contained within either [1] or [2]. From our perspective, we want to identify the connection between two facts. And what matters in the famous syllogism at hand is that the proposition, [3], is what joins fact [1] to fact [2] into joined and cogent sentences, the *equal* generates the *and* [thus: = < +].

The critical point is in the *equals*, since it is at that result that the point of the connection is both realized but also established. We see a connection between one item and the next because of the third item that the first two generate. In the logic at hand connection rests upon conclusion. And let me with emphasis state the central point: *that relationship, connection, is shown in a conclusion different from the established facts of two or more sentences that we propose to draw when we set up as a sequence two or more facts and claim out of that sequence to propose a proposition different from, transcending, the facts at hand.* We demonstrate propositions in a variety of ways, appealing to both a repertoire of probative facts and also a set of accepted modes of argument. In this way we engage in a kind of discourse that gains its logic from what, in general, we may call philosophy: the rigorous analysis and testing of propositions against the canons of an accepted reason. The connection produced by the cogent discourse of philosophy therefore accomplishes the miracle of making the whole more – or less – than the sum of the parts, that is, in the simple language we have used up to now, showing the connections between fact 1 and fact 2, in such wise as to yield proposition A. A simple, concrete example, within a repertoire of literally tens of thousands, derives from Sifré to Deuteronomy:

CCCXXVI:II

1. A.   "...when he sees that their might is gone, and neither bond nor free is left":
   B.   When he sees their destruction, on account of the captivity.
   C.   For all of them went off.

Let me make explicit, in terms of the first case, how I conceive the connections to be established, the conclusion to be drawn. A represents the conclusion, that is, the proposition we propose to prove. B, C present the facts that are connected. C is the first fact, namely, all of them went off into exile. B then is the second fact, that [1] when God saw that they had gone into captivity, and [2] were without arrogance or power, yielding the unstated conclusion, [3] he had mercy on them, and that then validates the proposition, A. Turned around, the second and third of the three sentences so work together as to make a point that neither one of them by itself establishes, and that is how such a syllogism works in general. Then a sequence of syllogisms of the same kind, not all of them fully spelled out and most of them as truncated as the first, make the same point, establishing the besought theorem by setting forth numerous demonstrations of that theorem: "When he sees...."

The second logic of of connection making and conclusion drawing is equally familiar. It is a teleological logic and takes the form of narrative, e.g., history. The logic invokes a fictive tension and its resolution. It appeals for cogency to the purpose and direction of an arrangement of facts, ordinarily in the form of narrative. Teleological or narrative logic further serves quite effectively as a mode of making connections between two facts, that is, linking two otherwise unrelated sentences, and presenting conclusions based on the linkage. In this mode of thought, we link fact to fact and also prove (ordinarily implicit) propositions by appeal to teleology, that is, the end or purpose of discussion that makes sense of all detail. The tension of narrative derives from the open-endedness of discourse. We are told a series of facts, or a problem is set forth, such that, only when we see in the sequence of the series of facts the logical, inevitable outcome do we find a resolution: that sense, that fittingness of connection, that makes of the parts a cogent whole. Accordingly, a proposition (whether or not it is stated explicitly) may be set forth and demonstrated by showing through the telling of a tale (of a variety of kinds, for example, historical, fictional, parabolic, and the like) that a sequence of events, real or imagined, shows the ineluctable truth of a given proposition. Whence the connection? The logic of connection demonstrated through narrative, rather than philosophy, is simply stated. It is connection attained and explained by invoking some mode of narrative in which a sequence of events, first this, then that, is understood to yield a proposition, first this, then that – *because of this*. That manufactured sequence both states *and also establishes* a proposition in a way different from the philosophical and argumentative mode of propositional discourse. The teleological logic of making connections and drawing conclusions is illustrated by a parable that supplies a simple example of how narrative links fact to fact in cogent discourse and further conveys with powerful logic a clear proposition:

The Fathers According to Rabbi Nathan XIII

2. A.   R. Simeon b. Yohai says, "I shall draw a parable for you. To what may the first Man be compared? He was like a man who had a wife at home. What did that man do? He went and brought a jug and put in it a certain number of dates and nuts. He caught a scorpion and put it at the mouth of the jug and sealed it tightly. He left it in the corner of his house.

   B.   "He said to her, 'My daughter, whatever I have in the house is entrusted to you, except for this jar, which under no circumstances should you touch.' What did the woman do? When her husband went off to market, she went and opened the jug and put her hand in it, and the scorpion bit her, and she went and fell into bed. When her husband came home from the market, he said to her, 'What's going on?'

   C.   "She said to him, 'I put our hand into the jug, and a scorpion bit us, and now I'm dying.'

   D.   "He said to her, 'Didn't I tell you to begin with, "Whatever I have in the house is entrusted to you, except for this jar, which under no circumstances should you touch."' He got mad at her and divorced her.

   E.   "So it was with the first man.

   F.   "When the Holy One, blessed be He, said to him, *Of all the trees of the garden you certainly may eat, but from the tree of knowledge of good and evil you may not eat, for on the day on which you eat of it, you will surely die* (Gen. 2:17),

   G.   "on that day he was driven out, thereby illustrating the verse, *Man does not lodge overnight in honor* (Ps. 49:24)."

Simeon's point is that by giving Man the commandment, God aroused his interest in that tree and led man to do what he did. The explicit proposition is the first point, we sin at our obsession. The implicit proposition is that God bears a measure of guilt for the fall of man. The issue of connection should be made explicit. Let us consider the sequence of sentences of the opening unit:

1. A man had a wife at home
2. He went and brought a jug
3. ...put in it a certain number of dates and nuts.

4. He caught a scorpion
5. ...put it at the mouth of the jug
6. ...sealed it tightly.
7. ...He left it in the corner of his house.

Nos. 1, 2, 3, + 4 bear no connection whatsoever. Nos. 4-7, of course, form a single sentence, but that sentence on its own stands utterly unrelated to the earlier of the two sentences, Nos. 1-3. However, we realize, the sequence of clauses and sentences, all of them discrete, in fact form a tight fit, since they bear the burden of the narrative. At the end, then, the narrative reaches its point and, retrospectively, establishes a very close connection between clause and clause, sentence and sentence. It is the goal, the teleology, of the composition, that joins the components of the composition to one another, and that happens only at the end. Our trust in the narrator's purpose is what allows us to suspend our suspicion that we are linking things that stand out of all relationship with one another. The linkage imparted at the end then makes sense of everything from the outset, and that is what I mean by a logic of teleology, as distinct from propositional logic that yields the making of connections and the drawing of conclusions.

This brings us to an utterly unfamiliar mode of establishing connections between sentences, which I call the logic of fixed association. My examples derive from a document other than the Bavli, but readers will rapidly recognize in simpler form precisely the modes of connection and conclusion characteristic of the Bavli. In this logic we find connection *without* conclusion, that is, the *and* but not the *equals* or the *therefore* [X + Y ≠]. In this logic, the two *and* the two do not *equal* anything. Then on what basis do we impute or introduce the *and* at all? The cogency of two or more facts [X + Y] is imputed and extrinsic. The *and* is not sensible, or intrinsic, propositional or purposive, syllogistic or teleological. But document after document appeals to precisely this logic of fixed association and testifies that, in the Jewish mind represented by diverse authorships, people do perceive cogency through fixed association without either syllogistic or even teleological proposition. That cogency, the connection lacking all proposition, derives from a sense of the order and proportion of data extrinsic to those at hand. All of these altogether too abstract descriptions will take on concrete meaning presently. *Fixed associations derive from an extrinsic and conventional list of items deemed joined for reasons pertinent to those items, and each fact or sentence finds its own relationship to that extrinsic connection, without the slightest connection to other facts or sentences that stand, in writing or in mental sequence, in the same context, fore and aft. Rather, discrete facts, propositions, or sentences hang together because they refer equally to an available protocol of associations.*

Clearly, the logic of fixed association contradicts the conception that connections between this and that derive from the traits of this and that, since the premise of fixed association is that we can connect A to B not because of any intrinsic traits but because of an extrinsic consideration. That extrinsic power that imposes connections not spun out of the traits of things is the Torah, which joins this to that though this bears no clear connection to that; appealing to the Torah and its sequence of things then yields connections that the things themselves do not yield. To revert to my opening theological observations, God connects what the human mind does not see joined at all. And, since, in the nature of things, what connects only by imputed connection yields no proposition we can discern within inherent characteristics, it must follow that God means for us to draw conclusions that, on our own, we cannot have reached. To show how this logic imparts coherence to otherwise incoherent sentences, we briefly follow a sustained passage, just as it occurs, in a sequence of sentences that bear no relationship, sequential let alone propositional, to one another. Proof of that fact is simple. Were the following items given in some other order, viewed in that other sequence, they would make precisely as much, or as little, sense as they do in the order in which we see them. That proves that the order of sentences has no bearing upon any proposition, and given the power of the correct ordering of facts/sentences in both syllogistic argument and teleological logic alike, the utter incapacity of order to impart meaning shows us that we have in hand a logic other than the philosophical syllogistic or the teleological. Now to our passage:

Sifré to Deuteronomy XXV:I

1. A. "What kind of place are we going to? Our kinsmen have taken the heart out of us, saying, ['We saw there a people stronger and taller than we, large cities with walls sky-high, and even Anakites']" (Deut. 1:25-28):
   B. They said to him, "Moses, our lord, had we heard these things from ordinary people, we should have never believed it.
   C. "But we have heard it from people whose sons are ours and whose daughters our ours."

Sifré to Deuteronomy XXV:II

1. A. "We saw there a people ...taller than we":
   B. This teaches that they were tall.
2. A. "...and greater...":
   B. This teaches that they were numerous.

Sifré to Deuteronomy XXV:III

1. A. "...large cities with walls sky-high, and even Anakites":
   B. Rabban Simeon b. Gamaliel says, "In the present passage, Scriptures speak in exaggerated language: 'Hear, O Israel, you are going to pass over the Jordan this day to go in to dispossess nations greater and mightier than yourself, cities great and fortified up to heaven' (Deut. 9:1).
   C. "But when God spoke to Abraham, Scripture did not use exaggerated language: 'And we will multiply your seed as the stars of the heaven' (Gen. 26:4), 'And we will make your seed as the dust of the earth' (Gen. 13:16)."

Sifré to Deuteronomy XXV:IV

1. A. "...and even Anakites did we see there":
   B. This teaches that they saw giants on top of giants, in line with this verse: "Therefore pride is as a chain about their neck" (Ps. 73:6).

Sifré to Deuteronomy XXV:V

1. A. "And we said to you":
   B. He stressed to them, "It is not on our own authority that we speak to you, but it is on the authority of the Holy One that we speak to you."

Sifré to Deuteronomy XXV:VI

1. A. "Do not be frightened and do not be afraid of them":
   B. On what account?
   C. "For the Lord your God is the one who goes before you."
   D. He said to them, "The one who did miracles for you in Egypt and all these miracles is going to do miracles for you when you enter the land:
   E. "'According to all that he did for you in Egypt before your eyes' (Deut. 1:30).
   F. "If you do not believe concerning what is coming, at least believe concerning what has already taken place."

That each unit of thought, signified by a Roman numeral, stands by itself hardly needs proof. Were we to present the several items in a different order, that shift would have no effect whatsoever upon the meaning of the several components of the passage. That proves that the individual sentences bear no relationship to one another. There is no *equals*. But there clearly is an *and*. That is to say, in the context of a document made up of a variety of intelligible propositions, such as is comprised by Sifré to Deuteronomy, the same overall sense for cogency that explains why a given passage makes a point also explains why another passage, which makes no point we can discern, nonetheless is deemed to form, also, and in its context, cogent discourse too.

The third logic therefore rests upon the premise that *an established sequence of facts, for example, words, extrinsic to the sense of what is said joins whatever is attached to those words into a set of cogent statements,* even though *said sequence does not form of those statements propositions of any kind, implicit or explicit.* The protocol of associated items, that is, the established sequence of words, may be made up of names always associated with one another. It may be made up of a received text, with deep meanings of its own, for example, a verse or a clause of Scripture. It may be made up of the sequence of holy days or synagogue lections, which are assumed to be known by everyone and so to connect on their own. The fixed association of these words, whether names, whether formula such as verses of Scripture, whether lists of facts, serves to link otherwise unrelated statements to one another and to form of them all not a proposition but, nonetheless, *an entirely intelligible sequence of connected or related sentences.* Fixed association forms the antonym of free association. There is no case in rabbinic literature, among the documents translated by me, in which the contents of one sentence stimulate a compositor to put down the next sentence only because one thing happens to remind the compositor of something else, that is, without all reference to a principle of association external to both sentences (our "fixed association"), and also without all reference to a shared proposition that connects the two (our "propositional cogency"). Not one case! Fixed association, it is clear, appeals to connections set forth in the Torah, so, as I said, God sees connections that we do not perceive, except through the eye of God.

To state matters in a more secular way, traditional writers will appeal to a prior, authoritative document to make connections between one thing and another: imposed and extrinsic connections that the authority of the authoritative document, embodying the tradition, sustains. Philosophical writers, setting forth a system on its own foundations and in its own terms, will appeal to cogency that is intrinsic not imputed, yielding a result that is propositional and syllogistic, not inert and merely informative. In the context of the Judaic canon, the Mishnah is a deeply philosophical writing, rarely appealing to authority, commonly forming its lists and their propositions by appeal to the inherent traits of things. Enough of Sifré to Deuteronomy has been cited to show us that the framers of that document, among many, have chosen a logic of fixed association, appealing to the Written Torah to connect thoughts that, on their own, would otherwise hardly intersect. And that brings us to the Talmud of Babylonia, which exhibits both traits of logic, and, I shall argue, also both traits of thought. It sets forth numerous propositions through a logic of cogent discourse that is fundamentally philosophical and syllogistic. But it joins these propositions through a logic of connection that is fundamentally fixed associative.

The ambiguity of the Bavli lies in the unanticipated intersection of a traditional form with a systemic statement. For while set forth in a manner that implicitly bears the attributes of a mere amplification of received truth, as a commentary to the Mishnah, the Bavli viewed in relationship to its sources emerges through a set of purposive choices and therefore is simply not a traditional document. Most of what the Bavli's authorship says simply expresses, in a cogent and coherent way, the topical, rhetorical, and logical choices, forming the well-crafted statement and viewpoint, of its authorship. Little of what the Bavli's authorship presents in a propositional form derives cogency and force from a received statement, and most of it does not. True, many of the propositions address the meaning of paragraphs of the Mishnah, and most of the document is laid out as a commentary to either the Mishnah or Scripture.

Three questions dictate our address to the Bavli. First, is the Bavli an autonomous system or has its authorship produced merely a dependent commentary? Second, does the Bavli utilize logic(s) congruent to its systemic program and purpose (if any)? Third, is the Bavli systemic or traditional, and how does the authorship of the Bavli represent its document in relationship to received writings, for example, as tradition or free-standing? The facts are these: first, the Bavli makes a coherent statement, second, forms a systemic document in traditional form, and, third, utilizes a mixture of logics remarkably suitable to the task of doing just that. The Bavli's statement comes to us within the logic of cogent discourse imparted by argumentation for a theorem and other modes of propositional cogency.

Precisely in what sense does the Bavli form both a systemic statement and also a traditional document? It is systemic in the presentation of a closed system, a whole, proportioned, and well-composed statement, one that in vast detail blatantly and repetitiously delivered the same self-evidently true answer to the same ponderous and urgent question. But it is traditional in the very real sense that its authorship constantly quotes and cites received writings, laying out its ideas in the form of commentaries to two of those writings, Scripture and the Mishnah, represented as the Torah in two media, written and the oral, respectively. The particular way in which the authorship of the Bavli accomplished this feat is through a fresh conception of the logic of cogent discourse. Specifically, it utilized [1] philosophical logic for the formation of propositions, that is to say, for the drawing of conclusions. But it also made ample and prevailing use of [2] the logic of fixed association for the linking of one proposition to another. In its syllogistic discourse the authorship presented the propositions that, all together, comprised its statement. In organizing that discourse within the discipline of the logic of fixed association, the authorship imparted to its statement the status of tradition, pretending that whatever it had to say constitutes a mere clarification of the received Torah, whether oral, in the Mishnah, or written, in Scripture.

I have already dwelt on the simple fact that the Bavli's authorship, standing at the outset of any sustained and cogent unit of discourse, knows precisely what it wishes to find out in any passage; it follows a clear-cut program, imposed throughout, a program to be discerned in devices of fixed rhetoric, persistent logical argument, and coherent analytical program, extending over the whole surface of the topical agenda that the authorship has selected. The break, already set forth, between the Mishnah's and the two Talmuds' systems, and the demonstration of the Bavli's system in comparison with the Yerushalmi's, shows us that the Bavli's authorship has made up its own mind and then imputed to a received document the consequence of its own independent thought. How then are we to demonstrate the autonomous and fresh character of so protean a statement as the Bavli, showing that that system is not continuous with the one of the Mishnah, but only connected to it? A simple experiment will amply prove the point. For the sake of argument, stipulating for the moment that the Bavli's authorship has indeed made a systemic statement, let us ask ourselves whether, on the basis of the system of the Mishnah, we can have predicted through extrapolation from the Mishnah's shape and structure the important components of the statement of the Bavli. The answer is partly affirmative, partly negative – and therefore negative. The affirmative side is simple to delineate. With only the Mishnah in hand, we can surely outline the main principles of the normative rules that the Bavli incorporates into, and utilizes as the medium for, its systemic statement. But if we knew only the Mishnah's program, we would vastly overstate the range and coverage of the Bavli's, which omits all reference to the Mishnah's first and sixth divisions (Agriculture, save only Blessings, and Purities, except for the rules of Menstrual Uncleanness). And that only suggests the vast disproportions between the Mishnah's authorship's estimates of the attention to be paid to a given range of law, and the decision of the Bavli's authorship on those same matters. The enormous volume of the Bavli's discussion of the three tractates of the Civil Law (Baba Qamma, Baba Mesia, Baba Batra), is out of all proportion to the place that those same tractates occupy within the composition and proportion of the Mishnah. The disproportions form only one indicator of the autonomous judgment exercised by the Bavli's authorship. For once they have chosen their own program of subjects and determined the attention they wish to devote to those subjects, they give evidence of a set of priorities and concerns that are their own and not inherited. Theirs is a fixed and methodical analytical inquiry, which wants to know the same thing about all things.

The form of the Bavli contradicts its intellectual program. For the form is highly traditional. The authorship of the Bavli leaves no doubt that it makes extensive use of extant materials, sayings and stories. The Bavli's authorship further takes as its task the elucidation of the received code, the Mishnah. More to the point, frequent citations of materials now found in the Tosefta as well as allusions to sayings framed in Tannaite Hebrew and attributed to Tannaite authority – marked, for instance, by TN' – time and again alert us to extensive reference, by our authorship, to a prior corpus of materials. Most striking of all, our authorship claims in virtually every line to come at the end of a chain of tradition, since the bulk of the generative sayings – those that form the foundation for sustained inquiry and dialectical discourse – is assigned to named authorities clearly understood to stand prior to the work of the ultimate redactors. Even if we preserve a certain reluctance to take at face value all of these attributions to prior authorities, we have to take full account of the authorship's insistence upon its own traditionality. In all of these ways, the authorship of the Bavli so represents itself as to claim that, assuredly, it stands in a line of tradition, taking over and reworking received materials, restating viewpoints that originate in prior ages. And that fact makes all the more striking the fundamental autonomy of discourse displayed by the document at the end.

8

The Bavli and the Bible: Two Solutions to One Problem

Two great religions emerged from antiquity, Judaism and Christianity. The principal document of Judaism was the Bavli, that of Christianity, the Bible. It is now possible to compare and contrast these foundation documents by imposing upon these unconnected and disparate documents a single program of analysis, one that asks about the *equal* and the *and*, the mode of making connections and drawing conclusions, that characterize the respective compilations.

To review the facts of the Judaic writing: the Bavli is made up of sizable systematic statements of propositions, syllogistic arguments fully worked out and elegantly exposed. Accordingly, two principles of logical discourse are at play. For the statement of propositions, sizable arguments and proofs, the usual philosophical logic dictates the joining of sentence to sentences and the composition of paragraphs, that is, completed thoughts. For the presentation of the whole, the other logic, the one deriving from imputed, fixed associations, external to the propositions at hand, serves equally well. The framers of the Bavli drew together the results of work which people prior to their own labors already had completed. Available as both completed documents and also sizable components, statements awaiting agglutination or conglomeration in finished documents, these ready-made materials were sewn together with only one kind of thread. Whatever the place and role of the diverse types of logics that formed the compositions circulating before and in the time of the Bavli – compilations of scriptural exegeses, the Yerushalmi, not to mention the exegeses of pentateuchal laws in Sifra and the two Sifrés, the Tosefta, The Fathers (Avot) and The Fathers According to Rabbi Nathan, Genesis Rabbah, Leviticus Rabbah, Pesiqta deRab Kahana, and on and on – the Bavli superseded them all and defined the mind of Judaism. It was through the Bavli that the entire antecedent canon reached the Judaism of the Dual Torah beyond the formative age.

Two principal sources of fixed associations served the Bavli's framers, the Mishnah and Scripture. The authorships of the tractates of the Bavli in general first of all organized the Bavli around the Mishnah, just as the framers of the Yerushalmi had done. Second, they adapted and included vast tracts of antecedent materials organized as scriptural commentary. These they inserted whole and complete, not at all in response to the Mishnah's program. They rarely created redactional compositions of a sizable order that focused upon given authorities, even though sufficient materials lay at hand to allow doing so. They joined the Mishnah to Scripture in such a way as to give final form and fixed expression, through their categories of the organization of all knowledge, to the Torah as it had been known, sifted, searched, approved, and handed down, even from the remote past to their own day. Accordingly, the Bavli's ultimate framers made the decision to present large-scale discussions along lines of order and sequence dictated not by topics and propositional arguments concerning them. Rather they selected the two components of the one whole Torah, oral and written, of Moses, our rabbi, at Sinai, and these they set forth as the connections that held together and ordered all discourse. That is how they organized what they knew, on the one side, and made their choices in laying out the main lines of the structure of knowledge, on the other.

The commentary form bore the message that the Bavli's authorship stood in a line of continuing tradition, even while that authorship presented a systemic statement of its own shaping. The logic of fixed association is what permitted the Bavli's authorships to appeal to two distinct repertoires of sequential items, the Mishnah and also Scripture. The use of the logic of fixed association served a critical theological purpose, specifically, facilitating the linkage into a single statement ("the one whole Torah") of the two Torahs, oral and written, that is, the Mishnah and Scripture. That is the effect of the Bavli's layout as a commentary to the Mishnah or to Scripture. As between the two kinds of logic relevant in this context – propositional and fixed associative – the Bavli appealed for ultimate composition, for the deep structure and cogency of all learning, therefore all thought worth thinking, to the fixed associative. The Bavli made room for propositional discourse at that middle range of knowledge that made of the parts autonomous statements of one thing or another, then also put all knowledge together in its own rather odd way, by the imputed and extrinsic associations dictated by Scripture and the Mishnah. Judaic thought therefore yielded not a series of treatises on topics and propositions, but a series of medium-length discourses that gain cogency imposed only from without. The upshot for the Bavli's authorship was to yield a systemic statement in the form of a traditional document.

What about the Bible? How does the Bavli's authorship's work compare to that of the Pentateuch's? If we make up a conversation between the Bavli's authorship and the framers of the Pentateuch, what sort of exchange can we imagine? Specifically, were the Jewish framers of the Pentateuch to confront the work of the authorship of the Bavli, would they have recognized a Jewish mind similar to their own? Properly introduced to what is at stake here, they would, I maintain, have said yes. What would have struck them as affirmative arguments? In the Bavli's anonymity, in its sustained discourse in behalf of "the community" or the consensus of sages, in its encompassing consistency and engaging mode of insistence on a single point in many particulars, yes, I think the pentateuchal authorship will have found their own traits of mind and discourse in the Bavli's framers' work. But I wonder whether they should also have accorded complete respect to an authorship that, so unlike themselves, claimed for its ideas second place, in a sequence of tradition tacking them on to a prior and received document.

After all, the great intellects of the Pentateuch will have wondered, why not do what their near contemporaries had done in rewriting J, E, JE, P, and D, to produce the Pentateuch (not to mention the nearly contemporary work of paraphrasing the books of Samuel and Kings in such a way as to produce the books of Chronicles)? For they had simply taken received materials and recast them in terms, and also in language, of their own. Why not, then, just rewrite the Mishnah, inserting, to take to be the case I introduced at the outset, the conception of an eschatological teleology represented by a Messiah in places where the theme does not appear? Or, lacking the boldness of the chronicler(s) (not to mention the pentateuchal compilers and revisers themselves!), the framers of the Bavli can at least allude to received materials without explicitly citing them in a way that preserved their distinct standing as an autonomous document. Many writers, both prior to, and in the time of, the pentateuchal ones did just that, making reference to established facts of life and thought without citing, in a slavish, academic way, the documents that preserved those facts. The authorships of the Pentateuch and of the Mishnah set forth systems in utter indifference to the category, tradition. And, I think it is clear, to the degree that the Essene library at Qumran represents a system, the writers there also made the same choice.

Why then did the Bavli's framers present as traditional what was, in fact, an independent and autonomous reshaping of inherited materials within a mold they themselves had made up? The answer to that question carries us into a set of issues that find resolution far beyond the sources on which we concentrate here. The form of commentary by itself is not pertinent to the answer, since it is the logic, not the form, that imparts cultural significance to modes of cogent discourse. But we can point to a problem that the Bavli's authorship successfully solved. How was a later generation to work out its received legacy of revealed truth without collapsing under the weight of tradition? The Bavli's framers found the way in which a set of philosophers, forming a system with its own generative principles of order, proportion, composition, and of course mode of logic to carry on cogent discourse, might relate its philosophical work to its larger historical context. And in solving that problem as they did, the Bavli's system builders discovered in the detail of their document the way for holding together in a fructifying tension continuity and change, permanence and spontaneity, charisma and routine (in terms our generation itself has received from its masters), culture and creativity, and, reaching outward beyond the limits of culture, nature, and nurture.

For philosophy and system building did not, and do not, take place fresh, even though, in logic and order, they are possible only when formed of the elaboration of first principles. On the contrary, thought forms a component of ongoing society, and systems restate received facts of everyday reality. Thought, after all, does not begin with thinking about thought, though it may end there. The Bavli then presents us with the answer that would characterize the Jewish mind from then to now to the question of how to hold together in fruitful tension tradition and system, history and philosophy, the continuity and change that unite past, present, and future. But that was not the only answer of the classical age, as we now see when we compare the Bavli to the Bible. For the invention of the Bible by Christianity – the Bible is the gift of the Church, after all – points toward antiquity's other important way of sorting out and holding together sustaining tradition and new thought. Receiving diverse systems of thought or fragments thereof, the intellect behind the Bible represented these diverse and contradictory writings as a single cogent system, essentially doing the opposite of what the Bavli's authorship did, while producing the same result: a traditional system. And for the intellects formed in the Bavli and in the Bible alike, that is how, for the history of the West, civilization would endure, with roots, but also growth and change.

In the case of the Christian mind, where do we look for a counterpart labor of system building through selectivity, such as the Bavli has given us? The answer, of course, is dictated by the form of the question. We turn to the work of canonization of available writings into the Bible.

There we see the counterpart, the making of choices, the setting forth of a single statement. When we compare the systemic structures represented by the Bavli and the Bible, therefore, we can appreciate how two quite distinct groups of intellectuals worked out solutions to a single problem, and did so, as a matter of fact, through pretty much the same medium, namely, the making of reasoned choices. Imputing the standing of tradition to what was in fact an original and fresh system shows us how intellectuals chose to gather together traditions and to impose upon them the form and structure of a system. And that is the way of holding things together in a stable composite that Christian intellectuals of the second and third centuries found in their question, out of writings deemed authoritative, of a single Christian truth, that is to say, what we should call a system. The comparison of the way of the Bavli to the manner of the Bible is apt not only because both led to a solution of a single perennial problem of ongoing society facing the advent of the permanently new.

We begin with a simple bedrock fact. Christianity finds in the Bible, meaning the Old Testament and the New Testament, the statement of the faith by the authority of God. And however diverse the readings of the Bible, Christian theologians, Catholic (Roman or Greek or Armenian or Russian in language) and Protestant alike define the foundations of all divine knowledge as the simple fact that there is a pattern of Christian truth, awaiting discovery and demonstration. So all Christianities appeal not to diverse traditions, insusceptible of harmonization, but to Christian truth, to the idea of orthodoxy (if not to the same Orthodoxy). Accordingly, Christian systems concur that there is more than tradition, there is also what we should call system, one Christian system, whatever it may be. And the Bible forms the statement of that system, however we choose to read it. Accordingly, the Bible for all Christianities forms traditions into a single system.

To understand why the framers of the Bavli effected the odd mixture of logics that they did to set forth their writing, we have to revert to their formal task, which was to set forth a commentary to the Mishnah. The Bavli's framers wished to present a system in the disguise of a tradition, and hence set a high priority upon relating their ideas to received writings. When we understand the character of the Mishnah and its relationship to the immediately prior system its authorship recognized, which was the Pentateuch (and Scripture as a whole), we shall grasp the choices confronting the Bavli's framers. The issue then was authority, and the position of the authorship of one system simply contradicts the datum of the authorship of the successor system. What the Bavli's framers did, then, was to subvert the received system by imposing upon it precisely the character the Mishnah's authorship had rejected, namely, that of a commentary to Scripture, a secondary expansion of Scripture. And – it would inexorably follow, quite by the way, the Bavli's framers then adopted for their own system that same form that they again and again imposed upon the Mishnah's system.

And that brings us directly to the problem of authority in the Mishnah: its relationship to *its* source, which in part was Scripture and in part was taxonomic logic. The Mishnah utilized a single logic to set forth a system that, in form as in inner structure, stood wholly autonomous and independent, a statement unto itself, with scarcely a ritual obeisance to any prior system. As soon as the Mishnah made its appearance, therefore, the vast labor of not only explaining its meaning but especially justifying its authority was sure to get under way. For the Mishnah presented one striking problem in particular. It rarely cited scriptural authority for its rules. Instead, it followed the inexorable authority of logic, specifically, the inner logic of a topic, which dictated the order of thought and defined the generative problematic that instructed its authors on what they wanted to know about a particular topic. These intellectual modalities in their nature lay claim to an independence of mind, even when, in point of fact, the result of thought is a repetition of what Scripture itself says. Omitting scriptural prooftexts therefore represents both silence and signals its statement. For that act of omission bore the implicit claim to an authority independent of Scripture, an authority deriving from logic working within its own inner tensions and appealing to tests of reason and sound argument. In that striking fact the document set a new course for itself. But its authorship raised problems for those who would apply its law to Israel's life. What choices lay before the Jewish intellect as it came to realization among system builders? From the formation of ancient Israelite Scripture into a holy book in Judaism, in the aftermath of the return to Zion and the creation of the Torah book in Ezra's time (ca. 450 B.C.) the established canon of revelation (whatever its contents) coming generations routinely set their ideas into relationship with Scripture. This they did by citing prooftexts alongside their own rules. Otherwise, in the setting of Israelite culture, the new writings could find no ready hearing. Over the six hundred years from the formation of the Torah of "Moses" in the time of Ezra, from ca. 450 B.C. to ca. A.D. 200, four conventional ways to accommodate new writings – new "tradition" – to the established canon of received Scripture had come to the fore.

First and simplest, a writer would sign a famous name to his book, attributing his ideas to Enoch, Adam, Jacob's sons, Jeremiah, Baruch, and any number of others, down to Ezra. But the Mishnah bore no such attribution, for example, to Moses. Implicitly, to be sure, the statement of M. Avot 1:1, "Moses received Torah from Sinai" carried the further notion that sayings of people on the list of authorities from Moses to nearly their own day derived from God's revelation at Sinai. But no one made that premise explicit before the time of the Bavli of the Land of Israel. Second, an authorship might also imitate the style of biblical Hebrew and so try to creep into the canon by adopting the cloak of Scripture. But the Mishnah's authorship ignores biblical syntax and style. Third, an author would surely claim his work was inspired by God, a new revelation for an open canon. But, as we realize, that claim makes no explicit impact on the Mishnah. Fourth, at the very least, someone would link his opinions to biblical verses through the exegesis of the latter in line with the former so Scripture would validate his views. The authorship of the Mishnah did so only occasionally, but far more commonly stated on its own authority whatever rules it proposed to lay down.

The solution to the problem of the authority of the Mishnah, that is to say, its relationship to Scripture, was worked out in the period after the closure of the Mishnah. Since no one now could credibly claim to sign the name of Ezra or Adam to a book of this kind, and since biblical Hebrew had provided no apologetic aesthetics whatever, the only options lay elsewhere. The two were, first, to provide a myth of the origin of the contents of the Mishnah, and, second, to link each allegation of the Mishnah, through processes of biblical (not mishnaic) exegesis, to verses of the Scriptures. These two procedures, together, would establish for the Mishnah that standing that the uses to which the document was to be put demanded for it: a place in the canon of Israel, a legitimate relationship to the Torah of Moses. There were several ways in which the work went forward. These are represented by diverse documents that succeeded and dealt with the Mishnah. Let me now state the three principal possibilities. [1] The Mishnah required no systematic support through exegesis of Scripture in light of mishnaic laws. [2] The Mishnah by itself provided no reliable information and all of its propositions demanded linkage to Scripture, to which the Mishnah must be shown to be subordinate and secondary. [3] The Mishnah is an autonomous document, but closely correlated with Scripture.

The final and normative solution to the problem of the authority of the Mishnah worked out in the third and fourth centuries produced the myth of the Dual Torah, oral and written, which formed the indicative and definitive trait of the Judaism that emerged from late antiquity. Tracing the unfolding of that myth leads us deep into the processes by which that Judaism took shape. The Bavli knows the theory that there is a tradition separate from, and in addition to, the Written Torah. This tradition it knows as "the teachings of scribes." The Mishnah is identified as the collection of those teachings only by implication in the

Bavli. I cannot point to a single passage in which explicit judgment upon the character and status of the Mishnah as a complete document is laid down. Nor is the Mishnah treated as a symbol or called "the Oral Torah." But there is ample evidence, once again implicit in what happens to the Mishnah in the Bavli, to allow a reliable description of how the Bavli's founders viewed the Mishnah. That view may be stated very simply. The Mishnah rarely cites verses of Scripture in support of its propositions. The Bavli routinely adduces scriptural bases for the Mishnah's laws. The Mishnah seldom undertakes the exegesis of verses of Scripture for any purpose. The Bavli consistently investigates the meaning of verses of Scripture, and does so for a variety of purposes. Accordingly, the Bavli, subordinate as it is to the Mishnah, regards the Mishnah as subordinate to, and contingent upon, Scripture. That is why, in the Bavli's view, the Mishnah requires the support of prooftexts of Scripture. By itself, the Mishnah exercises no autonomous authority and enjoys no independent standing or norm-setting status.

And this brings us back to the Bavli's authorship's explanation of its own position in relationship to the received "tradition," which is to say, to prior systemic statements, the Pentateuch's and the Mishnah's in particular. Their solution to the problem of the standing and authority of the Mishnah dictated their answer to the question of the representation, within a received tradition, of their own system as well. It was through pretending to speak only by a phrase-by-phrase commentary that the Bavli's authorship justified the Mishnah as tradition and represented it as a secondary elaboration of Scripture or as invariably resting on the authority of Scripture. And that same form, in the nature of things, bore the burden of their systemic statement as well. That form does what can be done to represent sentences of the Mishnah as related to sentences of Scripture. That mode of writing, moreover, accomplished what we may call the dismantling or deconstruction of the system of the Mishnah and the reconstruction of its bits and pieces into the system of the Bavli. For the Bavli's authorship never represented the Mishnah's system whole and complete, and rarely acknowledged that the Mishnah consisted of more than discrete statements, to be related to some larger cogent law that transcended the Mishnah. Having represented the Mishnah as it did, therefore, the Bavli's authorship quite naturally chose to represent its own system in the same way, that is to say, as a mere elaboration of a received tradition, a stage in the sedimentary and incremental process by which the Torah continued to come down from Sinai. And for that purpose the mixed logics embodied in the joining of philosophical and propositional statements on the principle of fixed association to a prior text served exceedingly well. That explains how, in the Bavli, we have, in the (deceptive) form of a tradition, what is in fact an autonomous system, connected with prior systems but not continuous with them. The authorship represented their own statement of an ethos, ethics, and defined social entity, precisely as they did the received ones, the whole forming a single, seamless Torah revealed by God to Moses at Sinai. So much for a system to which the standing of tradition is imputed through formal means. What about the Christians' problem and the solution they set forth in the formation of the Bible?

When we come to the counterpart religious world, we confront Christian intellectuals, dealing also with the inheritance of ancient Israel's Scriptures. Just as the authorship of the Bavli received not only what they came to call the Written Torah, but also the Mishnah and other writings that had attained acceptance, hence authority, from the closure of the Mishnah to their own day, so too did the Christian intellectuals inherit more than the Old Testament. They too had in hand a variety of authoritative documents, to which the inspiration of the Holy Spirit was imputed. So they confronted the same problem as faced the authorship of the Bavli, and it was in pretty much the same terms: namely, how to sort out received documents, each of which making its own statement take up a different problem and follow a different solution to that problem. The issue of the authority of contradictory traditions defined the task at hand. What the Christian intellectuals, working over several centuries from ca. 100 through ca. 400, did was to join together the received writings as autonomous books but to impute to the whole the standing of a cogent statement, a single and harmonious Christian truth. This they did in the work of making the biblical canon.[1] Joining diverse traditions into one, single, uniform, and, therefore, (putatively) harmonious Bible: God's word. And, once more, that explains my view that the Christian solution to the problem of making a statement but also situating that system in relationship to received tradition is to be characterized in this way: *imputing system to discrete traditions through a declared canon.* Thus, as in the title of this appendix, the comparison of the solutions that would prevail, respectively, in Judaism's Bavli and Christianity's Bible, are characterized as a system to which the standing

---

[1] I hasten to add, they did so not only in the process of the canonization of some writings as the Old Testament and the New Testament, the Bible. It seems to me the work of framing creeds, preparing liturgies to be used throughout the church(es), debating theology and the like, all attended to the same labor of stating the pattern of Christian truth out of the received writings, all of them claiming to derive from the Holy Spirit or to be consonant with writings that did, that competed for standing and that contradicted one another on pretty much every important point. Once more, I underline that in dealing only with the work of canon, I in no way pretend to address the broader issues implicit in the topic as I have defined it.

of tradition is imputed, as against traditions, to which the form of a single system is, through the canonization of scriptures as The Bible, imputed.

The legitimacy of my comparing the two intellects through their ultimate statements, the Bavli and the Bible, seems to me sustained by the simple theological judgment of Turner:

> The mind of the Church [in making the canon] was guided by criteria rationally devised and flexibly applied. There is no dead hand in the production of the Canon; there is rather the living action of the Holy Spirit using as He is wont the full range of the continuing life of the Church to achieve His purposes in due season.[2]

I can find no better language to state, in a way interior to a system to be sure, the claim that a writing or a set of writings constitutes a system: a way of life, a worldview, an address to a particular social entity. This too is made explicit by Turner, who I take to be a thoroughly reliable representative of Christian theology on the subject:

> There can be no doubt that the Bible is fundamentally an orthodox book, sufficient if its teaching is studied as a whole to lead to orthodox conclusions.... The Biblical data insist upon arranging themselves in certain theological patterns and cannot be forced into other moulds without violent distortion. That is the point of a famous simile of St. Irenaeus. The teaching of Scripture can be compared to a mosaic of the head of a king, but the heretics break up the pattern and reassemble it in the form of a dog or a fox....[3]

A master of the Bavli could not have said it better in claiming both the systemic character, and the traditional standing, of his statement. The Christian theologians took a sizable corpus of unrelated documents and turned them into the Bible, and they furthermore imputed to that Bible the character of a system and even claimed to uncover, within the Bible, structure, order, proportion, harmony, and, by the way, doctrine, hence: Christian truth. And the Judaic sages did no less, but they did it with different kinds of writings, for different reasons, and in a different way. The issue framed as discovering the pattern of Christian truth addressed the authority of received writings and their harmony, and that issue, I maintain, faced the Judaic sages in their encounter with the system of the Mishnah.

We compare things that are really not like one another. When scholars of the formation of the canon of Christianity use the word canon, they mean, first, the recognition of sacred Scripture, over and

---

[2]Turner, *Pattern of Christian Truth*, p. 258.
[3]Turner, p. 300.

beyond the (received) Hebrew Scriptures, second, the identification of writings revered within the Church as canonical, hence authoritative, third, the recognition that these accepted writings formed a Scripture, which, fourth, served as the counterpart to the Hebrew Scriptures, hence, fifth, the formation of the Bible as the Old and New Testaments. Now, as a matter of fact, none of these categories, stage by stage, corresponds in any way to the processes in the unfolding of the holy books of the sages, which I shall now describe in terms of Torah. But the word "Torah" in the context of the writings of the sages at hand in no way forms that counterpart to the word "canon" as used (quite correctly) by Childs, von Campenhausen, and others, and, moreover the word "Bible" and the word "Torah" in no way speak of the same thing, I mean, they do not refer to the same category or classification. But the difference is the very point of the comparison, for, after all, the generative problematic was the same: holding together received conceptions in a contemporary statement, answering new questions out of inherited truths, setting forth a system in such a way as to affirm its traditional authority (Judaism), setting forth tradition in such a way as to claim its systemic harmony (Christianity).

So the differences require underlining. First, the statement of the Bavli is not a canonical system at all. For in the mode of presentation of the Bavli's system, as a matter of fact, revelation does not close or reach conclusion. God speaks all the time, through the sages. Representing the whole as "Torah" means that the Bavli speaks a tradition formed in God's revelation of God's will to Moses, our rabbi. Ancient Israel's Scriptures fall into the category of Torah, but they do not fill that category up. Other writings fall into that same category. By contrast canon refers to particular books that enjoy a distinctive standing, Torah refers to various things that fall into a particular classification. There is a second, still more fundamental difference between Bible and Bavli. The Christian canon reached closure with the Bible: Old and New Testaments. The Judaic Torah never closed: revelation of Torah continued. The Torah is not the Bible, and the Bible is not the Torah. The difference in process leading to Bible and Bavli, respectively, has been spelled out in my brief summaries of two distinct histories. The Bible emerges from the larger process of establishing Church order and doctrine. The Torah ("Oral and Written") for its part derives from the larger process of working out in relationship to the pentateuchal system the authority and standing of two successive and connected systems that had followed, the Mishnah, then the Bavli. But the problem solved for Christianity by the Bible and for Judaism by the Bavli is one and the same problem. And that is one not of literature, let alone mere logic of cogent discourse. It is the problem of relating ongoing history to a well-composed culture, change to continuity, the newest generation to the enduring social world, and, in the deep reality of the heart and soul, daughters to mothers and sons to fathers.

Let me therefore conclude at the point at which I commenced, with the observation that thought proceeds always in a context, whether one of logic and process or proposition and proportion and composition. And context always is social. A long-standing problem faced all system builders in the tradition that commenced with the Pentateuch. From that original system onward, system builders, both in Judaism and, as we now realize, in Christianity, would have to represent their system not as an original statement on its own, but as part of a tradition of revealed truth. Not only so, but in the passage of time and in the accumulation of writing, intellectuals, both Christian and Judaic, would have to work out logics that would permit cogent discourse within the inherited traditions and with them. In the Christian case, the solution to the problem lay in accepting as canonical a variety of documents, each with its own logic. We note, for instance, that extraordinarily cogent communication could be accomplished, in some Christian writings, through symbol and not through proposition at all. Christian writings exhibit each its own coherent logical principles of cogency, with the making of connections and the drawing of conclusions fully consistent throughout.

The final solution of the canon sidestepped the problem of bringing these logics together within a single statement. If diverse logics work, each for its own authoritative writing, then I really do not have to effect coherence among diverse logics at all, and the canon, the conception of The Bible, would impose from without a cogency of discourse difficult to discern in the interior of the canonical writings. That decision would then dictate the future of the Christian intellectual enterprise: to explore the underbrush of the received writing and to straighten out the tangled roots. No wonder, then, that, in philosophy, culminating in the return to Athens, the Christian mind would recover that glory of logical and systematic order denied it in the dictated canon, the Bible. But the canon did solve the problem that faced the heirs to a rather odd corpus of writing. Ignoring logic as of no account, accepting considerable diversity in modes of making connections and drawing conclusions, the traditional solution represented a better answer than the librarians of the Essenes at Qumran had found, which was to set forth (so far as matters now seem at any rate) neither a system nor a canon.

The Bavli's authorship was the first in the history of Judaism, encompassing Christianity in its earliest phases, to take up, in behalf of its distinct and distinctive system, a position of relationship with the received heritage of tradition, with a corpus of truth assigned to God's revelation to Moses at Sinai. The framers of the Pentateuch did not do so; rather they said what they wrote was the work of God, dictated to Moses at Sinai. The Essene librarians at Qumran did not do so. They collected this and that, never even pretending that everything fit together in some one way, not as commentary to Scripture (though some wrote commentaries), not as systemic statements (though the library included such statements, as we noticed), and not as a canon (unless everything we find in the detritus forms a canon by definition). The authorship of the Mishnah did not do so. Quite to the contrary, it undertook the pretense that, even when Scripture supplied facts and even dictated the order of the facts, their writing was new and fresh and their own.[4] No wonder that the Mishnah's authorship resorted to its own logic to make its own statement in its own language and for its own purposes. No wonder, too, that the hubris of the Mishnah's authorship provoked the systematic demonstration of the dependence of the Mishnah on Scripture – but also the allegation that the Mishnah stood as an autonomous statement, another Torah, the oral one, coequal with the Written Torah. The hubris of the great intellects of Judaic and Christian antiquity, the daring authorships of the Pentateuch and the Mishnah, the great ecclesiastical minds behind the Bible, reached its boldest realization in the Bavli. This authorship accomplished, as we have seen, through its ingenious joining of two distinct and contradictory logics of cogent discourse the statement of the Torah in its own rhetoric, following its own logic, and in accord with its own designated topical program. But hubris is not the sole trait that characterizes the Jewish mind, encompassing its Christian successors, in classical times.

There is a second trait common to them all. It is that in all systemic constructions and statements the issues of logic responded to the systemic imperative and in no way dictated the shape and structure of that imperative. The system invariably proves to be prior, recapitulating itself, also, in its logic. And however diverse the issues addressed by various systems made up by the Jewish mind in classical times, all had to address a single question natural to the religious ecology in which Judaic systems flourished. That question, in the aftermath of the pentateuchal

---

[4]The best example is Mishnah-tractate Yoma, Chapters One through Seven, which follows the order of Leviticus 16 and reviews its rite, step by step, rarely citing the pertinent chapter of Scripture and never conceding that all that was in hand was a summary and paraphrase of rules available elsewhere. It is the simple fact that we cannot make any sense out of that tractate without a point-by-point consultation with Leviticus 16. But there are numerous other examples of a mere paraphrase, by Mishnah's authorship, of passages of Scripture (along with many more in which Scripture has nothing to say on topics dealt with in the Mishnah, or in which what Scripture thinks important about a topic is simply ignored as of no interest in the Mishnah).

system, concerned how people could put together in a fresh construction and a composition of distinctive proportions a statement that purported to speak truth to a social entity that, in the nature of things, already had truth. This framing of the issue of how system contradicts tradition, how the logic that tells me to make a connection of this to that, but not to the other thing, and to draw from that connection one conclusion, rather than some other – that framing of the issue places intellect, the formation of mind and modes of thought squarely into the ongoing processes dictated by the givens of society.

Why then characterize the Bavli's system builders as the climax of the hubris of the Jewish intellectuals? Why describe the emergence of Judaism as an act of extraordinary genius among a handful of intellectuals? The reason is that the Bavli's authorship was the first in the history of Judaism, encompassing Christianity in its earliest phases, to take up, in behalf of its distinct and distinctive system, a considered position of relationship with the received heritage of tradition, with a corpus of truth assigned to God's revelation to Moses at Sinai. Four centuries after the Mishnah, in their mind eighteen centuries after God revealed the Torah to Moses at Mount Sinai, the Bavli's authorship remade the two received systems, the pentateuchal and the mishnaic. In its own rhetoric, in accord with its own topical program, appealing to a logic unique to itself among all Jewish minds in ancient times, that authorship presented the Torah of Sinai precisely as it wished to represent it. And it did so defiantly, not discretely and by indirection. Not merely alleging that Moses had written it all down, like the pentateuchal compilers, nor modestly identifying with the direction of the Holy Spirit the choices that it made, like the Christians responsible for making the Bible, nor even, as with the framers of the Mishnah, sedulously sidestepping, in laconic and disingenuous innocence, the issue of authority and tradition entirely. Quite the opposite, the Bavli's intellectuals took over the entire tradition, scriptural and mishnaic alike, chose what they wanted, tacked on to the selected passages their own words in their own way, and then put it all out as a single statement of their own.

True, they claimed for their system the standing of a mere amplification of that tradition. But, as a matter of fact, they did say it all in their own words and they did set forth the whole of their statement in their own way, and – as above all – without recapitulating the received choices of ignoring or merely absorbing the received revelation, they represented as the one whole Torah revealed by God to Moses, our rabbi, at Sinai what they themselves had made up, and they made it stick. And that, I think, is the supreme hubris of the Jewish mind from the beginnings, in the Pentateuch, to the conclusion and climax in the Bavli.

I like to think that that hubris of theirs at least for the beauty of it explains the success of what they made up, on the simple principle, the more daring, the more plausible. For theirs was the final realization and statement in the formation of the Jewish intellect.

To conclude: Judaic and Christian thinkers in antiquity had to sort out the relationship between system and tradition. Both religions claim to present enduring traditions, a fundament of truth revealed of old. But both religions also come to realization in systematic and philosophical statements, which begin in first principles and rise in steady and inexorable logic to final conclusions: compositions of proportion, balance, cogency, and order. And, not only so, but the systemic statements formed within both religions address not only problems of thought but the structure of society, explaining why people conduct their lives in one way, rather than in some other. Accordingly, a system builder starts fresh to explain what is, in fact, the increment of the ages. Or so it would seem. For the Christian, the Bible responded to the issue, and, for the Judaic thinker, the Bavli provided a final solution. The issue continues to thrive, for how people sort out the demands of a received belief in the confrontation with the fresh conceptions of a new day assuredly continues to enjoy the attention of religious intellectuals. Tradition and change, inherited ideas in tension with the reconstruction and re-visioning of a contemporary mind – these point to the ongoing relevance of the issue of the place system builders make for themselves within a traditional order. Judaism is the religion of intellectuals, and that is as it should be (from their perspective), because God revealed not only a word but words, and the words lead from intellect to intellect, God's to ours. So when we engage our minds with the Torah, we enter God's mind, and, to conclude, that is how (within the theology of Judaism) Judaism emerges, for every day, in the language of the blessing when the Torah is read in the synagogue, God gives the Torah – not "gave" but "gives," here and now, in the encounter with the words. What accounts for the emergence of Judaism? *It is the power of the Judaism of the Dual Torah in its statement in the Bavli, to present as tradition what is in fact a system.*

Index

South Florida Studies in the History of Judaism